American Fiction in Transition

American Fiction in Transition

Observer-Hero Narrative, the 1990s, and Postmodernism

Adam Kelly

B L O O M S B U R Y

NEW YORK · LONDON · NEW DELHI · SYDNEY

Bloomsbury Academic

An imprint of Bloomsbury Publishing Inc

1385 Broadway
New York
NY 10018
USA

50 Bedford Square
London
WC1B 3DP
UK

www.bloomsbury.com

Bloomsbury is a registered trade mark of Bloomsbury Publishing Plc

First published 2013
This paperback edition first published 2014

Library of Congress Cataloging-in-Publication Data
Kelly, Adam.
American fiction in transition: observer-hero narrative, the 1990s, and
postmodernism/Adam Kelly.
pages cm
Includes bibliographical references and index.
ISBN 978-1-4411-1285-9
1. American fiction–20th century–History and criticism.
2. Narration (Rhetoric)–History–20th century. 3. Point of view (Literature)
4. Roth, Philip. Human stain. 5. Auster, Paul, 1947- Leviathan.
6. Eugenides, Jeffrey. Virgin suicides. 7. Doctorow, E. L., 1931- Waterworks.
8. Postmodernism (Literature)–United States. I. Title.
PS374.N285K45 2012
813'.540923–dc23

2012043598

ISBN: HB: 978-1-4411-1285-9
PB: 978-1-6289-2530-2
ePDF: 978-1-4411-7374-4
ePUB: 978-1-4411-3593-3

Typeset by Newgen Imaging Systems Pvt Ltd, Chennai, India
Printed and bound in the United States of America

For Anne and Liam

Contents

Preface

The image by Gregory Crewdson that appears on the cover of this book depicts an archetypal American scene. In a small town, in the middle of a street soaked by rain and artificial light, a man stands perplexed, having lost something obscure but important. Surrounded by gloom and shadow, the figure—perhaps a detective, perhaps a gangster, perhaps a salesman—is a morally ambiguous hero in the American grain, caught in a moment of transition between what has been done to him and what he is about to do in reaction.

The image is composed in a manner that does not allow the viewer entirely to enter the man's world, however. Its intermedial quality—this is a photograph, but it could easily be mistaken for a painting, a digital graphic, or a movie still—draws attention to its artificiality and staginess, as does its heightened color, stark lines, and ordered composition. And though it is taken with a camera, the image points less to a recognizably real world than to familiar artistic renderings of an imagined world. The modernist painter Edward Hopper is an obvious influence, with his distinctive use of light and shadow to evoke the isolation of human figures in the geometry of American urban space. Another influence is the postmodern filmmaker David Lynch, and indeed the title of the series from which the image is drawn, *Beneath the Roses* (2005), alludes to the opening of Lynch's *Blue Velvet* (1986), even if the scene depicted here is more redolent of the director's later *Lost Highway* (1997). Composed in what A. D. Coleman famously dubbed the directorial mode, Crewdson's photograph most of all recalls another genre of American postmodernism, the neo-noir film, particularly works from the early-to-mid 1990s by directors such as John Dahl, David Fincher, Carl Franklin, the Coen Brothers, and Quentin Tarantino. In retrospectively invoking these postmodern texts, Crewdson's image operates as a pastiche of a pastiche, neo-noir having drawn its characteristic motifs from the original film noir of the 1940s and 1950s. Published in the mid-2000s, a decade after the art it most clearly cites, this photograph is therefore not so much an embodiment of postmodernism as a comment upon it. In all its belated glory, it constitutes a playful reflection on the forms that American postmodernism adopted during the 1990s.

One final feature of Crewdson's image is important to the concerns of the present study. With leaves framing the shot in the top left-hand and right-hand corners, the photograph is carefully composed to suggest not the effaced camera eye of realism, but the subjective position of an observer, even a voyeur, a personage in position to capture this heightened moment in a man's life. And the figure captured by this observer is, at least in this moment, a person of consequence, a man whose anguish matters, who has lost something of value that sparks the observer's interest. The narrative dimension to the image brings these facets together: the observer is privy to this moment of transition, a moment when day becomes night both literally, in the darkening sky and the deepening rain, and figuratively, in the life of the hero. In *American Fiction in Transition*, my focus will be on a genre of the literary novel that chimes with this image.

Resurrecting an old critical term, I call this genre "observer-hero narrative," and in my introduction and four chapters, I contend that the genre's role in both the American literary tradition and the particular decade of the 1990s is a highly significant one.

Observer-hero narratives are hybrid affairs. This is true primarily because of their structure, which typically pits a narrator with skeptical modern impulses against a protagonist who is more mysterious and romantic in conception. The relationship between these two figures permits each novel in the genre to explore a clash of sensibilities, a clash that often reflects the transition from one historical, intellectual, or aesthetic epoch to another. Canonical American novels in this vein include *Moby-Dick*, *The Great Gatsby*, *All the King's Men*, and *On the Road*, and whenever a new novel is published that shares its narrative structure with these books, reviewers invariably draw comparisons to *The Great Gatsby* in particular. What is usually lacking is an adequate critical vocabulary with which to address the features these novels have in common. One purpose of this study, then, is to provide, or to rehabilitate, such a vocabulary.

My study also sees observer-hero narratives of the 1990s as hybrid in a further sense, and as doubly interested in the problem of transition. The novels by Philip Roth, Paul Auster, Jeffrey Eugenides, and E. L. Doctorow that I examine in this book are animated by a contrast not only between observer and hero, but also between different ways of telling, and understanding, the hero's story. Each novel sees the narrator oscillate between possible conceptions of a major decision the protagonist has made, and a range of representational modes—tragic, modern, postmodern—compete in the account the narrator offers. This anxiety in finding the correct way to narrate the hero's decision points in turn to a broader anxiety, bearing on the question of how transition should be conceived in a postmodern world that seems to put the notion of genuine historical change out of bounds. What these novels dramatize most of all, I will argue in this study, is a state of ongoing transition in our understanding of transition.

American Fiction in Transition thus has two principal goals. On the one hand, it draws attention to the important but neglected genre of observer-hero narrative. Exploring the origins and history of this genre, it seeks to understand the central place of observer-hero narrative in the American literary tradition, and to foreground its particular association with periods of transition between literary paradigms. On the other hand, the book is engaged with accounts of postmodernism and of what might come after it, looking to novels of the 1990s in order to explore these concerns. On a theoretical level, I draw on the conceptions of postmodern agency and temporality foregrounded in Fredric Jameson's work, and put these into dialogue with Jacques Derrida's work on undecidability and on a range of concepts—secrecy, testimony, narcissism, justice—that exhibit undecidability. Derrida's texts help us to conceptualize the storytelling oscillations that dominate 1990s observer-hero narratives, and to understand the new models of decision, transition, temporality, and agency that emerge from these novels. The novels in turn approach the problems of literary and cultural transition from a fresh perspective, allowing us to view both contemporary fiction and postmodern theory in a new light.

Parts of this study have appeared elsewhere in earlier forms. Chapter 1 is based on my article "Imagining Tragedy: Philip Roth's *The Human Stain*," published in *Philip*

Roth Studies 6.2 (Fall 2010). Chapter 4 draws on material from "Society, Justice and the Other: E. L. Doctorow's *The Waterworks*," published in *Phrasis* 47.1 (Spring 2006). My article "Moments of Decision in Contemporary American Fiction: Roth, Auster, Eugenides," published in *Critique: Studies in Contemporary Fiction* 51.4 (Summer 2010), offers an earlier version of the arguments of the book, and material from the article appears in various places throughout *American Fiction in Transition*. I am grateful to the editors of these three journals for permission to draw upon this work.

The writing of this book would not have been possible without the support of various institutions, colleagues, friends, and family. The project began life as part of a doctoral dissertation completed at University College Dublin, where John Brannigan and Ron Callan provided expert guidance and moral and intellectual support. I owe them both immense thanks. The book was revised and completed at Harvard University, where I have had the great privilege to visit as a postdoctoral fellow for two years. My gratitude goes to the Irish Research Council for the funding opportunity that made my time in the United States possible, and to Werner Sollors and James Simpson in the English Department for supporting my candidacy and making me welcome. While at Harvard, my understanding of dialectical thought has been enhanced by the Hegel Reading Group, organized by Will Baldwin, and my appreciation of all things literary American has been furthered by the American Literature Colloquium, with thanks especially owed to Kathryn Roberts, Nick Donofrio, Maggie Doherty, and Maggie Gram. At University College Dublin, friends and colleagues who had a particular influence on the project include Tom Murray, always an incisive interlocutor on political questions, Sharae Deckard, so often the voice in my head when I write about Fredric Jameson, and Seferin James, with whom I had the great pleasure to share many a conversation on the thought of Jacques Derrida as well as the organizational responsibilities for the Derrida and America conference we hosted at UCD in 2009. I also wish to acknowledge senior colleagues at other institutions who have supported me and my work, particularly Derek Attridge at the University of York, Stephen Burn at Northern Michigan University, Philip Coleman at Trinity College Dublin, Tony Hutchison at the University of Nottingham, and Tim Woods at Aberystwyth University. For discussions of the cover image, I thank Robin Kelsey at Harvard. Haaris Naqvi and the staff at Bloomsbury have been a pleasure to work with, and I would also like to acknowledge the helpful comments made by the two anonymous readers to whom the press sent my proposal.

Many friends and colleagues read parts of the manuscript as it moved toward completion. In addition to the aforementioned Ron Callan, Maggie Gram and Seferin James, I am also thankful to Mark O'Connell and Martin Hägglund. These people all gave generously of their time and expertise to help me improve my text. One person read the manuscript in its entirety: Ríona Nic Congáil, who not coincidentally happens to be the person with whom I am honored to share my life away from writing. I owe her more gratitude than I can express here. And finally, I want to acknowledge my family: my sister Fiona, my brother Mark, and my mother and father, Anne and Liam Kelly. This book is dedicated to my parents, who have supported me through every transition in my life thus far. I am glad to have made them proud, and hope to continue to do so into the undecidable future.

Introduction

If, indeed, the subject has lost its capacity actively to extend its pro-tensions and re-tensions across the temporal manifold and to organize its past and future into coherent experience, it becomes difficult enough to see how the cultural products of such a subject could result in anything but "heaps of fragments" and in a practice of the randomly heterogeneous and fragmentary and the aleatory.

Fredric Jameson, *Postmodernism*, 25

The passive decision, condition of the event, is always in me, structurally, an other event, a rending decision as the decision of the other. Of an absolutely other in me, of the other as the absolute who decides of me in me.

Jacques Derrida, *The Politics of Friendship*, 68

In Thomas Pynchon's *Gravity's Rainbow* (1973), the would-be hero, Lieutenant Tyrone Slothrop, starts out as a figure of parodic omnipotence, of mysteriously excessive agency. Slothrop's penile erections around London during World War II form a pattern with sites of V-2 rocket explosions, and this strange predictive capacity soon makes him the object of scrutiny by larger forces. Pursued by two obscurely located opposing powers, the Firm and the Counterforce, Slothrop becomes the prey of a system that seems at once all-powerful and strangely haphazard, and by the novel's end he has been stripped of any temporal coherence and intimations of agency that he might have possessed. Moreover, Slothrop is not alone in his fate; the world he inhabits is one characterized more generally by what Timothy Melley has termed "agency panic." This is a world in which events are perceived to lie beyond human control, in which "Decisions are never really *made*—at best they manage to emerge, from a chaos of peeves, whims, hallucinations and all-around assholery" (Pynchon 676). This sentence—which comments reflexively upon the construction and texture of Pynchon's own novel, its replacement of high modernist seriousness with a narrative voice that arbitrarily and joyfully indulges peeves and whims—provides a characteristic example of the author's mix of somber antihumanist vision and knockabout comic farce. *Gravity's Rainbow*'s virtuoso combination of these attributes has seen the novel widely canonized as the central document of American literary postmodernism, the fictional text that most clearly and compellingly exemplifies the postmodern worldview.

It is no coincidence, then, that the fate of Pynchon's protagonist in *Gravity's Rainbow* resonates strongly with the account of contemporary subjectivity provided by Fredric Jameson in *Postmodernism, or, The Cultural Logic of Late Capitalism* (1991), the text that could be called the central document of American theoretical postmodernism. Applying to Pynchon's novel the terms of my opening epigraph from Jameson, we might say that while Tyrone Slothrop's "cultural products"—those sexual escapades that offer him his nearest approximation of self-expression—already appear "heterogeneous and fragmentary" at the beginning of *Gravity's Rainbow*, by the end of the novel the protagonist has himself become a "heap of fragments": "The plan went wrong. He is being broken down instead, and scattered" (Pynchon 738). For Jameson, Slothrop's disintegration would be a metaphorical figure for the plight of the human subject under late capitalism, an economic world-system that remains unrepresentable at the scale of subjective consciousness and destroys the subject's organic relation to "the temporal manifold," extinguishing the possibility of organizing "past and future into coherent experience."[1] While in Pynchon's novel the underlying cause of the damage is not quite as identifiable as it is for Jameson, this is the case in part because the temporal relationship between cause and effect has itself been irreparably damaged in the world of *Gravity's Rainbow*.[2] Pynchon and Jameson appear to be singing from the same hymn-sheet in this respect, at least, in that in both writers what we have come to call postmodernism is defined by a concern with *events* rather than *decisions*. "Decisions are never really *made*," Pynchon writes, and the story he and Jameson both tell—that a de-centering of the human subject has rendered individuals incapable of organizing time, that a narrative sense of one's destiny has been imperiled by grand historical shifts and contemporary economic and technological developments—has become the central fable of postmodern literature and theory.

In *American Fiction in Transition*, I read four US novels of the long 1990s as responses to this postmodern fable, as fresh engagements with questions of temporality, agency and decision at the human scale. Philip Roth's *The Human Stain* (2000), Paul Auster's *Leviathan* (1992), Jeffrey Eugenides's *The Virgin Suicides* (1993), and E. L. Doctorow's *The Waterworks* (1994) are all examples of a genre of the novel that, following the critic Lawrence Buell, I call "observer-hero narrative." In this genre, a dramatized first-person narrator retrospectively tells the story of an important figure in his or her life who has died. In these 1990s novels, the deceased figure seems to embody a certain kind of heroism, in that his or her life seems to offer a model of decision and temporal agency set against a postmodern backdrop that has placed these qualities out of bounds. I say "seems" here, however, because the real drama in these novels concerns how best to represent and explain, how best to tell the story of, the life and decisions of the hero in question. The classic narratological divide between story and discourse is embodied in these novels by the division between the hero and the observer, and a range of

explanatory paradigms and representational modes—tragic, modern, postmodern—
are brought to bear by the narrator on his storytelling task. Each novel becomes in
large part the story of the problem of telling the story, the problem of explaining the
seemingly inexplicable decisions the hero takes, the key transitions to which his life
bears witness. And understanding the transitions of an individual life, finding a model
to narrate the decisions implied by the events of the plot, has a larger significance: I
read these novels as allegorical engagements with the problem of transition understood
more broadly, at the historical and theoretical levels.

For Jameson, postmodernism not only names a historical deep freeze, wherein
human agency no longer appears as the motor of historical transition, but the term
also signifies the difficulty of gaining sufficient critical distance to address that freeze.
"Postmodernism, postmodern consciousness," he declares, "may then amount to not
much more than theorizing its own condition of possibility, which consists primarily in
the sheer enumeration of changes and modifications" (ix). The possibility of agency and
decision grounded in subjective experience, a possibility central to nineteenth-century
realism and still operative for Jameson in the individuating character of high modernist
style, has been eroded in both postmodern life and postmodern texts.[3] Replacing this
possibility is a list of phenomenological symptoms that aid the maintenance of the
systematic status quo—in *Postmodernism*, Jameson writes of the loss of historical
consciousness, the sense of a perpetual present, the waning of affect, the replacement
of the temporal by the spatial, the annexing of the natural by the cultural. These facets
make up the "cultural dominant" of the late twentieth century, and in Jameson's view
literary texts can no longer maintain a critical relation to that dominant.[4]

Jameson's own critical response to this situation involves a renewal of the dialectical
method, and I will return to it later in this introduction. But in the chapters of this study,
I take an alternative route, seeing in observer-hero narratives of the 1990s a response
by literary texts to the postmodern condition and the twinned problems of individual
agency and historical transition. In taking this route, I argue that a key question facing
any discourse—literary or theoretical—that wants to respond to the postmodern
situation, is how to rethink the notion of the event to bring it closer to the notion of the
decision. This is one way to describe the project undertaken by Jacques Derrida in his
late work, where, as we shall see in Section V of this introduction and in the chapters
that follow, he treats the decision precisely as an event both connected to and breaking
with the prior determinations of structure, both linked to the freedom of a subject and
breaking with any determined account of that freedom. It is this double gesture that
makes Derrida's philosophy a suitable frame for understanding the double movement
of contemporary observer-hero narratives, where the story of inexplicable decisions
made by the protagonist-hero, framed through the narrator's point of view, provides
a literary correlative for what Derrida calls "the decision of the other in me." Reading
this overlooked narrative genre, and focusing on the theme of transition, I explore
the contemporary American novel for its engagement with important aspects of the
intellectual context of the late twentieth century. Framing my readings in Derridean
terms, throughout *American Fiction in Transition* I take the literary novel seriously
as a site of contemporary resistance to postmodern fragmentation and stasis, a place

where the postmodern diagnosis we find most clearly articulated in Jameson can be incorporated and staged as simply one possible mode of interpretation among others.

In the present introduction, I lay the groundwork for my four literary case studies by explicating central concepts and elaborating on a range of contexts already alluded to in brief. I begin by reviewing nascent debates about American fiction of the 1990s, focusing on recent scholarship that argues for a transition beyond postmodernism in the fiction of that decade. By sketching out the critical background in this way, I aim to clarify my intervention in a rapidly expanding field. In the second section I introduce the genre of observer-hero narrative in fuller terms, by reconstructing a critical debate now over three decades old. Here the theme of transition also gains in definition, as I argue for a transitional role for this narrative genre in literary history. In the third section I outline the specific importance of observer-hero narrative in the American literary tradition, while in the fourth section I seek to anticipate critical concerns with my methodology and selection of literary case studies, particularly with regard to questions of genre, gender, and race. The final section then outlines in broader detail the implicit theoretical debate between Jameson and Derrida that underlies my inquiry. This is where many central claims of my study are highlighted, and the key tenets of my reading method clarified. I conclude the introduction with a brief overview of a forerunner to my study, Jerry H. Bryant's *The Open Decision* (1970). This text, like my own, reads the novels of its era as exemplifying a series of concerns in the realms of culture and ideas; the differences between Bryant's methods and mine, however, offer an instructive comparison between critical conceptions of the relationship between literature and literary theory in our respective eras.

I Postmodernism in eclipse: American fiction in the 1990s

Scholarship on American literature and culture in the 1990s is still in its nascent phase, but if critics have so far agreed on one thing, it is that the decade marked a period of transition. For historicist critics, the post-Cold War and pre-9/11 status of the 1990s made this transitional quality inevitable. Against Francis Fukuyama's famous neoconservative argument that the fall of communism heralded the end of history as the "end point of mankind's ideological evolution" (Fukuyama 4), Phillip E. Wegner, in *Life Between Two Deaths*, views the long 1990s as "one of those transitional phases" (9), a time offering utopian possibilities that now risk being forgotten, "a moment of heated debate over the direction of the future" (1). Samuel Cohen, in *After the End of History*, argues that the decade was characterized by "a markedly retrospective quality" to American culture (10), a quality evident in a spate of historical novels—by major figures including Pynchon, Roth, Don DeLillo, and Toni Morrison—that "connect the past to a future whose tenuousness places it at the center of the contemporary American historical imagination" (4). For critics writing primarily about literary-historical rather than historical formations, the period likewise offers a tale of transition. Andrew Hoberek, for instance, has located in American novels of the 1990s the beginnings of a "contemporary transformation of what counts as serious fiction" ("Cormac" 485), a turn by recognizably literary writers, such as Cormac McCarthy and Michael Chabon, to the wholesale appropriation of genre as respectable terrain for creative work. Hoberek calls this "a transition in parentheses: not finished but increasingly visible as an emergent phenomenon" (486), a sentiment that echoes Daniel Grassian's claim that the 1990s witnessed "a period of literary eclecticism and hybrid fictions, which utilize a wide variety of literary approaches, have conflicting viewpoints and blend media and technological forms" (2).

The specific strand of this scholarly conversation with which I am most concerned bears on the idea that the 1990s witnessed the signs of a transition beyond postmodernism, variously understood. By the early 2000s, critics were already sounding the death-knell of postmodernism: in the 2002 reprint of her influential study *The Politics of Postmodernism*, Linda Hutcheon called postmodernism "a twentieth-century phenomenon, that is, a thing of the past" (165), while on the opening page of *Postmodern Debates*, from 2001, Simon Malpas suggested that if postmodernism named a space of critical debate, then the debate had already moved elsewhere (1). These declarations, and others like them, depict the 1990s as the decade when postmodernism was on the wane.[5] As a consequence, critics have coined new terms to classify the period's literary output: Jeremy Green has suggested "late postmodernism" to characterize American fiction of the pre-millennial moment; Christian Moraru has identified the emergence of what he calls "cosmodernism" during the decade, conjoining cosmopolitanism with modernist aesthetics; Rachel Adams has written of the eclipse of postmodernism by "American literary globalism." Other critics have favored the term "post-postmodernism": while Grassian avoids the phrase because it "suggests we have moved past postmodernism" (17), Stephen Burn uses post-postmodernism to categorize 1990s fiction by writers such as Jonathan Franzen, Richard Powers, and David Foster Wallace, writers who self-consciously engage with their postmodern forebears in their work. Explaining the emergence of this movement and this term, Burn comments: "Looking back from the perspective of the millennium, the 1990s appears to have been a transitional decade for American fiction, torn between the emergence of a generation of writers seeking to move beyond postmodernism and the prolonged vitality of many writers—Barth, Gaddis, Pynchon, Coover—associated with the rise of the movement" (9–10).

Burn's narrative of generational succession in the 1990s recalls the situation in the American 1950s, when postmodern writers including Barth, Gaddis, and Pynchon were emerging at a time when by-then-canonical modernists such as Faulkner and Hemingway were still dominant figures. In his introduction to a journal issue entitled *After Postmodernism*, Andrew Hoberek confirms the sense of shared valence between these two decades, declaring that "American fiction has entered a phase of as-yet-uncategorized diversity similar to the one that prevailed following World War II" ("Introduction" 240). In a move that will resonate with my methods in *American Fiction in Transition*, however, Hoberek adds a caveat: the task of conceptualizing a transition away from the dominance of postmodernism may well involve rethinking the very notion of transition itself. Hoberek draws particular attention here to Jameson's characterization of the thinking of transition as a peculiarly modern problem, further exacerbated within the postmodern era as Jameson conceives it. Whereas modernism, in Jameson's words, "also thought compulsively about the New and tried to watch its coming into being," postmodernism, concerned less with the temporal than the spatial,

> looks for breaks, for events rather than new worlds, for the telltale instant after which it is no longer the same; for the "When-it-all-changed," as [William] Gibson puts it, or better still, for shifts and irrevocable changes in the representation of things and of the way they change. (*Postmodernism* ix)[6]

In the American context that anchors Jameson's postmodern diagnosis, recent events such as the September 11 attacks, the election of Barack Obama, and the economic crisis of 2008 have all offered popular candidates to signify a new moment "when-it-all-changed." When it comes to considering "the representation of things and of the way they change," however, Hoberek advises a critical approach toward this fascination with immediately visible, ostensibly paradigm-altering events. With the comparison to the earlier postwar decade in mind, he contends that "if contemporary fiction is indeed post-postmodern, this does not exemplify some singular, dramatic, readily visible cultural transformation—the search for which in fact constitutes a postmodern preoccupation—but grows out of a range of uneven, tentative, local shifts" ("Introduction" 241). Studying these local shifts will enable us to think more clearly about larger ones, argues Hoberek, and thus the proper critical response to contemporary transition consists "neither of assertions of postmodernism's continued relevance nor of sweeping declarations of a potential successor but rather of concrete analyses of literary form and the historical conditions that shape it" (240). In his contribution to *After Postmodernism*, Timothy Bewes goes further, directly contesting Jameson's diagnosis of "a certain spatial turn" in the postmodern. According to Bewes, Jameson's own formulations—which emphasize fragmentation and stasis as the by-products of postmodernism's spatial dominant—constitute an obstacle to historicizing the contemporary and to thinking transition: "The task of theorizing what comes after the postmodern, then, may well have to begin by challenging the spatialized notion of the postmodern as an epoch that may be succeeded by anything at all" (274). In order to provide this challenge to the Jamesonian emphasis on space, in his essay Bewes looks to cinematic tropes in the later fiction of Paul Auster.[7]

The critical approach adopted by Hoberek and Bewes—with contemporary literary fiction read against a background of Jamesonian theory—offers a good example of the way present debates about postmodernism regularly oscillate between theoretical ground and artistic practice.[8] The complex history of the term itself indicates one reason for the prevalence of this critical dynamic. While "postmodernism" initially gained prominence as a characterization of stylistic innovations in the work of US fiction writers of the 1960s and 1970s, its breadth of cultural reference would later extend almost unstoppably, not least in the synthetic work of Jameson, the first to describe postmodernism as a cultural dominant.[9] A legitimate response to subsequent confusions around the term is offered by Burn, who argues that "such tangled histories and often conflicting usages" make futile the attempt "to explore what the end of *postmodernism* might mean in an interdisciplinary sense" (3). Burn therefore retains postmodernism as a descriptive category for literary aesthetics while bracketing its cultural and theoretical overtones. Yet if we wish to persist in reading literature as an index to wider culture—if, as Hoberek puts it, we want to see "stylistic shifts in works of literature" as indexing "larger cultural changes" ("Introduction" 237)—then it remains important to connect changes in contemporary literary form to postmodernism understood in its expanded sense as a cultural dominant.

In *American Fiction in Transition*, I therefore follow critics such as Hoberek and Bewes by attending to local manifestations of literary change in contemporary writing, and by suggesting the way these literary changes challenge certain characteristic features of cultural and theoretical postmodernism. Moreover, my aim in this book is to move the debate forward through a focus on four case studies in a genre of the novel—observer-hero narrative—that historically specializes in monitoring transition, in dealing with breaks and exemplifying shifts "in the representation of things and of the way they change." In the next two sections, I define this literary genre, outline its history, and point to some features that make it an apt lens through which to view the problem of transition in late-twentieth-century American literature and culture.

II Observer-hero narrative: Defining the genre

In order to introduce observer-hero narrative as a literary-critical term, it is necessary to reconstruct an all-but-forgotten scholarly debate now more than 30 years old. Conceived in its narrowest terms, the debate concerned the best generic designation of a recognizable group of novels, including such canonical works as *Moby-Dick*, *Heart of Darkness*, *The Good Soldier*, *The Great Gatsby*, and *Doctor Faustus*. In 1971 Kenneth Bruffee published an article putting forward his proposed coinage for the genre, "Elegiac Romance," following the article with a book-length study of the same name in 1983. In 1979, and apparently without knowledge of Bruffee's earlier essay, Lawrence Buell published a discussion of much the same group of works under the title "Observer-Hero Narrative." Here is the definition that begins Buell's piece:

> This genre may be defined in brief as a story told by a dramatized first-person narrator about a significant relationship or encounter he has had with another person. The two figures are both opposites and counterparts, the second person perceived both as contrasting with the first in outlook or life-style and as embodying in purer or more extreme form qualities which the observer has or sympathizes with in moderation. The observer's world seems more like our world, while the second person's seems more intensely focused and more romantic by comparison. The structure of the narrative is built upon the interplay of these psychic universes. (93)

To this structural outline Buell adds a number of other features common to examples of observer-hero narrative. At the level of character, the hero tends to exert a pull on the mind of the observer that lies deeper than any rational explanation (95). At the level of discourse, the observer's account of the hero is always biased in some way, and the former always acts as both admirer and judge (97). At the level of story, the action is almost entirely concentrated in the hero—"the hero is a do-er and a be-er, whereas the observer is a thinker and a seeker" (96)—and that action always ends in the same result: "As a rule, the action centering in the hero ends conclusively and tragically, with his death, while the witness pauses on the brink and philosophizes" (100). At the level of meaning, finally, the narrative induces a certain nostalgia (albeit usually of an ambivalent kind) for the values of a more noble past: "The hero is characterized in such a way as to renew the observer's (and the reader's) faith in the possibility of a degree of grandeur that we had more or less assumed to have faded from the contemporary world" (101). With these common features in mind, Buell includes a section in his essay justifying the designation of observer-hero narrative as a distinctive literary genre.

Not all contributors to the debate agree with Buell's use of the category of genre: Walter Reed, for instance, rejects the term in characterizing his four nineteenth-century "meditations on the hero" as forming not a genre but rather "an imaginative structure of thought" (9). Addressing this problem directly, Kenneth Bruffee begins *Elegiac Romance* with a prologue on the question of genre, citing the work of a range of postwar critics who constitute the field of modern genre theory, from Wayne C. Booth and Northrop Frye to Claudio Guillén and Alastair Fowler.[10] Bruffee goes on to contend not only that Buell's observer-hero narrative is "a coherent category of twentieth-century fiction" (30), but that what Bruffee calls elegiac romance in fact constitutes the major subset of Buell's larger genre, "the epicenter of the class" (27). Elegiac romance represents "the fourth and most recent phase in the evolution of the quest romance tradition" (32), comprising "an effort to dispense with heroes and heroism entirely" (55), and featuring a narrator who is "a new and distinctively twentieth-century figure" (51). For Bruffee, this narrator is the central figure in every example of elegiac romance, the character who grows and changes as the tale is told; hence, he argues, elegiac romance fictions demand to be read as the narrator's story, as "pseudo-autobiography concealed as pseudo-biography" ("Elegiac" 467). Bruffee is also committed to a Freudian understanding of the genre, in which the narrator is involved in "symbolic projection" and the conscious detail of the story eventually gives way to the discovery of an "inner truth" associated with the narrator's unconscious (*Elegiac* 68). The story represents the narrator's attempt to work through material he has repressed: "By revealing and understanding the trauma, through telling his tale, he resolves the neurosis" (134). This working through of past repression—which Bruffee suggests is Oedipal in source (148)—helps the narrator to recover "the coherence of his inner world" (52); this makes "the 'thread of logic' underlying this new understanding" into the "ultimate subject" of elegiac romance (135). Conceived in this way, elegiac romance represents, according to Bruffee, "a neglected resource for understanding 'modernism'" (57).

By comparison with Bruffee's analysis of elegiac romance, Buell's description of observer-hero narrative is not simply broader in scope, it is also less prescriptive as regards content and interpretation. One advantage of his nomenclature, for my purposes here, is that it foregrounds the formal and structural qualities of the genre, its division into two primary character roles, only then suggesting its varying possible meanings. Citing René Wellek and Austin Warren's *Theory of Literature* as support, Buell claims that "most outer forms [. . .] seem to suggest a certain angle of vision on reality." In the case of observer-hero narrative, this implies a particular epistemology—"objective reality is unknowable"—and suggests, at its ethical core, "an ambiguous evaluation of heroism" (103). Recognition of this epistemological skepticism and ambivalence regarding heroism makes Buell more circumspect than Bruffee, for whom the observer-narrator is always in the end a pragmatic realist who "exposes and copes with the delusion of hero-worship and outgrows it" (*Elegiac* 15). As I will show in the chapters that follow, Bruffee's modernist understanding of the genre as a quest resolved on the symbolic level is merely one interpretive possibility put forward by observer-hero narratives of the 1990s, to be placed next to older and newer understandings.

It is apt, then, that unlike Bruffee, Buell declines to consign his version of the genre to strict historical limits as an offshoot of modernism's inheritance of the quest romance tradition. Rather, he outlines a number of nineteenth-century genres that shared (and continue to share in their present-day forms) technical features with observer-hero narrative, including Gothic fiction, framed tales, the historical romance, the bildungsroman, the familiar essay, and the biographical reminiscence (103–7). Buell remarks further that on a thematic level the genre's emergence in the nineteenth century was the product of two connected trends in western literature since the Renaissance, namely "the gradual disappearance of the traditional hero, and the rise of interest in subjective consciousness as a literary subject" (103). While Buell refuses to overly delimit possible interpretations of the texts he names, he does, nevertheless, suggest that the juxtaposition of two psychic worlds found in observer-hero narratives tends to mark the genre as a transitional one; as he puts it, the genre "reflects a pervasive malaise in the culture that keeps harping on it" (108).

Although Buell does not go on to make the point, it might be added that periods which our established stories of literary history usually associate with aesthetic transition have indeed been marked by the publication of a number of significant texts fitting the description of observer-hero narrative. For example, Robert Marler has shown how the emergence in US magazines of the modern short story from the traditional tale can be traced to the 1850s; it was during this decade that Herman Melville, in observer-hero narratives such as "Bartleby, the Scrivener," "Jimmy Rose" and *Moby-Dick*, was fusing aspects of the decaying romance tale with features of the realist mode that would flourish after the Civil War.[11] Similarly, in the period between the dominance of realism and the era of high modernism, the key transitional figures in the Anglo-American sphere, Joseph Conrad and Henry James, both experimented with the genre, the former producing some of its signature texts.[12] Most strikingly of all, the late 1950s and early 1960s, the period traditionally considered the run-up to the emergence of postmodernist fiction in the United States, produced a surfeit of observer-hero narratives. Mark Harris's *Bang the Drum Slowly* and James Baldwin's *Giovanni's Room* were published in 1956, while Jack Kerouac's *On the Road* was issued in 1957, though it was completed earlier in the decade. Truman Capote's *Breakfast at Tiffany's* and John Barth's *The End of the Road* appeared in 1958, and these were followed in 1959 by three important texts exploiting the observer-hero structure: "Seymour: An Introduction" by J. D. Salinger, *Henderson the Rain King* by Saul Bellow, and *A Separate Peace* by John Knowles. In 1962, two more significant examples appeared, Vladimir Nabokov's *Pale Fire* (which overtly parodies certain conventions of the genre, for instance the passive/active construction of the observer/hero), and *One Flew Over the Cuckoo's Nest* by Ken Kesey. By contrast, the periods that critics normally associate with the dominance of literary realism, high modernism, and postmodernism produced few examples of the genre. Those that did appear in these periods, such as F. Scott Fitzgerald's *The Great Gatsby* and Willa Cather's *My Mortal Enemy* in the mid-1920s, or Gore Vidal's *Burr*, Bellow's *Humboldt's Gift*, and Joan Didion's *A Book of Common Prayer* in the mid-1970s, were written by authors not usually associated with the more experimental formal trends in their respective eras.[13]

Two hypotheses follow from the above observations. The first is that, as the example of Joseph Conrad suggests, writers of fiction might be thought of as aesthetically transitional (at least through the relevant parts of their careers) precisely to the extent to which they favor the genre of observer-hero narrative. Applying this insight to the case of *Pale Fire*, for instance, helps to account for the critical disagreement regarding the classification of Nabokov's work as postmodernist or not, a disagreement also to be found in scholarship on Auster, Roth, and (to a lesser extent) Doctorow at the other end of the postmodern epoch. Moreover, in recent critical work on John Barth, the one author named above who is definitely considered a postmodernist, *The End of the Road* tends to be allocated a transitional place in his corpus. The flexibility of the observer-hero structure of the novel is testified to by one critic—"By putting his own aesthetic formalism on trial in *The End of the Road*, Barth produced a text more dialogically robust than the aesthetically ordered worlds of the postmodern novels that followed" (Conti 83)—while the general scholarly consensus is that it was not until the mid-1960s that Barth's work shifted, as another critic puts it, "from the existentialist style of novels such as *The End of the Road* to the more obviously postmodern works like *Lost in the Funhouse* (1968), *Chimera* (1972), and *Letters: A Novel* (1979)" (Punday 596).

A second hypothesis (indeed, something of a corollary to the account of literary history provided above) is that periods of aesthetic transition might be identifiable through the number of significant observer-hero narratives they produce. The evidence for this becomes especially compelling when we take into account those features of the genre that suggest two representational modes in conflict. At the level of content, the two-character narrative structure, in offering an extended comparison of differing personalities channeled through the representing consciousness of one, allows for a correlative contrast between worldviews, a contrast that can be taken as exemplary on a wider level than simply the lives of individuals. Hence, the contrast between narrator and hero can register the pressure of the new against the resistance of the old, or it can offer something more like a dialectic of two intellectual tendencies in a particular era. It can provide a contrast between two modes of social life, or between more fundamental modes of perception or ontology. Registering at the level of discourse, the contrast can suggest how particular conventions of representation struggle to depict certain ideas and figures, and the narrative arc of a specific observer-hero text can demonstrate a shift toward new modes of understanding and new representational possibilities. These shifts are often explicitly felt and described by the narrator, meaning that, as Buell notes, "observer-hero narratives are forever moving beyond the narrative level into discursive meditation," a realm in which "plot becomes eclipsed by commentary" (99). In this way, observer-hero narratives often attempt to allegorize their own interpretation, suggesting "their ulterior significance or implication" within the text itself (100), and thus allowing historical variations in the narrator's interpretive assumptions and representational moves to indicate the major concerns, and contradictions, of different periods.

For example, Marlow's depiction of Kurtz in *Heart of Darkness* allows the narrator (and the reader) to glimpse the possibilities of amoral power that the official colonial narrative of the late nineteenth century wished to deny, while simultaneously invoking the epistemological uncertainty that will come to be associated with the modernist worldview. Similarly, Nick Carraway, in his evocation of Jay Gatsby, comes to recognize the social contradictions masked by the pursuit of the American dream at the same time as he privileges an epiphanic modernist aesthetic, most notably in the scenes at Gatsby's parties. In *Doctor Faustus*, Adrian Leverkühn embodies for Serenus Zeitblom the painfully ambiguous relation of art and politics in an era of creeping totalitarianism, and Zeitblom's plodding tale of genius likewise suggests the incommensurability of two kinds of art. In *The End of the Road*, the contrast between Jacob Horner and Joe Morgan has its roots in their competing philosophical orientations toward the world, displayed in their inhabitance of different language games. In all of these cases, the novel in question can be seen both as a presaging of change and as a symptom of that change, marking in the contrasts between observer and hero the tensions, both cultural and representational, that informed the context in which the text was written.

Both Bruffee and Buell underplay these historical shifts in the meaning and morphology of observer-hero narrative, preferring to describe the genre in terms that emphasize aspects that all its examples share. This is to some extent a byproduct of the need to classify the genre for the first time, to participate in what Wellek and Warren, in their theory of genre, call "the discovery, and the dissemination, of a new grouping, a new generic pattern" (227). Both Bruffee and Buell see the genre as developing in response to a set of identifiable historical factors in the nineteenth century, but then treat it as a relatively static formation throughout the twentieth century. In doing so, they also favor epistemological concerns over ideological ones, more or less ignoring socio-cultural perspectives on genre that were emerging in the period in which their work appeared, for instance in the growing influence of Bakhtinian theory, the political criticism of Jameson, or perspectives on the relation between genre and gender offered by the work of feminist critics.[14] Most notably for my immediate purposes here, Bruffee, and to a lesser extent Buell, overlook the particular role played by the genre of observer-hero narrative in the American literary tradition. In choosing to begin his history of elegiac romance with a discussion of Conrad, rather than Hawthorne, Melville or Poe 50 years earlier, Bruffee can make a case for the genre as a specifically twentieth-century phenomenon, and therefore coincident with a post-heroic period: "heroism and hero-worship have ceased to be viable themes in Western literature. Together they are a (largely nineteenth-century) delusion, and both have been discredited in the twentieth century" (*Elegiac* 15). It is no coincidence that in downplaying the hero's role in favor of the observer, the "exemplary modern figure," and in relegating nineteenth-century examples in favor of post-Conradian ones, Bruffee also glosses over the American dimension. The theme of heroism has played a particularly important role in the US context, and as the prominence of novels written by American authors in the discussion above indicates—and as Buell recognizes in an aside (94)—observer-hero narrative has played a conspicuous role in the American literary tradition.

III Observer-hero narrative: The American dimension

David Minter's *The Interpreted Design as a Structural Principle in American Prose* (1969) offers a close analog to the studies by Bruffee and Buell discussed above, but one that focuses, as its title suggests, solely on American texts. Alluding to characters from Hawthorne's *The Blithedale Romance*, Minter explains that "interpreted design" is his term for "works structured by the juxtaposition of two characters, one a man of design or designed action, a Hollingsworth, who dominates the action of his world, the other a man of interpretation, a Coverdale, through whose interpreting mind and voice the story of the man of design comes to meet us" (3–4). Unlike Bruffee and Buell, who are concerned solely with a formal structure in narrative fiction, Minter's study treats as examples of interpreted design not only novels by Hawthorne, Fitzgerald and Faulkner, but also a range of Puritan jeremiads, as well as autobiographies by Edwards, Franklin, Thoreau and Henry Adams (in these autobiographies, Minter explains, "the characteristic dialectic is between older (investigating-interpreting) and younger (designing-acting) versions of the same man" [21]). Although Minter makes clear that interpreted design should be understood as a response to "cultural and intellectual developments that are modern rather than merely American" (7), he nonetheless notes the genre's relevance to "America's faith in a fluid world that invites man to shape his fate" (23), and also to "America's uneasiness with her success" (25). Minter even goes so far as to generalize interpreted design as a figure for the history of America itself: "A part of what has troubled America is closely related to the themes central to the interpreted design: namely that in building, perhaps grandly and at least stupendously, her builders have succeeded only by failing; that they have built as they have only by failing repeatedly to build as they had intended" (23).

This critical tendency to generalize outward, from claims about literary texts to claims about "America" as a homogenous concept and unified historical agent, should remind us that we are in the territory here of the myth-and-symbol school of literary criticism, an approach that dominated the discipline of American Studies while it was at its height in the early postwar era. Critical texts of this period such as Henry Nash Smith's *Virgin Land* (1950), R. W. B. Lewis's *The American Adam* (1955), and Ihab Hassan's *Radical Innocence* (1961) established the figure of the quester-hero as central to the mythology of America and "the American mind." Theodore Gross's *The Heroic Ideal in American Literature* (1971) is a study almost parodically in this vein, opening with a series of breathless declarations: "Literary heroes dramatize the moral texture of a country. Creations of the imagination, they embody the unspoken ideals, the undesired terrors, the dream life and the mundane existence of their readers. Heroes represent a people, and by discovering the meaning of their character, by returning to the roots of their behavior, we discern the moral figure in the tapestry of a nation" (v). The grand abstractions found in these sentences, which implicitly connect modern American literature with Greek and Roman epic, were already under serious critical pressure by the time Gross published his book. In 1972, Bruce Kuklick published "Myth and Symbol in American Studies," a hard-hitting critique of the philosophical idealism of the myth-and-symbol school, and in "Paradigm Dramas," a 1979 essay that inaugurated what would become an institution in American Studies—the synthetic state-of-the-field article—Gene Wise argued that "American Studies has never recovered from the earthquake-like jolts of the sixties, and the consciousness those events forced upon the culture" (314). The theme of heroism, in the new post-sixties context of cultural pluralism, began to look more like a repressive ideological fiction than an expression of the moral imagination of a nation. As a consequence, rather than celebrate the figure of the hero, critical treatments on the theme published in more recent years—such as David Simmons's *The Anti-Hero in the American Novel* (2008) or Jonathan Mitchell's *Revisions of the American Adam* (2011)—have tended to analyze the function of heroic representations in particular periods, adopting a historicist methodology that firmly denies R. W. B. Lewis's claim that the American hero is "an individual emancipated from history" (5).

To invoke the theme of the hero in a discussion of American literature, consequently, is to tread perilously close to a set of now rejected assumptions about the relationship between literature and national character. And yet, as many recent studies also testify, the ideology of the heroic individual has had a serious role to play in American culture, right up to the present day.[15] It is with this in mind that it becomes possible to regard observer-hero narrative—with the critical distance it offers through its narrative division between story and discourse—as a genre ideally suited to express, and to critically engage with, the anxieties that accompany American culture's hagiographic streak. One does not have to view the hero as a representative of the soul of the American people, as Minter does, to understand the cultural work the genre can accomplish.[16] Taking this attitude toward observer-hero narrative also allows us to specify further the historical conditions of the genre's emergence, building upon Buell's analysis. Such a move is required because although, as Buell argues, the Romantic interest in consciousness, allied with a range of technical developments in related genres, can be held responsible for the wider emergence of observer-hero narrative in the nineteenth century, this set of factors hardly explains the striking fact that so many of the genre's major early exponents—Irving, Poe, Hawthorne, Melville—hailed from the United States.

This fact may, instead, owe something to the comparatively *late* arrival of Romantic ideology in the United States. Romanticism, with its emphasis on individual selfhood and private interiority, was preceded in American culture by the ideology of republicanism, which constrained representations of the self through an emphasis on the civic, the public, the representative man. There were no American romantic autobiographers contemporary with Goethe, Rousseau, or Wordsworth; instead, early biographies and autobiographies of founding fathers such as Washington and Franklin presented them primarily as public figures, with depictions of their private selves shaped ideologically to emphasize consistency with the ends of civic virtue. These men were represented as heroes of action, akin to the heroes of ancient Greece and Rome, yet they existed in a modern republic in which, as Clive Bush argues in *The Dream of Reason* (1977), official thinking had it that "representative ideology had supplanted the social role of the hero" (17). This was far from the truth, according to Bush, a fact demonstrated by the hagiographic character of the early national period's biographies, public portraits, statues, and philosophies of history. Recognizing an inaugurating paradox of early American republicanism—that the founding fathers were exceptional men, but also men who were supposed simply to represent qualities embodied by the collective—Bush is led to ask a series of broader questions: "What is the role of the hero in democracy? What is the nature of individual and social sovereignty? What is meant by *representation* in art and in the drama of state? Are they connected? What is the relation of the spectator to the drama of representative democracy?" (x). With the emergence of American Romanticism, these questions and others like them would be addressed by the work of writers who had been born into this early national, republican milieu: by Emerson's *Representative Men* (1855), for instance, where Napoleon plays the new role of hero as omnipotent bureaucrat; by Hawthorne's *The Scarlet Letter* (1850), so obviously concerned with the disparity between public and private perceptions of individual selves, and the effect this disparity can have on a community; and, most notably of all, by Herman Melville's *Moby-Dick* (1851).[17]

It is this latter novel, the first full-length example of American observer-hero narrative, that provides what Bush deems "the most complex and interesting insight into the representative hero's role" (51). Oddly, however, in discussing Ahab's character Bush ignores Ishmael's function as the narrative prism through which the ambivalent hero is presented to us. Among the many recent considerations of the novel that correct this oversight, Anthony Hutchison's *Writing the Republic* (2007) sees in *Moby-Dick*'s divided narrative a paradigm for the political novel as it would go on to develop in the United States. Hutchison begins with a problem of content rather than form, from an interest in defining "the political novel as a discrete entity" in US literature (xviii). He nonetheless finds a specific narrative structure—what I have been calling observer-hero narrative—arising again and again in the political novels that are his object of study: not only in *Moby-Dick*, but in Lionel Trilling's *The Middle of the Journey* (1947), Gore Vidal's *Burr* (1973), Russell Banks's *Cloudsplitter* (1998), and Philip Roth's "American trilogy" (1997–2000). Hutchison does not give a specific name to this divided narrative structure, but his study offers a thoughtful analysis of its function in the American political setting. Quoting the "essential republican principle" given in the work of William R. Everdell—"that no one person shall rule the community, that everyone shall have a part in the public's business" (176)—Hutchison writes that the idea of republicanism, a founding political doctrine in the United States, is figured in these novels in "the tension between what we might describe as a 'conflicted narrator' and an ambivalently viewed central character who is the prime focus of the narrative" (174).

Hutchison explains how this structure, and the tension it exemplifies, distinguishes the American novel from its most prominent counterparts. Whereas the European political novel is "democratic" in its depiction of middle-class values and social manners, and the Russian political novel is "tsarist" in its tendency to prioritize the single individual as the source of moral and aesthetic power, "what makes American political novels primarily 'republican' rather than democratic in character is their foregrounding of this central tension between the two narrating and narrated personages: the man of action and the man of thought, the novel's 'executive' power and its (unacknowledged) legislator" (182).[18] Hutchison's conception of how this narrative structure functions in an American political context—with the narrator as metaphorical senator and the hero as president—allows him to explain basic conventions of the observer-hero genre in his own terms: "Such novels, furthermore, insofar as they seek to distribute or 'balance' narrative power, deploy their narrators in a way that recalls the upper chamber's most important responsibility in a republic—to provide the final barrier against dictatorship. This might go some way to explaining why, though the narrated character usually dies by the close of the narrative, the narrator almost always survives" (177).

Hutchison's description of this genre as "republican" is not intended to suggest that the political values of divided American narratives remain always the same. Rather, "republican" designates for Hutchison the way a mainstream tradition of liberalism clashes with a range of competing values at different historical moments: "American ideals, whether republican, liberal, Protestant, radical, or neoconservative, are filtered through this novelistic form as a means of digesting the meaning of social and cultural change for the health of the polity" (184). Hutchison's study is significant, therefore, for the way it tracks the changing political meaning of the observer-hero genre in American literature. From its nineteenth-century emergence to the late twentieth century and beyond, each instantiation of the genre will figure a different set of historical–political values in conflict, a different set of problems to solve. *Writing the Republic* provides a good example of how the genre of observer-hero narrative can be regarded in morphological terms, as employing a set of conventions in a flexible manner to engage with different stages in American society and culture, addressing the core intellectual concerns of each era. It is with something like this model in mind—though leaving to one side the particular categories of political thinking that Hutchison employs—that I wish to argue for novels of the 1990s as representing a new and important departure for the observer-hero genre in American literature. Before moving to the specific intellectual and theoretical concerns I want to foreground in relation to these novels, however, there remains a further important set of issues in need of addressing.

IV Critical issues: Race, gender, genre

The main critical studies cited in the previous two sections—Bruffee's *Elegiac Romance*, Buell's "Observer-Hero Narrative," Reed's *Meditations on the Hero*, Minter's *The Interpreted Design*, Hutchison's *Writing the Republic*—are written by white males and are overwhelmingly concerned with literary texts written by white males. *American Fiction in Transition*, in taking as its four case studies novels by Roth, Auster, Eugenides, and Doctorow, does not disrupt this pattern.[19] Moreover, issues of race are not touched upon by any of the above-named critics, and only Bruffee makes reference to questions of gender. "Elegiac romance," he writes, "appears to be, until recently at any rate, a conspicuously 'male' form of fiction, used to work out peculiarly male problems of hero-worship, rivalry, fear of impotence, and fear of adult relations and responsibilities" (*Elegiac* 211). Nevertheless, he warns, "to say that elegiac romance is a form of fiction limited to stories about distinctively male sorts of problems and anxieties would severely misrepresent the genre," given that it also deals with a set of universal experiences: "death, loss, regeneration, and emotional maturation" (212). It certainly seems true, with these qualities in mind, that there should be nothing to prevent writers who are not white and/or not male from employing the genre to deal with their concerns. And it is clearly the case that there exist examples of observer-hero narratives written by non-white and non-male authors, with characters who are non-white and non-male (I have named a number of these already). Nevertheless, the vast majority of well-known examples of the genre are by and about white men. Why is this the case? Is there something about observer-hero narrative that makes it especially suited to representing the lives and concerns of white men, as Bruffee suggests? Or is there a gender and racial bias operating in this criticism, which leads it to ignore the claims to canonicity of observer-hero narratives written by non-white and non-male authors? Or, thinking more radically and reflexively, is the retrospective construction of a genre itself a critical phenomenon with Anglocentric and patriarchal overtones? And does my own gesture of associating observer-hero narrative with aesthetic transition simply reproduce a patriarchal story of literary history?

These are large questions, and in attempting to address them in this section I consider two observer-hero narratives, one by an African–American male, Ernest Gaines, the other by a white American woman, Joan Didion. The aim here is not to have these examples stand in for all texts by non-white or non-male authors. Rather, I wish to consider the challenges these particular texts present both to the specific concerns of my study and to generic analysis more broadly, and whether and in what ways these challenges can be generalized beyond the particular examples invoked. This critical maneuver will lead me in the final part of this section to questions about the literary category of genre itself: how we should understand the term, and what we are doing when we consider a range of texts as examples of a particular genre, in this case the genre of observer-hero narrative.

Turning first to the issue of race, I do so through the lens of a novel of the 1990s that might well have formed a larger part of this study had my concerns been slightly different. Ernest J. Gaines's *A Lesson Before Dying* (1993) is narrated by Grant Wiggins, a college-educated black schoolteacher in rural Louisiana, and is set a few years after the Second World War. Wiggins tells the story of the trial and execution of Jefferson, a poor and uneducated local man in his early twenties, who accidentally becomes involved in a robbery in which a white storekeeper is shot and killed. At the trial, which opens the novel, Jefferson's white lawyer defends his client's innocence by insisting on his base stupidity and racial inferiority, his status as "a thing that acts on command" (7). The lawyer tells the jury that he "would just as soon put a hog in the electric chair" (8), and the comparison of himself to a farm animal echoes in Jefferson's consciousness throughout his time in prison as he awaits his execution. Wiggins, the narrator, does not attend the trial in person, but the novel opens with a line that could function as a synecdoche for the narrator's role in observer-hero narrative more generally, in the way it frames a mode of narration that will combine first-person meditation with third-person reportage: "I was not there, yet I was there" (3).

A Lesson Before Dying is certainly a novel obsessed by questions of heroism. Most obviously, Jefferson's name, in recalling one of the republic's founding fathers, suggests a potential grandeur to his character. Yet the name is evidently also chosen for its thorny racial overtones, bearing in mind Thomas Jefferson's slave-holding and alleged fathering of children with one of his female slaves.[20] This is typical of how heroism is treated in the novel—it is a complicated affair—and much of this complication derives from the way the character of Jefferson fails to match the dominant conventions of the observer-hero genre. While Wiggins plays the traditional role of thinker and seeker in the novel—"I'm still trying to find out how a man should live," he tells his lover Vivian—Jefferson cannot play the usual role dictated by the genre, a fact Wiggins summarizes in the same breath: "Am I supposed to tell someone how to die who has never lived?" (31). Jefferson is not "a do-er and a be-er," in Buell's terms, nor a "figure of design," in Minter's; he is instead an innocent and passive victim. Yet the entire story turns for Wiggins on the question of whether Jefferson can come to face death in a heroic manner.

Wiggins's concern with this question escalates throughout the novel. While at university Wiggins had heard a lecture on James Joyce's *Dubliners* by a visiting professor, a "little Irishman" who praised in particular the story "Ivy Day in the Committee Room": "Regardless of race, regardless of class, the story was universal, he said" (89). Wiggins initially reads the story with frustration: "I read the story and reread the story, but I still could not find the universality that the little Irishman had spoken of." It is only years later, after so many visits to bars, barbershops, and community events, that Wiggins comes to understand the meaning of the Irishman's words: "Then I began to listen, to listen closely to how they talked about their heroes, how they talked about the dead and about how great the dead had once been. I heard it everywhere" (90). While Wiggins is relatively alienated from his community—he will not go to church, and often complains bitterly about the faults of his neighbors—this talk of heroes past speaks powerfully to his racial consciousness. The reader learns that in his bedroom, "A photocollage of Frederick Douglass, Abraham Lincoln, and Booker T. Washington hung over the mantel" (104), and during one conversation with Vivian, Wiggins laments the history of his race, and particularly the performance of its men:

> We black men have failed to protect our women since the time of slavery. We stay here in the South and are broken, or we run away and leave them alone to look after their children and themselves. So each time a male child is born, they hope he will be the one to change this vicious circle—which he never does. [. . .] What [Jefferson's grandmother] wants is for him, Jefferson, and me to change everything that has been going on for three hundred years. (166–7)[21]

Wiggins's characteristic response in the novel to the racial and masculine inheritance he here articulates is a combination of bitter cynicism and angry violence. In one early scene, while teaching in his classroom in the local church, he strikes a child's head from behind with a wooden ruler. In his lack of evident remorse for this action, and in his harsh verbal treatment of a young cousin of Jefferson who is also in the class—"I didn't apologize for what I had said, nor did I show any sympathy for her crying" (40)—the reader sees the depths of Wiggins's anger and frustration, while not being allowed to sympathize wholly with him. Later, Wiggins is involved in a violent brawl in a bar, and as she tends his wounds Vivian angrily chides his false heroism. But when she tells him "You could have walked out of there," he replies, "Can Jefferson walk out of where he is?" (205), and the reader realizes the central role Jefferson's plight now plays in Wiggins's psyche. Indeed, as the execution draws nearer, Wiggins begins to associate his own secular redemption with Jefferson's willingness to face death with bravery. While the narrator declines to attend the execution, Reverend Ambrose, a pious local pastor who has been Wiggins's colleague and rival in the attempt to teach Jefferson a lesson before dying, is there in person, and the narrator remarks: "He is brave, braver than I, braver than any of them—except you, I hope. My faith is in you, Jefferson" (249). At the novel's conclusion, Wiggins's faith is rewarded, when Jefferson's white warden Paul (named no doubt for the converted disciple of Jesus) tells the narrator of the "transformation" he has witnessed at the execution scene: "Straight he walked. I'm a witness. Straight he walked" (254). Yet if Jefferson's transformation into a noble hero at the end of his life is the core event of the story, then the observer-narrator's own transformation is also confirmed by the novel's closing lines, which return us to the scene of Wiggins's earlier violence as he takes his leave of Paul and re-enters the school: "I turned from him and went into the church. Irene Cole told the class to rise, with their shoulders back. I went up to the desk and turned to face them. I was crying" (256).

Preoccupied by heroic themes, Gaines's novel also highlights some of the epistemological concerns that will frame my primary case studies in *American Fiction in Transition*. The battle between the religious and secular worldviews of Ambrose and Wiggins—a battle we will see staged again in *The Waterworks*—is played out as a problem of knowledge when the question of Jefferson's interior state of mind arises. "Him? What's he thinking?" Reverend Ambrose asks Wiggins. "What's he thinking deep in him? Deep in you, what you think?" Wiggins's reply acknowledges his ongoing struggle to understand his own depths, not to mention the depths of another: "Who knows what someone else is thinking? They say one thing, they may be thinking something else—who can tell?" (100). Yet despite the emergence, at various points in the novel, of these concerns with the limits of knowledge regarding oneself and others, it is significant that the complexity of the hero's motivations in acting as he does—a complexity at the center of the novels I deal with in my four chapters—plays no real role in *A Lesson Before Dying*. The hero's key action, when it does come in Jefferson's final brave confrontation with death, is portrayed in religious and political terms, certainly, but it is not understood to be a mysterious thing, an event offering endless problems to the interpretive goals of the narrator (as will be the case, for instance, in *The Virgin Suicides*).

Furthermore, *A Lesson Before Dying* does not transfer its epistemological concerns into formal questions of narration and representation to the extent that the novels my chapters focus upon do, and Gaines's novel is even less engaged by the postmodern themes and debates I highlight. The rural Louisiana "quarter" in which most of the novel takes place does not resemble the urban and suburban settings of the novels by Roth, Auster, Eugenides, and Doctorow, and the racial concerns that occupy Gaines draw little on postmodern ideas of identity performance; indeed, in *A Lesson Before Dying* notions of racial inheritance are relied upon to provide the core drama of the story (whereas in *The Human Stain*, for instance, such notions will be problematized). At the level of style—and as the allusion to *Dubliners* might suggest—Wiggins's narrative is one of "scrupulous meanness," in Joyce's phrase, exemplifying the minimalist conventions re-popularized in American writing by Raymond Carver's fiction of the 1970s and 1980s. Although mostly sidelined, questions of representation are thematized at one moment in the novel, however, when in the third-to-last chapter Gaines breaks the narrative frame to offer the reader an unmediated excerpt from the prison diary Jefferson had begun writing at Wiggins's instigation. In the tradition of Twain, Faulkner, and Zora Neale Hurston, the prose in this chapter mimics the spoken African–American voice: "mr wigin you say you like what i got here but you say you stil cant giv me a a jus b cause you say I aint gone deep in me yet an you kno i can if I try hard an when i ax you what you mean deep in me you say jus say whats on my mind so one day you can be save an you can save the chiren" (228).

This juxtaposition of Wiggins's crisp prose and Jefferson's struggles with linguistic self-expression indicates that *A Lesson Before Dying* is indeed interested in transition, but that such transition is to be understood primarily in terms of race and class progress.[22] Rather than a novel overtly concerned with the implications of its own narrative form and sequencing—a description applicable to the novels by Roth, Auster, Eugenides, and Doctorow—*A Lesson Before Dying* might better be read as employing the observer-hero genre in order to reflect upon what Erica Edwards, in a recent study, identifies as "a tension that has shaped African American letters over the last century: a simultaneous investment in and critique of charismatic leadership" (xiii).[23] On this reading the subject matter would mandate the form, rather than the other way around, but further questions would be raised. Is *A Lesson Before Dying* then to be read as nostalgic for traditional masculinity, and thus guilty, in Edwards's terms, of "reducing a heterogeneous black freedom struggle to a top-down narrative of Great

Man leadership" (xv)? Alternatively, does the novel critique this model—"register[ing] the faultlines," as Edwards puts it (xvi)—by positing a true hero as something other than a charismatic leader figure? Or to frame this dichotomy slightly differently: is it better to say that Gaines *employs* the resources of a literary genre to do cultural work in *A Lesson Before Dying*, or rather to say that his novel *subverts* the genre by departing from some of its norms? Although critical work in race studies would offer plenty of tools to address this question, I turn now to the issue of gender, in large part because a prominent strand of recent scholarship has focused on the nexus of gender and genre.

One significant observer-hero narrative that has occasioned debate on gender grounds is Joan Didion's *A Book of Common Prayer* (1977). When Bruffee states in *Elegiac Romance* that the narrative genre he calls elegiac romance should not be seen as "a form of fiction limited to stories about distinctively male sorts of problems and anxieties" (212), he is explicitly responding to an article on Didion's novel by Patricia Merivale. In her essay, Merivale considers *A Book of Common Prayer* in light of Bruffee's description of elegiac romance, but argues that the novel subverts this "almost exclusively 'masculine' genre" in important ways (45). Making an extended comparison to Graham Greene's *The Quiet American*—an archetypal elegiac romance/ observer-hero narrative that, like Didion's novel, features an American protagonist displaced to the "squalid tropics" (47)—Merivale claims that *A Book of Common Prayer* is by far the more difficult novel to interpret: "the elliptical style and deliberate ambiguities of both author and narrator make plot, let alone significance, less than instantaneously accessible" (45). In *The Quiet American*, Thomas Fowler tells his story of Aiden Pyle for clear reasons—complicity, contrition, confession, in Merivale's summary—and the form of the novel is straightforward: "Fowler simply writes a book, which is, in itself, a quite unproblematic activity for him" (52). In *A Book of Common Prayer*, Grace Strasser-Medina's reasons for narrating the story of Charlotte Douglas are not nearly so palpable, and the process of telling appears far more intractable. "I will be her witness," Grace informs the reader in the novel's opening line (Didion 11); "I have not been the witness I wanted to be" is how the novel concludes (272). Yet why Grace should want to be Charlotte's witness is never made fully clear, nor is it obvious why she feels she has failed in that task. Merivale's conclusion is that "Didion's is not only a far more ironic text than Greene's but also a more self-reflexive one. Fowler's book is true, as far as he knows the truth. Grace's is about what she cannot discover or make sense of; if there is one mystery even darker to her than Charlotte's nature, it is her own" (52).[24]

Merivale consequently suggests that *A Book of Common Prayer* does not simply replace the conventional male observer-hero relationship of elegiac romance with an exact female equivalent: rather, many formal and semantic elements of the genre are subverted by what she terms Didion's "distinctively 'feminine' variant of the contemporary identity quest" (45). According to Bruffee, however, "[c]ertain characteristics of Didion's novel seem more typical of its genre than Merivale allows," and he goes on to list these characteristics, concluding that the novel conforms to the central generic device whereby the narrator, through telling her story, exposes "elements of her inner self that had heretofore lain safely hidden from conscious awareness" (214n9). Bruffee's discussion of *A Book of Common Prayer* forms part of a chapter of *Elegiac Romance* entitled "Radical Variations," but how radical these variations are permitted to be is open to question: Bruffee wants to resist the notion that the genre is truly subverted by them.[25] Rather, he reabsorbs Didion's novel back into the generic frame by dividing elegiac romance into Thomas Rosenmeyer's two currents of pastoral elegy—one where nature revives, the other where nature dies in sympathy for the person who has died. *A Book of Common Prayer* belongs in the second of these two currents, and, in keeping with his Frye-an methodology, Bruffee speculates as to whether Grace's closeness to death in telling her tale might be a constitutive mythic feature of the feminine version of the genre. He calls for more investigation of this line of inquiry (214n9).[26]

This quarrel between Merivale and Bruffee plays out a characteristic critical debate concerning the politics of gender in the analysis of literary genre. In an essay surveying this territory, Mary Eagleton notes that "[f]eminist criticism tends to be divided between those who see the shift from hero to heroine as an important political move, and those who doubt whether a change of personnel alters fundamentally the aesthetic and social values of the form" (253). Merivale adopts something like the first position, arguing that Didion's appropriation of the genre—"Didion seems to be the first to make that central relationship a female bonding," Merivale notes (46), ignoring the claims of, among others, Willa Cather—results in a reshaping of elegiac romance to feminist ends. Bruffee, in a kind of non-feminist confirmation of the second position, argues that the aesthetic and social values of the form trump the gender of the author or characters. "What some critics find more subversive," Eagleton continues, "is feminism's questioning of realist forms of writing. To query the truth, coherence and resolution of realism is to undermine the symbolic order" (253). Taking this approach (an understated version of which we can also ascribe to Merivale) would lead us to say that Grace's inability to draw clear lessons from the story she tells of Charlotte's life and death would block the urge toward meaning and mourning characteristic of a patriarchal metaphysics: "the meaning of that sojourn continues to elude me," as Grace acknowledges (Didion 21). What this more radical interpretation would share in common with other feminist positions, however, is the view that observer-hero narrative (or elegiac romance) is constitutively a masculine genre. From a feminist perspective, then, the patriarchal subject positions of observer and hero necessarily become displaced in various ways when female authors employ—or subvert—the genre, and/or when the key narrative roles are filled by female characters.

It is only a step from here to the claim that the very notion of genre is itself a patriarchal construct. This is the position adopted by Mary Jacobus in a well-known essay-review of Alastair Fowler's *Kinds of Literature: An Introduction to the Theory of Genres and Modes* (1982). Critiquing the use of the word "theory" in Fowler's subtitle, Jacobus claims that "Fowler's book is an instance of the refusal of theory in the interests of maintaining an ultimately conservative view of literary history" (47). Rather than be aligned, the terms "genre" and "theory" should instead be opposed to one another, claims Jacobus: "Genre in effect does away with the need for theory since it organizes literature in the forms in which we already know it; recognizability and an unbroken line of descent are the final criteria, and literary hierarchies remain unchanged" (47).

Such a repetition of established hierarchies through patriarchal descent makes the politics of genre "implicitly conservative" (55); likewise, Fowler's appropriation of Wittgenstein's notion of "family resemblance" as a tool for establishing genres fails to acknowledge that "genre is always impure, always 'mothered' as well as fathered, and that 'lodged within the heart of the law itself [is] a law of impurity or a principle of contamination'" (56).

What does it mean for a genre to be "mothered" as well as "fathered"? The quotation embedded in Jacobus's last line here is taken from "The Law of Genre," an influential 1980 essay by Jacques Derrida that also provides Jacobus with the epigraph to her review. In this essay, Derrida begins playfully by stating a law and promising to obey it: "Genres are not to be mixed. I will not mix genres" (223). The law that "genres are not to be mixed" demands, according to Derrida, a logic (such as Fowler's) that would strictly classify genres in order to maintain order and separation: "As soon as the word *genre* is sounded, as soon as it is heard, as soon as one attempts to conceive it, a limit is drawn. And when a limit is established, norms and interdictions are not far behind" (224). These norms, interdictions and limits represent the law of the father, yet for something to come into being, to be given birth to, there must be a prior intermixture of mother and father, rather than descent from the father alone. When genres are "mothered" in this way, they ironically give birth to the law—"or more exactly, to begin with, to the representatives of law, to those who wield authority" (246)—and this law in turn prohibits acknowledgment of the very intermixture necessary for such birth to occur.

But for Derrida, this law—this principle of non-contamination, of generic purity—is inevitably put into question by what he calls "the logic of the example" (227). Every text that is birthed can only become an example of a genre by inscribing itself with a mark or gesture that does not itself belong to the genre in question; as Derrida puts it, "The trait that marks membership inevitably divides" (227). The need to mark itself, or to be marked, as part of a genre means that any text is both inside and outside that genre at the same time: "The re-mark of belonging does not belong" (230). And so, for Derrida, the question of genre is never one of belonging, but of participation:

> a text would not *belong* to any genre. Every text *participates* in one or several genres, there is no genreless text, there is always a genre and genres, yet such participation never amounts to belonging. And not because of abundant overflowing or a free, anarchic and unclassifiable productivity, but because of the *trait* of participation itself, because of the effect of the code and of the generic mark. In marking itself generically, a text unmarks itself. (230)

What, then, are the implications of treating observer-hero narrative as a literary genre? Despite the inevitability of "norms and interdictions" in any critical inclusion and exclusion of certain texts, if the novels read in *American Fiction in Transition* are considered participants in a genre, rather than members or strict examples of it, then we can see these texts as transitional in one further way—they mark the transitional state of genre in general, its citation of a law only to participate anew in resisting that law's application. This means that the distinctions I have been asking about in this section, for example whether a racially inscribed or gendered text might be employing or subverting the genre, can be queried on the basis that they imply a set of static conventions identified with an institutional law. If we conceive of texts as singular acts of participation, then we should reconceive the notion of genre as a dynamic concept, put to work differently and remade with each example.

In a similar way, my readings of individual novels in the chapters of this study should be understood not simply as exemplifying an overarching theoretical methodology, but as acts that participate in a developing critical process. Each of my four chapters begins with a prologue highlighting a concept investigated in Derrida's texts—secrecy, testimony, narcissism, and justice, respectively. The reading of each novel in five main parts then attempts to follow Derrida in treating literary criticism as an event of countersignature, a response to the singularity of a work that cannot be dominated by a pre-formulated set of laws. Such a response to singularity centrally involves an attempt to do justice to literary form, because while, as Derrida notes, literary texts always inscribe metaphysical theses in their content, and can thus be analyzed rigorously in terms of that content, in formal terms "poetry and literature have as a common feature that they suspend the 'thetic' naivety of a transcendent reading" ("This Strange" 45). Taking to heart Derrida's privileging of the formal practice of writing over the content of an abstractable argument—"Sometimes theoretical arguments as such, even if they are in the form of critique, are less 'destabilizing,' or let's just say alarming, for 'metaphysical assumptions' than one or other 'way of writing'" (50)—should result in a methodology that is continuously in transition, open to reshaping by the very examples it cites in order to propagate its lawfulness.

V The intellectual background: Derrida, Jameson, narrative, and decision

The novels I am concerned with in *American Fiction in Transition* participate in the genre of observer-hero narrative in the manner described above, drawing on some of the genre's core features while extending its possibilities. In each text, the observer-narrator assumes a mediating responsibility for the story he tells, collating and interpreting information, and thus acting as a surrogate for both the reader and the writer of the text. *The Human Stain* features Philip Roth's regular narrator Nathan Zuckerman telling the story of his late friend Coleman Silk. *Leviathan* is the story of one novelist, Benjamin Sachs, told by another, Peter Aaron. In *The Virgin Suicides*, the lives and deaths of the Lisbon sisters are narrated by a group of middle-aged men who were once their youthful contemporaries. *The Waterworks* tells of three protagonists, a journalist, a scientist, and a detective, each competing for the role of hero in the tale told by an old newspaper editor, McIlvaine.

As we can see from these single-line summaries, my study moves not in chronological order of publication, but from what might be considered a classic observer-hero narrative in *The Human Stain*, to increasingly less standard versions of the generic frame in succeeding chapters. In addition, my chapters move backward in time, with the action of each novel set earlier than the one before. The novels by Roth, Auster, and Eugenides are all narrated from a point in the 1990s, but the story of the hero takes place, respectively, in the 1990s, the 1980s, and the 1970s, with historical incidents from each decade framing the events of the narrative and deepening the concern with transition. *The Waterworks* then jumps back a century, to a set of events from the 1870s narrated retrospectively from an indeterminate point about 30 years later. Putting consideration of Doctorow's novel to one side for now, it is also notable that the first three novels named above share an overtly tragic outline. Each contains five chapters, mimicking the five-act structure of a Shakespearean tragedy. Each features a hero figure who attains a high status in the eyes of the narrator, before falling from that height (often literally) and ending in death. But although each narrator, dwelling frequently on questions of agency and fate, highlights the tragic vein in his telling, and in certain ways attempts to make the narrative adhere to this outline, each finds that the story he tells comes to challenge the tragic alignment. In each case, the narrator self-reflexively comments upon this challenge, drawing attention to a crisis he confronts, a crisis that centers most crucially on the problem of representing and comprehending a major decision the protagonist has made. Alternative possibilities for representing the decision, and incorporating it into a narrative, are foregrounded; broadly speaking, tragic and modern perspectives clash. And in the failure of either of these two perspectives to dominate and resolve the problem, a third possibility presents itself, one that emphasizes the potential incoherence of all attempts to narrate and understand the decision in a linear, realist, causal fashion. This possibility can be described, in Jamesonian terms, as a postmodern understanding of the moment of decision as the "when-it-all-changed," the pure event.

American Fiction in Transition asks how we should read the relationship between these different perspectives on the hero's decision as they are framed through the narrator's point of view. My contention is that, rather than present the postmodern understanding as trumping other possibilities, these four novels oscillate between these perspectives on moments of transition in an individual life, and do so in ways that index the problem of conceiving transition more broadly, at the levels of theory, history, politics, and culture. It is with respect to these levels, in the final part of this introduction, that I wish to sketch a comparison between Jameson and Derrida that clarifies my choice to frame this study with reference to these thinkers. Both are major figures in the intellectual history of the late-twentieth-century United States, but I do not intend to draw a direct line of influence between their work and the novels that are the focus of my chapters. Instead, I want to argue that these American novels can be understood as immanent responses to a cultural situation defined by Jameson as postmodern, but that their response to that situation is better framed through Derrida's emphasis on undecidability than through Jameson's dialectical method. In order to make this argument, however, we need to understand in broader terms what is meant (at least in the case of these two thinkers) by dialectics and by undecidability, and how the two relate to one another.

Fredric Jameson is not interested simply in diagnosing the event-oriented consciousness of postmodernity; he also wants to offer a set of tools for dealing with its effects. In *The Political Unconscious*, his most influential work of criticism in this vein, Jameson affirms as his goal "a dialectical or totalizing, properly Marxist ideal of understanding" (10). This ideal is to be achieved using a method that identifies the forces of history as the repressed content of a literary text, figured for the critic by the text's surface antinomies and deeper contradictions. Throughout his *oeuvre*, Jameson utilizes a variety of terms to describe this approach, referring in different places to "totalization," "metacommentary," "dialectical criticism," and "cognitive mapping." While far from synonymous, these terms nonetheless point toward a structuring commitment or belief underlying all of Jameson's work. By achieving a totalizing or dialectical conception of the world-system, and by seeing it as one moment "within the unity of a single great collective story" (*Political* 19), Jameson contends that we will eventually be empowered to overturn that system. Yet in the discursive means used to achieve this goal lie a paradox, what in *Postmodernism* Jameson recognizes as a "Sartrean irony":

> What happens is that the more powerful the vision of some increasingly total system or logic—the Foucault of the prisons book is the obvious example—the more powerless the reader comes to feel. Insofar as the theorist wins, therefore, by constructing an increasingly closed and terrifying machine, to that very degree he loses, since the critical capacity of his work is thereby paralyzed, and the impulses of negation and revolt, not to speak of those of social transformation, are increasingly perceived as vain and trivial in the face of the model itself. (5–6)

Jameson's retort to what amounts here to an implicit gesture of self-criticism is to continually reiterate, across a great many of his texts, his belief that it is only through such processes as totalization, cognitive mapping, and the dialectic that we can find the grounds for a response. "I have felt," begins the paragraph following the quotation above, "that it was only in the light of some conception of a dominant cultural logic or hegemonic norm that genuine difference could be measured and assessed" (6). Yet the terms in which Jamesonian totalization has often been taken up and criticized—as overly hegemonic, as a repression rather than a valid assessment of difference—demonstrate the fine line the dialectical process threads.[27] Nevertheless, it is to this path that Jameson remains firmly committed: "If we do not achieve some general sense of a cultural dominant, then we fall back into a view of present history as sheer heterogeneity, random difference, a coexistence of distinct forces whose effectivity is undecidable" (6). The claim is that identifying the cultural dominant, in this case postmodernism, through a process of totalization will allow the emergence of "a capacity to act and struggle which is neutralized by our spatial as well as our social confusions" (54), the emergence of what Perry Anderson in his commentary on Jameson calls "[t]he collective agency necessary to confront this disorder" (Anderson 66).[28]

Yet how this response is to emerge, how transition can occur through the force of collective agency, is not entirely evident from Jameson's work. And this is not something Jameson denies: instead he sees it as a necessary symptom of the sociocultural situation of the postmodern present. Jameson's position here is clearest in the account he offers of the contemporary function of utopia. In *Postmodernism*, Jameson remarks that "the question of Utopia would seem to be a crucial test of what is left of our capacity to imagine change at all" (xvi). In a later text, he expands as follows: "The very political weakness of Utopia in previous generations—namely that it furnished nothing like an account of agency, nor did it have a coherent historical and practical-political picture of transition—now becomes a strength in a situation in which neither of these problems seems currently to offer candidates for a solution" (*Archaeologies* 232). Utopian thinking here replaces accounts of agency and transition, and Jameson often looks in his work to excavate the utopian content of popular culture as a kind of aesthetic figuration for the political resistance made impossible within the eternal present of postmodernity. Rather than naively celebrate its transforming positive force, however, Jameson has been careful to retain utopian thinking as a predominately negative mode of analysis. As he explained to an interviewer, "[m]y method in this area and in the utopian area generally has been a negative one, that is, it's to examine the blockages on the future and on the utopian impulse rather than to propose positive new utopian visions of the type the nineteenth century in its crucial utopian moments projected so brilliantly, from Fourier to Morris" ("Live Jameson" 131). This critical method leaves the reader not in a fundamentally altered future, as a conventional reading of the various science fictions Jameson discusses might suggest, but once again in the present, with our consciousness of political limitation heightened by the contact with utopia. As such, for Jameson, "Utopia's deepest subject is precisely our inability to conceive it, our incapacity to produce it as a vision, our failure to project the Other of what is, a failure that, as with fireworks dissolving back into the night sky, must once again leave us alone with *this* history" ("Of Islands" 101).

We are back again in our position of "Sartrean irony," where the vision Jameson articulates of an increasingly total system makes responses to that system an all-or-nothing game. It is here that the postmodern search "for events rather than new worlds, for the telltale instant after which it is no longer the same" begins to look like the only desperate response possible to the scenario Jameson outlines. But in the novels I examine in *American Fiction in Transition*, this is not the only model of transition available. These novels in fact witness an oscillation between this model of transition—where real change, if it ever occurs, will be radical, inexplicable, and sudden—and older tragic and modern conceptions of transition. This oscillation, I argue, is best understood on the model of Derrida's conception of undecidability rather than Jameson's dialectics, because Derrida does not posit one underlying explanation where "History" would name the succession of modes of production and would define ongoing class struggle as the "single great collective story." Instead, Derrida rejects the structural necessity of a dialectical overview before a decision can be made; such an overview would provide the necessary corollary of Jameson's belief that genuine agency could in the final analysis only involve a challenge to the prevailing mode of capitalist production. Derrida instead theorizes a generalized experience of undecidability that foregrounds decisions made all the time, decisions that take place in the absence of full knowledge and calculation, but nonetheless take place.

Derrida's position vis-à-vis the dialectical one is most explicitly stated in his "Afterword" to the debate with John Searle, in which Derrida outlines "at least three meanings" of the term undecidability:

1. One of them determines in a manner that is still too *anti*dialectical, hence too dialectical, that which resists binary or even triplicity (see in particular *Dissemination*).
2. The other defines, still *within the order of the calculable*, the *limits* of decidability, or calculability or of formalizable completeness.
3. The third remains *heterogeneous* both to the dialectic and to the calculable. In accordance with what is only ostensibly a paradox, *this particular* undecidable opens the field of decision or of decidability. It calls for decision in the order of ethical-political responsibility. It is even its necessary condition.

"In none of these three meanings," Derrida concludes, "is any completeness possible for undecidability. The effect of the latter is precisely to render all totalization, fulfillment, plenitude impossible" (*Limited* 116).[29] Derrida's resistance to dialectic and totalization here echoes his consistent refusal of a transcendent outside from which one could ever regard the totality of a structure. As he puts it in his foundational *Of Grammatology*, "one always inhabits, and all the more when one does not suspect it" (24). This inhabiting places us always, as it were, in the midst of things, making incalculable and structurally blind decisions on a constant basis:

> However lucid it is, [. . .] a decision [. . .] must advance where it cannot see. This blindness is *not* a lack of knowledge—I repeat, it has nothing to do with what could in principle come to know [sic]—it is the *very structure* of *any* decision, what relates all decisions, immediately, to the undecidable. If there is no "experience" of the undecidable at the moment of decision, then the decision will be nothing but the mechanical application of a rule. ("Nietzsche" 232)

Within Derrida's analysis, with its resistance to the notion of a prior law that governs the undecidability of a decision, there is nothing like the status Jameson offers to the concept of History as "ground and untranscendable horizon" (*Political* 102).[30] Ian Buchanan makes the contrast between the two thinkers on this point explicit, if not wholly dichotomous: "For Jameson (contra Derrida) history *is* outside the text, and indeed the outside of text, yet (in partial agreement with Derrida) only accessible to us in textual form and therefore very much inside the text too. This is the essential paradox the concept of the political unconscious must resolve" (58–9). Yet for Derrida, Jameson's conception of "History," and his notion of "the political unconscious," would in fact serve as metaphysical idealisms that act to constitute the very paradox they are ostensibly trying to solve. Likewise, a process such as cognitive mapping would posit the metaphysical possibility of a transcendent outside to the system, a point from which to survey it. That this may in fact *reduce* the political potential of the concept is an insight not only offered by Derrida's work; Perry Anderson also acknowledges it at a rare critical moment in his otherwise celebratory account of Jameson's thought: "Here some deeper difficulties may be at work. Jameson's marriage of aesthetics and economics yields a wondrous totalization of postmodern culture as a whole, whose operation of 'cognitive mapping' acts—and this is its intention—as a placeholder of dialectical resistance to it. But its point of leverage necessarily remains in that sense outside the system" (132).

Not alone does Derrida's insistence on an "experience" of undecidability heterogeneous to dialectical thought constitute a refusal of any metaphysical outside to the system from which the decision emerges, but he explicitly associates this undecidability, in the third meaning cited in the "Afterword" passage above, with "ethical-political responsibility." This responsibility, argues Derrida, can only inhere in a singular decision beyond the calculation of totalizing rules and dialectical understanding. Here is where his answer to the theoretical problem Jameson identifies as the "winner loses logic" of "Sartrean irony" lies. For Derrida, any conception of totality, including that offered by "theory," must always be suspended in the singular incidence of the decision, which breaks with all totality and dialectics in favor of an undeterminable future. That Derrida frames this in terms of ethics (and elsewhere in terms of hospitality, the gift, justice, etc.) marks his difference from Jameson in a still clearer manner, because Jameson has always resisted a discourse of ethics in his work, seeing such a discourse as little more than ideological mystification. In his book on Wyndham Lewis, for instance, he remarks that "ethics, wherever it makes its reappearance, may be taken as the sign of an intent to mystify, and in particular to replace the complex and ambivalent judgments of a more properly political and dialectical perspective with the comfortable simplifications of a binary myth" (*Fables* 56).[31] Interestingly, this skepticism of ethics is shared by Paul de Man, the most influential American exponent of deconstruction, who gives it a more Nietzschean slant in *Allegories of Reading* when he remarks that "ethicity" is "the referential [. . .] version of a linguistic confusion" (206). By contrast, although Derrida has on occasion resisted the designation of "ethics" as a descriptive term for aspects of his later work, he retains it in the "Afterword" quotation and in many other places as the marker of an otherness beyond totalization that it remains crucial to preserve.

Finally, by comparison with Jameson, Derrida remains wary of utopia as a useful way of thinking critically about present conditions. In an interview given the title, "Not Utopia, the Im-possible," he contrasts his skepticism concerning the former term with his embrace of the latter:

> Utopia has critical powers that we should probably never give up on, especially when we can make it a reason for resisting all alibis and all "realistic" or "pragmatic" cop-outs, but all the same I'm wary of the word. There are some contexts in which *utopia*, the word at any rate, can be too easily associated with dreams, or demobilization, or an impossible that is more of an urge to give up than an urge to action. The "impossible" I often speak of is not the utopian. Rather, it gives their very movement to desire, action, and decision: it is the very figure of the real. It has its hardness, closeness, and urgency. (131)

This statement shadows the most direct textual dialogue between Derrida and Jameson, which occurs in the volume *Ghostly Demarcations*, a symposium of contributions by prominent Marxists on Derrida's *Specters of Marx*, with a long contribution by Derrida responding to their arguments. The interchange between Jameson and Derrida is the most friendly in the collection, with Jameson dubbing Derrida "the world's most eminent living philosopher" ("Marx's" 26), and Derrida consistently claiming an affinity with the points Jameson makes, maintaining on a number of occasions that he does not receive the latter's remarks as objections (Derrida, "Marx" for example, 239, 246). Nonetheless, the two thinkers part ways when it comes to the application of the term "utopia" to Derrida's work in *Specters*. Jameson suggests that Derrida's text includes a "subterranean Utopianism" that he claims Derrida prefers to dub "a weak messianic power," following Walter Benjamin's formulation ("Marx's" 33). Responding directly to this remark, Derrida argues as follows: "*Anything but Utopian*, messianicity mandates that we interrupt the ordinary course of things, time and history *here-now*; it is inseparable from an affirmation of otherness and justice" ("Marx" 249).

Derrida's resistance to the term "utopia," here and elsewhere, clarifies the way the core structures of his thought reject that designation in their constant theorization of impurity and contamination. One could say, indeed, that Derrida is the great post-utopian thinker of the postmodern age, while Jameson, by contrast—and as he freely admits—holds onto the prospect of the utopian as an alternative to accounts of agency and political transition which he sees as having become redundant in a postmodern present. For Derrida, decisions always occur here and now, ushering an undeterminable future into a present in constant transition, whereas for Jameson, decisions are forever postponed by the subject's fragmentation and cognitive inability to map the whole. Derrida is explicit in his belief that the cognitive mapping envisaged by Jameson could never offer the basis for a decision, but that this does not stop us constantly making decisions, here, now. In "Not Utopia, the Im-possible," he offers one of innumerable formulations of this position that appear throughout his late work:

> A decision, while it remains "mine," active and free, as a phenomenon, must not simply be the deployment of my potentials or aptitudes, of what is "possible for me." In order to be a decision, it has to cut off this "possible," tear up my history, and thus be first of all, in a particular and strange way, the decision of the other in me: coming from the other with regard to the other in me. Paradoxically it must carry a certain passivity that in no way lightens my responsibility. These are paradoxes that are difficult to integrate into a classical philosophical discourse, but I don't think that a decision, if there ever are decisions, is possible in any other way. (128–9)

What does a debate at this level of theoretical abstraction mean for our conception of literary narrative? My main suggestion in *American Fiction in Transition* is that the observer-hero structure of 1990s novels, and the oscillation between various conceptions of decision and transition that they stage, figure in illuminating ways many of the paradoxes, "difficult to integrate into a classical philosophical discourse," that

Derrida refers to in the above quotation. This process plays out differently in each novel, and it is difficult to generalize across them; nonetheless, an opening observation would be that the central relationship in these novels between hero and observer renders a decision to act and a decision to narrate inseparable, two sides of the same literary coin. It is the decisiveness of the life of the hero, his or her apparent ability to exhibit agency in an era anxious about that very possibility, that attracts the narrator to the story in the first place, and causes him to attempt to represent that decisiveness. At a certain point in each novel the decision to tell the story is itself thematized by the narrator, and is represented as a decision simultaneously "active and free" but nonetheless somehow demanded. The struggle to write "the decision of the other in me" pushes the narrator against and beyond "the deployment of [his] potentials or aptitudes," eventually forcing him to explore his indecision concerning how the story should be told. The role of narrator thus carries, as Derrida puts it, "a certain passivity that in no way lightens my responsibility." The oscillation between the different possibilities of representing the form and meaning of the hero's decision—an oscillation that marks the novels of this epoch as themselves transitional—shows how the observer's struggle to tell the story forms his response to an experience of paradox, and also to an anxiety about whether "there ever are decisions." In summary, observer-hero narrative, with its division of story and discourse into two embodied characters, offers the literary figuration of a set of ideas that are difficult and paradoxical to grasp in a philosophical register. The complex temporalities at play in each novel—where the hero's decision both pre-exists its narrative articulation but is simultaneously shaped into the decision it is by the narrative decisions of the observer—figure in literary form the temporal paradoxes that underlie Derrida's philosophical explication of undecidability.

A problem of periodization remains. Derrida's conception of the decision, as presented above, does not involve a historical claim about how decision works in any particular era, but a claim operational on a (quasi-)transcendental level. It cannot therefore simply be periodized as postmodern, nor as applying specifically to the postmodern era. Indeed, Derrida's own sole major periodizing term, "the end of the book and the beginning of writing," which he outlines in *Of Grammatology* and *Dissemination*, provides for a new temporality of reading and writing that defies conventional narratives of literary history by invoking the "untimeliness" of literary texts, the challenge they present to the notion of bounded historical contexts and periods. Although in certain ways concurrent with the postmodern era (in that Derrida announced its arrival in 1967), the epoch of writing that Derrida conceives of is not dominated by Jamesonian conceptions of space or a perpetual present. Instead this epoch is characterized by dissemination—which Derrida describes as "the theory and practice of the *graft* without a body proper, of the *skew* without a straight line, of the *bias* without a front" (*Dissemination* 11)—and by *différance*, which he defines as "the becoming-space of time and the becoming-time of space" (*Grammatology* 68). Strictly speaking, then, the positing of dissemination and *différance* does not mark a historical claim, and these concepts do not therefore provide much help in coming to terms with developments in contemporary writing.[32]

So a legitimate question would be, why Derrida, and why now? One answer, elaborated upon in this introduction and throughout my chapters, is that I see in Derrida's conception of undecidability an important model for thinking about the structures of literary narrative, and particularly the characteristics of the genre I am calling observer-hero narrative, as I find them operating in novels of the 1990s. This is the formalist answer. The more historicist one is that I also take Derrida's work to stand in for the larger movement in recent intellectual history usually referred to as "theory," a movement whose shaping of contemporary conceptions of language and thought, and whose specific influence on the American novel, are subjects of increasing debate in contemporary criticism.[33] Jameson has regularly claimed theory as the closest replacement for the modernist avant-garde, and has suggested that in the postmodern era it is no longer the work of art but the work of theoretical interpretation that, as he resoundingly puts it, "takes place within a Homeric battlefield" (*Political* 13).[34] Against this background, it makes sense to see the literary novel of the 1990s as responding to wider intellectual trends, even if the authors themselves would not always acknowledge the influence of those trends. In each of my readings, therefore, I attempt to show how these literary texts do not ignore their postmodern inheritance, but instead respond to it in immanent ways. Herein lies the importance of periodizing. In summary, one might say that each of these novels inscribes a response to postmodernism as a period through an engagement with postmodernism as an interpretive model.

One final answer to the question of my methodological reliance on Jameson and Derrida can be offered by citing a critical forerunner to *American Fiction in Transition*. Jerry H. Bryant's study *The Open Decision: The Contemporary American Novel and its Intellectual Background* (1970) carries out a survey of American fiction of the postwar era through a framework Bryant constructs from the existentialism of Sartre, Marcel, and Camus, and the process philosophy of Whitehead. The novels and plays of the postwar—works by Mailer, Ellison, McCullers, Percy, Bellow, Heller, Albee, and others—are read by Bryant as framing the existential plight of the solitary individual in an America where social institutions and prior ethical codes offer no guidance to the goal of self-fulfillment. What Bryant calls "the open decision," a concept he adapts from Max Scheler, captures in his estimation not only the now-classic existentialist position on human choice and freedom, but also "the logic of the larger intellectual climate to be found in present-day physics, philosophy, sociology, psychology and other disciplines of study." This climate is "unified by a particular view of reality," a reality in which the human being is at the center, and, in Sartrean terms, the existence of things is understood to precede their essence (4). This widespread view of reality in turn provides the contemporary "language game" in which the American novelist writes, a language game that "constitutes the perceptual patterns according to which our novelists grant priority to issues" (8).

Published in 1970, *The Open Decision* is—like the work of Bruffee and Buell—a late document of the pre-"theory" age. In his focus on existential issues, Bryant accepts an unproblematic and relatively untheorized view of language and representation, focusing almost solely on story and character in the novels he examines. In "Periodizing the 60s," Jameson explicitly names existentialism as the "ideological supplement" to high modernism, in that both operate according to the "supreme fiction" of the "meaninglessness of the contingent object-world unredeemed by the imagination" (199). By analogy, we might say that what Jameson calls "theory" (a term which takes in structuralism, poststructuralism, psychoanalysis, cultural studies, etc.) is the ideological supplement to postmodernism, because in both the art and theory of the postmodern period the notion of a centered imaginative subject gives way to a de-centering focus on language and systems. While it may or may not be true that the writers Bryant examines themselves minimized linguistic and representational concerns in their work, this was not the case with the high postmodernists who directly succeeded those writers, and it is certainly not the case with the writers featured in this study, who relate to their postmodern inheritance in new and valuable ways. These writers are also concerned to explore, in the stories they tell, the consequences of the theoretical de-centering of the subject, and to offer intimations of human agency that can challenge that worldview. In undertaking these tasks, the novels I read in *American Fiction in Transition* also offer important intimations of transition in its many guises: aesthetic, intellectual, cultural, and historical. It is the work of this study to articulate these intimations of transition in critical terms.

Tragedy and Secrecy: Philip Roth's
The Human Stain

Indeed, the dance that sealed our friendship was also what made his disaster my subject. And made his disguise my subject. And made the proper presentation of his secret my problem to solve. (45)

Prologue

If one were asked to nominate a work from the philosophical tradition that contributes to the genre of observer-hero narrative, Søren Kierkegaard's *Fear and Trembling* would be a prime candidate. Narrated by Johannes di Silentio, and consisting of his interpretive retelling of the biblical story of Abraham and Isaac, *Fear and Trembling* is included by Walter Reed as one of the four nineteenth-century "meditations on the hero" that make up his study of that name.[1] Reed outlines many aspects of Kierkegaard's text that would be relevant to its consideration as an observer-hero narrative, but of most immediate interest to the present chapter is the contrast drawn in *Fear and Trembling* between Abraham and the tragic hero of classical antiquity. According to di Silentio, the actions of a tragic hero—even one such as Agamemnon who, like Abraham, is called upon by the gods to sacrifice his own child—can always be understood within the sphere of ethical life, as a response to a transcendently ordered universe: "the ethical is the divine, and thus the paradox therein can be mediated in the universal" (*Fear* 60). Although the suffering of the tragic hero is immense, that suffering expresses forms of universal motivation and social desire, allowing the observer to "forget his own sufferings in those of the tragic hero" (61). The actions of Abraham, by comparison, cannot be understood in this ethical and universalizing manner, for they speak not of order but of contingency and chaos: "Abraham is at no time a tragic hero but is something entirely different, either a murderer or a man of faith" (57). As a consequence, the figure of Abraham induces not catharsis but shock or awe in the observer, and offers a pronounced challenge to reading, writing, and thinking: "I *think* myself *into* the hero. I cannot think myself into Abraham" (33). *Fear and Trembling* constitutes one long meditation on the impossibility of thinking oneself into this kind of hero. Kierkegaard's text is haunted by the silence that comes of the observer's attempt to articulate the paradox of faith at the heart of Abraham's story, even when this silence issues, as it would in a Beckett novel, in an endless stream of words.

Jacques Derrida's commentary on *Fear and Trembling* remains one of the best known of his later texts. In offering his own interpretation of the Abraham story to complement Kierkegaard's post-Romantic and anti-Hegelian reading, Derrida's *The Gift of Death* departs from Kierkegaard on a number of important points. For instance, in a move that looks forward to my own readings in this study, Derrida highlights the way the central paradox of Abraham's decision is precisely what generates the demand for narration, and influences the form such narration takes: "The account of Isaac's sacrifice can be read as a narrative development of the paradox that inhabits the concept of duty or of absolute responsibility" (*Gift* 67). In addition, Derrida focuses less on the dumbstruck silence of the observer, as Kierkegaard does, than on Abraham's own silence, his non-response to the conventional requirements of justification and explanation. This silence "does not consist in hiding *something*, in not revealing the truth" (122); the secret Abraham holds is not inaccessible only to the observer, but also to the hero himself: "he is sworn to secrecy because he is in secret" (60). Were Abraham to try to tell his story, he could only repeat this central secret without revealing it. According to Derrida, this is in fact the best explanation of the words Abraham does speak in the biblical account: "He says God will provide. God will provide the lamb for the holocaust. Abraham thus keeps his secret at the same time as he replies to Isaac. He doesn't keep silent and he doesn't lie. He doesn't speak nontruth" (59–60).[2] In being told in this way, Abraham's remains a secret that puts in question all telling—it generates a narrative with a hermeneutic deficit that cannot be transcended in the direction of final revelation. As Derrida asks toward the end of *The Gift of Death*, "A secret can be transmitted, but in transmitting a secret as a secret that remains secret, has one transmitted at all? Does it amount to a history, to a story? Yes and no" (80).

Derrida departs from Kierkegaard most radically, however, when he positions Abraham not as a singular knight of faith, acting above and beyond the capability and understanding of normal humans, but as an exemplary everyman, faced with the choice between incompatible demands. For Kierkegaard, the fundamental paradox of the Biblical story lies in Abraham's faith, his belief that he will get Isaac back despite the absurdity of that idea. "Faith," maintains Kierkegaard, "is precisely the paradox that the single individual as the single individual is higher than the universal" (55), and it is this faith in the absurd, as Derek Attridge has noted of *Fear and Trembling*, "that resolves everything" ("Derrida's" 20). For Derrida, however, the paradox is tauter, because God and Isaac make competing and fundamentally incompatible claims. Maintaining that "*tout autre est tout autre*"—every other is wholly other—Derrida denies that God can be a priori privileged over Isaac, or vice versa; he argues that a decision worthy of the name can only occur when ethical rules are suspended in the moment of action.

And, crucially, this is the case not only for Abraham, but for all of us, every day, facing decisions that we cannot justify, decisions that introduce an irrevocable violence into the project of ethical life. Abraham's decision on Mount Moriah, a decision made not in certain faith but in blindness and a lack of knowledge, is exemplary for every decision:

> He decides, but his absolute decision is neither guided nor controlled by knowledge. Such, in fact, is the paradoxical condition of every decision: it cannot be deduced from a form of knowledge of which it would simply be the effect, conclusion or explication. It structurally breaches knowledge and is thus destined to non-manifestation; a decision is, in the end, always secret. (*Gift* 78)

With this secrecy in mind, on several occasions in *The Gift of Death* Derrida follows Kierkegaard in contrasting Abraham with the tragic hero: "The tragic hero has access to mourning. Abraham, on the other hand, is neither a man of mourning nor a tragic hero" (66); "The tragic hero, on the other hand, can speak, share, weep, complain. [. . .] Abraham can neither speak nor commiserate, neither weep nor wail" (74); "Whereas the tragic hero is great, admired, and legendary from generation to generation, Abraham, in remaining faithful to his singular love for the wholly other, is never considered a hero. He doesn't make us shed tears and doesn't inspire admiration" (79). Yet there is a deceptive inconsistency to Derrida's formulations here: if, as he maintains throughout this text, we are all Abrahams, forever engaged in impossible decisions that cannot find justification in ethical generality, then there should be no place for the tragic hero in Derrida's schema. If we are always on Mount Moriah, then we are never in ancient Greece, and the collective mourning of the tragic hero, as Kierkegaard understands him, is never available to the maker of any decision, eternally alone in his singularity. The tragic hero should therefore function not as an alternative *within* Derrida's story of ethical decision, but as an alternative *to* that story, an alternative that would argue for continuity and order over rupture and change. The story that emerges from Derrida's radical reading of Abraham's actions is a story of perpetual, moment-to-moment transition, a story that simultaneously calls for narration and makes narration impossible: "Does it amount to a history, to a story? Yes and no" (80). It is this "yes and no," this undecidability haunting the tragic narration and its conception of ordered transition, that captures succinctly the central narrative quandary of Philip Roth's *The Human Stain*, in which Nathan Zuckerman undertakes to tell the story of the ambiguous hero Coleman Silk.

I Tragic allusions

Roth makes no secret of his intention that *The Human Stain* be read with reference to classical tragedy. From the epigraphic citation of *Oedipus Rex*, to the five-chapter structure capped by a final act entitled "The Purifying Ritual," to a plot that reads like an exercise in Sophoclean homage—talented hero doggedly refuses to acknowledge a terrible act he has committed, only to succumb to an ironic and mysteriously inevitable fate years later—all the signs point to a sustained effort by the author to fully exploit the narrative conventions and thematic hallmarks of tragedy: seriousness, high rhetoric, a powerful central protagonist, an ambiguous play of agency and fate, a movement toward revelation and death, and the lingering sense of what A. C. Bradley famously termed tragedy's "painful mystery" that resists analysis (29). Add in the consistent allusions throughout the novel to canonical tragic texts—including *The Bacchae*, *The Iliad*, *Hamlet* and *Death in Venice*, in addition to *Oedipus*—and it is clear why, in the growing critical literature on *The Human Stain*, almost all treatments mention the tragic element.[3] Indeed, a handful of essays have taken that element as their central concern. Bonnie Lyons declares that the late trilogy of which *The Human Stain* is the third part "establish[es] Roth as our most important author of significant American tragedies" (125). Elaine Safer suggests that the comic elements of the novel prepare the reader for a shift to tragedy, and sees the central characters as tragic figures. Patrice Rankine notes that "[a]llusions to Greek epic and tragedy are the driving force of the novel" (103), and argues that Roth utilizes tragic references in order to deepen the implications of the protagonist Coleman Silk's decision to pass as Jewish-American.

Rankine's essay delineates many of the implicit and explicit allusions to tragedy in *The Human Stain*, highlighting the sheer range of intertextual and generic references throughout the text. Nonetheless, his treatment shares with those of Lyons and Safer a lack of attention to the way the relationship between established motifs of tragedy and the particular story of Coleman Silk is itself treated as a significant subject in Roth's novel. In other words, the predominant critical take on *The Human Stain* reads the novel simply as an embodiment of tragedy, rather than as a reflection upon that mode and an examination of the processes and assumptions it encodes. It is no coincidence that the novel's narrative structure does not play a large role in the arguments of the above-named critics, for it is here, and particularly in the role of Nathan Zuckerman as narrator, that this examination and reflection primarily take place. As I outlined in my introduction, *The Human Stain* has the structure of an observer-hero narrative, a fact that bears greatly upon its intertextual engagement with the history of tragic literature, as well as upon its treatment of moments of decision and transition in the story being told.[4]

With this in mind, the critic who has produced the most compelling exploration of tragedy in the novel thus far is Geoffrey Bakewell. Acknowledging Zuckerman as the ostensible writer of the story we read, Bakewell points out that within the frame of the novel, "*The Human Stain* is ultimately [Zuckerman's] creation and composed almost entirely of his empathetic reconstructions and imaginings" (42). As the self-appointed storyteller, Zuckerman also takes on the mantle of tragic poet, "applying to Coleman's life the standard explanatory categories of accident and inevitability, destiny and fate" (43). Consequently, rather than being simply, as Lyons claims, "a newer novelistic version of the dramatic Chorus" (126), Zuckerman is also dramatist, messenger, and actor in his own drama. And to his credit, Bakewell goes further than this, recognizing that in Zuckerman's layered reflections upon the application of tragedy to Coleman's life and story, another kind of interrogation is ongoing in the novel, an interrogation that, as we shall see, touches upon questions of epistemology, ontology, and the basic possibility of tragedy itself. In a footnote, Bakewell hits upon a major question *The Human Stain* puts to its readers, a question he states without attempting to answer it: "If it really is a 'foolish illusion' to apply to 'real life' the forms and patterns of Greek tragedy, why does Nathan make this mistake so frequently?" (43n48). Answering this question forms an important aspect of my own exploration of Roth's novel in the present chapter.

Bakewell's reference to the "foolish illusion" of applying the forms of tragedy to "real life" is drawn from Zuckerman's remarks upon witnessing Mark Silk's emotional breakdown at the funeral of his hated father. Watching the hysterical scene, the observer speculates that, just like a writer trying to complete his story, Coleman's son desires "a just and perfect consummation," a form of closure that, "outside the classical tragedy of the fifth century B.C.," it would be foolish for any individual to expect (*Human* 315). The passage appears late in the novel, and serves in its context a self-reflexive function, because by this point the narrator's own application of the forms of tragedy to the story he tells has itself been rendered problematic for the reader. Earlier on, however, and particularly in the opening two chapters of *The Human Stain*, tragic parallels are cited and highlighted in a less self-conscious manner.

As a professor of classics at Athena College, New Hampshire, Coleman Silk is introduced to the reader in full flow, declaiming on Homer's *Iliad* to his students: "there, for better or worse, in this offense against the phallic entitlement, the phallic *dignity*, of a powerhouse of a warrior prince, is how the great imaginative literature of Europe begins, and that is why, close to three thousand years later, we are going to begin there today . . ." (5). Precious little, it seems, has changed over time. We begin *The Human Stain* with a latter-day warrior prince, who in an academic context has leveled the field before him, powerfully asserting his will in the reconstruction of a college faculty that he dredges from oblivion to high-level achievement. That this process makes him enemies, who then turn spitefully against him in his hour of need, is a reversal characteristic of tragic storytelling. The plot turns on Coleman's unexpected disciplining for a stray remark in class, when he refers to two absent students as "spooks," only for those (black) students to lodge complaints on racial grounds. Coleman's visceral reaction to the slights that come his way speak to his new companion Zuckerman of "the great man brought low" (18), of "the derangement of [. . .] the monarch deposed" (23). When the narrator remarks, "There is something fascinating about what moral suffering can do to someone who is in no obvious way a weak or feeble person. [. . .] Its raw realism is like nothing else" (12), the reader is forcibly reminded of the sufferings of Lear and Othello, blindsided by their own flaws and the treachery of those in whom they place their trust. Indeed, throughout the opening chapter of *The Human Stain*—as in almost all of Roth's best writing—subtlety is eschewed in favor of directness. In contrast to a modernist work such as *Ulysses*, in which Joyce indicates the mythic reference point in little more than the novel's title, Roth's novel could not begin with a more overt paralleling of Coleman's story with those of the canon of tragic heroes before him.

It is, however, only when Coleman's big secret is revealed to the reader early in the second chapter that the full and complex irony of his position becomes clear. Born an African–American, Coleman has spent his entire adult life passing as a Jew, and Zuckerman emphasizes throughout this part of the text that Coleman is where he is as the result of a decision, an assertion of agency in the face of his racial fate, displaying in response to prejudice what Arthur Miller attributed to every tragic hero, "the inherent unwillingness to remain passive in the face of what he conceives to be a challenge to his dignity, his image of his rightful status" (Miller 4). The title of the chapter, "Slipping the Punch," refers to the first significant decision of Coleman's teenage years, when, in a fitting betrayal of the Shakespeare-loving but violence-hating father who had given him the middle name Brutus, he secretly takes up boxing. This choice will lead directly to his decision to pass for the first time: on the advice of his coach Doc Chizner, in his first major fight Coleman mentions nothing about his race, a suppression of information that inspires him "to be more damaging than he'd ever dared before" (99). He puts this drive down to the power of having a secret: "He did love secrets. The secret of nobody's knowing what was going on inside your head, thinking whatever you wanted to think with no way of anybody's knowing" (100). "Everyone Knows," the ironic illusion of public knowledge invoked by the title of the novel's opening chapter, and by Delphine Roux's scurrilous letter therein, here become "nobody knows," as the secret enters the novel as a major trope. Coleman's desire for secrecy will motivate his later decision to split with Ellie Magee, who knows he is black, and take up with his future wife Iris Gittelman, who doesn't. The boxing analogy reasserts itself as this decision is explained: "But here he comes roaring out of his corner—he has the secret again. [. . .] He's got the elixir of the secret, and it's like being fluent in another language" (135–6).

This emphasis on secrecy is constant throughout the text; as Debra Shostak argues in her authoritative book on Roth, *The Human Stain* is a novel "framed around secrets" (*Philip* 257). The novel opens with Coleman's revelation to Zuckerman of his secret affair with Faunia Farley, a secret that, in a letter supposed to keep her own identity secret, Delphine Roux will later declare that "everyone knows." At the finale, likewise, Les Farley's putative murder of Coleman and Faunia remains an unconfessed secret, though one Zuckerman will nonetheless expose to the logic of "everyone knows" in a book that bears the same title as the novel we are reading. Then there is Coleman's secret decision to pass as a Jew, his decision to keep his history a secret, a secret only revealed to an astonished Zuckerman after his friend's death. Furthermore, as Shostak points out, these secrets revealed at the level of the plot open onto other more profound ones, secrets that do not give themselves up so easily to revelation: the secrecy of Coleman's motivations for his decision; the secrecy of Zuckerman's own motives, the desires that drive him to investigate the story; the secrecy of the artistic process, of the writer's methods for bringing order to chaos in his narrative. And, of course, there is the secret involved in tragedy more generally, the terrible and seemingly inexplicable metaphysical destiny of the human being in a painful world.

Quoting Northrop Frye's remark that "tragedy seems to elude the antithesis of moral responsibility and arbitrary fate," Rita Felski has noted a critical agreement in contemporary scholarship that "what distinguishes tragedy is an uncanny unraveling of the distinction between agency and fate, internal volition and the pressure of external circumstance" (xii). In Shostak's view, nevertheless, tragedy in Roth's novel can be decoded in the final analysis through the lens of fate as historical determinism. "Coleman," she suggests, "has built his life around the premise that secrets offer an escape from history" (*Philip* 258), but history is precisely what returns with tragic force to defeat him, both in the guise of his own personal history of racial denial, and in the guise of a larger American history, marked in the figure of his supposed killer, the crazed Vietnam war veteran Les Farley. Indeed, Shostak goes so far as to conclude her discussion with the claim that "Les *is* the secret" (265); he is the "*vrai*" that Zuckerman has been searching for ever since the narrator's first appearance in Roth's early novella *The Ghost Writer* (1979).

Shostak's position here is representative of the prevailing critical line on the novel, which sees its tragic themes as generated in response to historical forces.[5] Despite the persuasiveness of her reading, however, the relationship Shostak outlines between tragedy and secrecy, and history and decision, does not do full justice to the intricate structure of *The Human Stain*. Zuckerman discovers the secret of Coleman's race, and comes to ponder the secret of his decision, only after the latter's funeral, depicted in the final chapter; yet the novel's arrangement, with the narrative revelation of Coleman's secret coming as early as the second act, shifts the emphasis away from the reader's discovery of Coleman's passing (which could form the focus of a suspense novel, for example, or a melodrama) to an inquiry into the motive and meaning of his choice. It is Bakewell, once again, who best connects this structural feature of the novel to Roth's tragic concerns. While acknowledging that *The Human Stain* is "Sophoclean in theme: it addresses our cultural taboos, and how we deal with those who violate them," Bakewell sets out to examine how Roth "reshapes his Oedipal inheritance," borrowing from established tragic patterns in a critical manner (30).

Specifically, Bakewell argues that Roth reverses the epistemological structure of Sophocles's drama, so that gradual and painful self-discovery on the part of the hero is replaced in *The Human Stain* by the revelation of the hero's consciously hidden secret to the reader. And, we could add, by the revelation of that secret to the observer-narrator too, who then retrospectively shapes the story we are told. The reflexive attention this structure draws to the way the novel is narrated allows the reader to see how *the conventions of tragedy offer secrecy a form*, how those conventions map the secret in a way that removes aspects of its hiddenness in favor of the revelatory drive of epistemological desire. Highlighting the power of this desire, Shostak concludes that "*The Human Stain* [. . .] demonstrates repeatedly that secrets exist only to be told" (*Philip* 258). Yet, unless telling is to be distinguished from revelation in the manner Derrida outlines in his reading of Abraham, this is not, in my view, the final message of Roth's novel. Rather, as I argue in this chapter, *The Human Stain* maintains a secrecy beyond representation, a secrecy that generates the very narratives of decision and transition that aim, and yet fail, to achieve revelation.[6]

II Tragic illusions

In telling the story of Coleman's life, Zuckerman is clearly intent on giving his narrative a tragic outline. Alongside the parallels and allusions that litter the text, however, the narrator also adds another layer by having Coleman display a conscious relationship to tragedy, and a vexed awareness of how tragic themes and tropes might apply to the circumstances of his own life. This is certainly a complex matter: sometimes tragic references are used to support agency, while sometimes they emphasize fate and accident; sometimes Coleman correctly recognizes parallels, and sometimes he does not; sometimes his knowledge of tragedy aids his understanding and action, and at other times he becomes puzzled, indignant, and resistant to the lessons of his own field of specialism. An early turning point in his life is the death of his father, an event that ignites Coleman's sense that it is time to begin "making up" his own story (107), a story in which "[h]e was Coleman, the greatest of the great *pioneers* of the I" (108). This traditional American hero of self-invention will not fall prey to his father's tragic sensibility: "'Beware the Ides of March.' Bullshit—beware *nothing*. Free. [. . .] Free to enact the boundless, self-defining drama of the pronouns we, they, and I" (108–9). Soon, however, Coleman will find that it is often at those moments when he feels most strongly the power of his own self-creation that his certainty is most starkly undone. When he invites his first white girlfriend Steena Paulsen to dinner at his family home, thereby revealing his secret to her, the text focalizes his thoughts: "His decision to invite her to East Orange for Sunday dinner, like all his other decisions now [. . .] was based on nobody's thinking but his own" (118). This profession of decisive agency, forceful though it seems, is quickly complicated by the scene that occurs a few pages later, in which Coleman meets Steena again, four years after their break-up over the revelation of his race:

> The way it might have ended—the conclusion against which reality had decisively voted—was all he could think about. Stunned by how little he'd gotten over her and she'd gotten over him, he walked away understanding, as outside his reading in classical Greek drama he'd never had to understand before, how easily life can be one thing rather than another and how accidentally a destiny is made . . . on the other hand, how accidental fate may seem when things can never turn out other than they do. That is, he walked away understanding nothing, knowing he could understand nothing, though with the illusion that he *would* have metaphysically understood something of enormous importance about this stubborn determination of his to become his own man if . . . if only such things were understandable. (125–6)

This is a rich passage, foregrounding the themes of agency, destiny, and secrecy that are central to the novel, and doing so through a moment of *anagnorisis* for the protagonist. Struggling to grasp the metaphysical meaning of his sudden recognition, Coleman is brought back to the Greek texts with a kind of baffled insight, and is left with an experience of contingency that his own decisions, "based on nobody's thinking but his own," had seemed designed to counteract. Now he realizes that "[w]hat happened with his mother and Walt could as easily never have occurred. Had Steena said fine, he would have lived another life" (126). At the close of the section, the link that these thoughts have to tragic themes is made even more explicit: "He thought the same useless thoughts—useless to a man of no great talent like himself, if not to Sophocles: how accidentally a fate is made . . . or how accidental it all may seem when it is inescapable" (127).

While the Greek parallels may appear uncanny, if useless, to Coleman in the above passage, at other moments he willfully rejects the trappings of tragedy, feeling that bare reality must contrast with the narrative conventions he teaches in class. For instance, as Coleman watches Faunia jokingly interact with her co-workers on the Athena campus lawn, he suddenly regrets the path his life has taken, and vows to change:

> To live in a way that does not bring Philoctetes to mind. He does not have to live like a tragic character in his course. [. . .] Jokingly dancing with Nathan Zuckerman. Confiding in him. Reminiscing with him. Letting him listen. Sharpening the writer's sense of reality. Feeding that great opportunistic maw, a novelist's mind. Whatever catastrophe turns up, he transforms into writing. Catastrophe is cannon fodder for him. But what can *I* transform this into? I am stuck with it. As is. Sans language, shape, structure, meaning—sans the unities, the catharsis, sans everything. (170)

Coleman here projects as his other Zuckerman the writer, whose narrative imaginings are taken to contrast with the unformed reality of his real existence, an existence that ought to offer freedom to live outside the bounds of novelistic convention. Yet it is not difficult to see that this repudiation of narrative form itself occurs within a narrative designed by Zuckerman (and of course by Roth), where "language, shape, structure, meaning" are provided by the narrator in an echoing of the tragic conventions that Coleman wants to reject. This illusion of a space of autonomy for a character to reflect on his experience outside narrative, all while the reader is made aware of the writtenness of the scene, is a typical trope of Roth's fiction, characteristic of his particular approach to the boundary between "the written and unwritten world" (Roth, *Reading* xiii).[7] In this case it performs a specific role, preparing the reader for a moment a few pages later when Coleman's refusal to absorb the lessons of tragedy will lead him to become bewildered by his own story, hanging grimly onto the conviction that everything is explicable in rational terms when his experience repeatedly suggests otherwise. This moment occurs when Coleman considers the possibility that his son Mark hates him because he knows his secret:

> That made no sense at all as a grievance—it could not be! Yet Coleman wondered anyway, irrational as it might be to associate Markie's brooding anger with his own secret. [. . .] If the children who carried his origins in their genes and who would pass those origins on to their own children could find it so easy to suspect him of the worst kind of cruelty to Faunia, what explanation could there be? [. . .] Retribution was not unconsciously or unknowingly enacted. There was no such quid pro quo. *It could not be.* And yet, after the phone call—leaving the student union, leaving

the campus, all the while he was driving in tears back up the mountain—that was exactly what it felt like. (176-7)

Coleman has been accustomed to reading classical tragedy in an allegorical manner—he is not prepared to have its "irrational" or "unconscious" anti-logic of retribution presented to him as the best causal explanation for his son's hate. Yet his repressed recognition here points to forces beyond his understanding, forces that indelibly connect him to generations before and after in a manner no ideology of agency, no attempt to grasp "the alternate destiny, on one's own terms" (139), can fully suppress.

While these passages foreground weighty themes, balance is offered by other passages in the opening three chapters that stress the more humorous side of Coleman's recognition and misrecognition of tragic parallels and references. Early on, after learning from a phone call to his beloved daughter Lisa that his son Mark may have spread unfounded gossip about him, we are told that it took "no less than the prophylaxis of the whole of Attic tragedy and Greek epic poetry, to restrain him from phoning on the spot to remind Markie what a little prick he was and always had been" (63). The bathetic tone here provides a counterweight to the grandeur elsewhere associated with tragedy, and the same is true of a conversation between Iris and Coleman concerning Iris's unfortunate friend Claudia, duped by her husband for several years: "'Where is the intimacy,' she says, 'when there is such a secret?' [. . .] 'Yes,' Coleman said, 'it's like something out of the Greeks. Out of *The Bacchae*.' 'Worse,' Iris said, 'because it is not out of *The Bacchae*. It's out of Claudia's life'" (178-9). In addition to this comic denial on Iris's part of any interrelation between tragic art and everyday life, and to the ironic shadow which Coleman's own secret places over their exchange, Bakewell detects a further irony in Coleman's misrecognition of the correct parallel in the scene: "As her Hellenist husband should have known, the *locus classicus* for a wife not knowing crucial particulars about her husband is surely *Oedipus Rex*" (Bakewell 34). This kind of confusion often afflicts Coleman at moments of heightened drama—in the above scene, he had been intending to tell Iris his secret before hearing of her furious reaction to the secret-keeping of a friend's husband.

Iris also plays a key role in the moment when Coleman's sense of agency is most dramatically undermined, the moment at the finale of chapter two when he faces down his mother to inform her that he has chosen to disown her and her racial heritage. While Coleman had once again conceived this decision as a powerful expression of his agency, while he is informing his unsurprised mother a sense of the ridiculous nevertheless overcomes him: "If anyone was surprised it was Coleman, who, having openly declared his intention, all at once wondered if this entire decision, the most monumental of his life, wasn't based on the least serious thing imaginable: Iris's hair" (136). In his wish to deny his past, Coleman suspects at this moment that he has chosen his Jewish wife owing solely to the kinky hair that could explain any similar growth among his children. Clearing his mind of such thoughts, Coleman tries to reiterate his sense of destiny—"To get that from life, the alternate destiny, on one's own terms, he must do what must be done"—but the tragedy of this choice is once again both underlined and undercut by his mother's earthy rejoinder: "You think like a prisoner. You do, Coleman Brutus. You're white as snow and you think like a slave" (139). At the finale of chapter two of *The Human Stain*, the task of assessing Coleman's existence is still an open question. Is his decision the powerful act of the tragic hero, or the weak betrayal of a slave?

III Narrative connections

To this point, I have been writing as if—whatever the weight, tone, and variation of tragic influence upon his life and consciousness—Coleman Silk's character is consistent and his story is basically explicable as a sequence in the manner described. I have done so because this is what the early acts of *The Human Stain* would have us believe; later in the novel, however, we encounter a thorough unraveling of this logic of locatable cause and demonstrable effect, an unraveling that puts questions like the culminating one of Section II above in sharp relief. The realism of the novel's first three chapters is challenged by the epistemological speculations of the fourth and the revelations of the fifth. The reader gradually realizes fully just how much motivation Zuckerman has invented, and how much mapping and patterning he has had to carry out on an inexplicable life. Now the narrative changes tack, and it is this very inexplicability that is foregrounded, presenting the reader with a retrospective challenge to Zuckerman's tragic conception of Coleman's life and major decision.

In chapter four, while attending a summer concert in the Berkshires, Zuckerman spots Coleman and Faunia leaning to talk to one another "about what, of course, I did not know." This prompts the narrator into an angry condemnation of the presumption to know that he finds everywhere in contemporary life:

> Because we don't know, do we? *Everyone knows* . . . How what happens the way it does? What underlies the anarchy of the train of events, the uncertainties, the mishaps, the disunity, the shocking irregularities that define human affairs? *Nobody* knows, Professor Roux. [. . .] What we know is that, in an unclichéd way, nobody knows anything. You *can't* know anything. The things you *know* you don't know. Intention? Motive? Consequence? Meaning? All that we don't know is astonishing. Even more astonishing is what passes for knowing. (208–9)

Although this diatribe is nominally directed at Delphine Roux, the manner in which the sentiment reflects on Zuckerman's own narrative project is striking. All the reader's knowledge to this point, the illusion that "everyone knows [. . .] what happens the way it does," has been provided not by Roux but by Zuckerman's own mix of reportage and imaginings. Indeed Delphine herself, whom Zuckerman never meets, is almost entirely the creation of the latter's pen. Narrative is a primary vehicle for transmitting knowledge; in telling Coleman's story, as well as those of Faunia, Delphine, and Lester Farley, Zuckerman stands guilty of allowing imagination take the place of truth, of inventing "intention, motive, consequence, meaning." But while the narrator at times freely admits this guilt, and hence permits provisional truth claims to be contextualized by the epistemological uncertainty that surfaces in passages such as the above, in the closing movement of the novel a more profound problem begins to emerge.

When, in the fifth and final chapter, Coleman's sister Ernestine reveals the truth of her brother's birth to Zuckerman, she admits that she cannot comprehend his baffling decision to cast off his identity and family: "Coleman never in his life chafed under being a Negro. Not for as long as we knew him. This is true. Being a Negro was just never an issue with him. [. . .] Mother would propose reasons, but none was ever adequate" (324–5). Here the stress on the unlocatability of causes and the inexplicability of actions emphasizes the unknowability of the other person, the very otherness of the other. But what also begins to suggest itself to Zuckerman in these late passages is something more radical: a basic discontinuity to life, a fragmentation that results when a coherent notion of subjectivity fractures and breaks down. Understandably, a stunned Zuckerman cannot resist attempting to connect the Coleman he knew, who had with "furious determination" resigned from Athena College, with the young black man abruptly leaving his family behind 40 years earlier: "Not that I was sure there was any connection, any circuitry looping the one decision to the other, but we could try to look and see, couldn't we? How did such a man as Coleman Silk come to exist? What is it that he was? [. . .] Can such things ever be known?" (332–3). But finding that this mental inquiry leads nowhere, Zuckerman admits his thorough perplexity:

> I couldn't imagine anything that could have made Coleman more of a mystery to me than this unmasking. Now that I knew everything, it was as though I knew nothing, and instead of what I'd learned from Ernestine unifying my idea of him, *he became not just an unknown but an uncohesive person.* (333, my emphasis)

All of a sudden, we witness a shift from an epistemological problem to an ontological one. With the dawn of Ernestine's revelation it is as though Coleman ceases to submit to any notion of a unifying subjectivity, becoming "uncohesive," his life a series of decisive, performative events unconnected by any underlying core of self. Not only can the connections that would indicate "what [it is] that [Coleman] was" not be discovered, Zuckerman now realizes, but they may not exist at all. Moreover, this twinning of racial revelation with ontological incoherence on Zuckerman's part encourages the reader to see the tragic coherence of the early chapters of *The Human Stain* in a new light, as a kind of narrative imposition. In condemning the gossipers of Athena, Zuckerman at one point notes ironically that a label performatively effected upon a person may be divorced from any cause: "No motive for the perpetrator is necessary, no logic or rationale is required. Only a label is required. The label is the motive. The label is the evidence. The label is the logic" (290). The label, presumably, is not the truth. Yet Zuckerman's own label for the events that have befallen Coleman, "tragic," has by now become equally questionable as a truthful description of the story he is attempting to tell.

In *Fear and Trembling*, Søren Kierkegaard had contrasted the collective mourning available to the tragic hero with the absolute, terrifying inwardness of the modern individual. A century later, in the work of dramatists such as Arthur Miller and Jean-Paul Sartre, these poles had collapsed, and tragedy tended to be articulated in existential terms. Nonetheless, in Miller, as in Brecht and his followers, tragedy still retained its instructive role, which for Antonin Artaud, another great exponent and theorist of tragedy, was necessary for the genre: "We are not free. And the sky can still fall on our heads and the theater has been created to teach us that first of all" (Artaud 79). For tragedy to assume this pedagogic role requires, according to Miller, "the finest appreciation by the writer of cause and effect" (*Theatre* 6). The assumption underlying this claim is that cause and effect can be known, and for Miller the inner secrets of humanity, including the key dialectic of free will and determinism, are to be expounded by the keen artistic mind.

Yet in Roth's novel, the undermining of the tragic pattern is manifest. The central character becomes, for the tragic poet, "an uncohesive person." His decisions no longer appear to have continuity: they do not occur due to particular and identifiable character traits, but register instead as contingent events. This might seem to bring us back, perhaps ironically, to a more Aristotelian view of tragedy—the imitation of an action and not of a character. Zuckerman mostly knows, after all, what Coleman *does* in his life, if not the reasons why he does it. But in his theory of tragedy in the *Poetics*, Aristotle was still centrally concerned with the fate of the protagonist—"people possess certain qualities in accordance with their character, but they achieve well-being or its opposite on the basis of how they fare" (11)—and could not have countenanced an unknowable or uncohesive central presence in the drama. Thus Zuckerman's narrative examination of cause and effect runs aground here; but another mode of understanding, one of traditional importance in literary art, shadows this search for causality throughout *The Human Stain*, and is offered at certain points as a supplement or alternative. Aware that narrative coherence fails to account for Coleman's life, in his search for the kind of coherent insights that tragedy seems to require, Zuckerman at times turns overtly to symbolism, the hermeneutic backbone of so much modern art. Understanding the way symbols function in the novel is a crucial aspect of its reading, and a treatment of this topic is required before this chapter moves toward its conclusion.

IV Symbolic connections

The first major symbol in *The Human Stain* is the tattoo that Coleman receives on "the worst night of his life" (180, 184), the night he is forcibly removed from the white whorehouse in Norfolk for being black. In an extraordinary scene, Zuckerman imagines the voice of Coleman's dead father coming back to remind him of the immensity of his racial defection: "A world of love, that's what you had, and instead you forsake it for this! The tragic, reckless thing that you've done!" (183). Coleman promises his father's spirit that if he gets through to his navy discharge he will "never lie again" (182). Yet what becomes of this promise is another in a long line of discontinuities. The narration switches from free indirect discourse to a detached recounting of Coleman's discovery by shore patrol the next morning, with a fresh US Navy tattoo imprinted on his arm. In considering the symbolic potential of this tattoo, we move back inside Coleman's mind:

> [I]t was the sign of the whole of his history, of the indivisibility of the heroism and the disgrace. Embedded in that blue tattoo was a true and total image of himself. The ineradicable biography was there, as was the prototype of the ineradicable, a tattoo being the very emblem of what cannot ever be removed. The enormous enterprise was also there. The outside forces were there. The whole chain of the unforeseen, all the dangers of exposure and all the dangers of concealment—even the senselessness of life was there in that stupid little blue tattoo. (184)

The tattoo is a synecdoche *par excellence*—not only does it stand for the totality of Coleman's life, but it also contains all the "outside forces" that complete the tragic pattern to which his life is subjected in the book. It seems to enclose all the meaning that the narrative as a whole meditates upon. And yet the coherence offered is illusory: nothing can be learned from such symbolic positing that can bring us closer to real understanding. This we can intuit because at this very moment we witness perhaps the most abrupt shift in the entire novel: the narrative moves immediately from the above passage to an introduction to the vexed relationship between Coleman and Delphine that begins years later. The symbolic tattoo has proven an epistemological dead-end—it is as though Zuckerman cannot decide where else to go after the enclosing totality that it represents. His tragic narrative is attempting to map an authentic temporality, whereas the basic relation of symbolism, as Paul de Man has argued, "is one of simultaneity, which, in truth, is spatial in kind, and in which the invention of time is merely a matter of contingency" ("Rhetoric" 207). Refusing an illusory spatial coherence, Zuckerman cannot here countenance understanding the world or Coleman's life in a manner that negates the importance of time and temporal development.

To strengthen this reading, we can look to other examples of potentially all-encompassing symbols in the text. In Zuckerman's culminating confrontation with Les Farley, much of the palpable tension of the scene on the ice is created by the presence of Farley's threatening drilling tool, the auger. This unfamiliar word is no doubt utilized to exploit its visual and aural similarity to "augur," another term resonant with tragic potential. That the auge(u)r may hold the promise of wisdom is confirmed when Zuckerman responds to the presence of the drilling tool a few inches from his face: "Here. Here was the origin. Here was the essence. Here" (359). In this instant, the auge(u)r would seem, like the tattoo before it, to encapsulate the meaning of the entire narrative; and yet that meaning proves more obscure than ever. Again, it is the very secrecy of meaning we are witnessing, and it is fitting that Farley himself should recap on this theme in his eulogy to his "secret spot" in the mountains: "That's how secret it is. Maybe I end up tending to be a little dishonest. But this place is like the best-kept secret in the whole world" (349).

"And now I know," responds Zuckerman. But despite his confidence here, Zuckerman knows nothing, neither about this secret nor the others he has struggled with in his narrative. Roth would seem to be mocking the symbolic mode even while paying homage to it, never more so than in the final two lines of the novel, in which the entire scene becomes an ironic image of purity and peace:

> There it was, if not the whole story, the whole picture. Only rarely, at the end of our century, does life offer up a vision as pure and peaceful as this one: a solitary man on a bucket, fishing through eighteen inches of ice in a lake that's constantly turning over its water atop an arcadian mountain in America. (361)

Here, at the novel's millennial finale, is Roth's conclusive puncturing of a symbolic explanation of events. Denied "the whole story" through the lack of knowledge and certainty offered by narrative connections, here we are offered "the whole picture." Yet a moment of reflection reveals this sense of an ending to be a grand forgery—there is nothing pure and peaceful about Les Farley or what he represents to Zuckerman, and behind this Thoreauvian image of arcadia lies a murderous and disturbing reality.

This symbol of the human mark on the arcadian landscape—"like the X of an illiterate's signature on a sheet of paper" (361)—recalls once again what would seem to be the master symbol of the text, the one that gives the book its title both within the covers and without—the human stain itself. As a tragic trope it recalls the notion of *hamartia*, although the image, as it is explored in the novel, suggests a more universal application than as a straightforward analogy with the hero's fatal flaw. The passage within which the phrase occurs has Faunia Farley considering the deficiencies of a hand-raised crow she has become fond of:

> "That's what comes of hanging around all his life with people like us. The human stain," she said, and without revulsion or contempt or condemnation. Not even with sadness. *That's how it is*—in her own dry way, that is all Faunia was telling the girl feeding the snake: we leave a stain, we leave a trail, we leave our imprint. Impurity, cruelty, abuse, error, excrement, semen—there's no other way to be here. Nothing to do with disobedience. Nothing to do with grace or salvation or redemption. It's in everyone. Indwelling. Inherent. Defining. [. . .] All she was saying about the stain is that it's inescapable. That, naturally, would be Faunia's take on it: the inevitably stained creatures that we are. (242)

Here, it initially seems, we have the final word on the tragic meaning of the novel. The quest for purity, a quest that Coleman appears to engage in throughout the novel, is a fantasy, a lie. It finds its image in the stain, a fundamental mark common to all humans. Critics and commentators have been near-unanimous in proclaiming this as the novel's central message.[8] Yet the final line of the above quotation should give us pause: "That, naturally, would be Faunia's take on it: the inevitably stained creatures that we are." To this point in the novel, Zuckerman has been at pains to imagine Faunia as a kind of hyper-materialist. For her, all forms of metaphysical thinking are at fault for the sins of the world.[9] That a view ascribed to her should contain the core message of a novel so obsessed with metaphysical questions is not impossible, but more likely Zuckerman means to indicate that the stained nature of humanity is just one of a number of possible interpretations to place in the epistemological vortex that the novel has by now become.

V Narrative beyond tragedy

Summarizing my analysis thus far, I would now like to suggest that Zuckerman's project of narrating the life and decisions of Coleman Silk in *The Human Stain* brings three representational frameworks into conflict. The first is the classically tragic perspective, in which the hero disregards his determinate heritage in a doomed attempt to defy the gods. Walter Reed defines the hero as "that singular and energetic individual whose character contains his fate" (1), and it is this version of Coleman, "the greatest of the great *pioneers* of the I," that Zuckerman promotes throughout the majority of *The Human Stain*. As the text's narrator, however, Zuckerman himself represents a second, more modern view of the self, a man who rather than raging against fate reconciles himself to his accidental place in the sphere of life and attempts to understand himself as fully as possible, particularly through reflection upon his own psychology. In the short passages where he details the current circumstances of his life—living and writing alone in the Berkshires, impotent after a prostate operation "several years ago"—Zuckerman is careful to clarify for the reader that he understands very well the causal processes at work in the decisions that have led him to this point: "I want to make clear that it wasn't impotence that led me to a reclusive existence. [. . .] The operation did no more than to enforce with finality a decision I'd come to on my own" (36–7).

In *Elegiac Romance*, Kenneth Bruffee suggests that the observer-narrator is the "exemplary modern figure" of the genre (15), and his modernity is tied to the kind of reflective investigation in which Zuckerman engages: "The narrator recovers the coherence of his inner world by drawing the past out of himself in telling his tale" (52). Moreover, this search for coherence is linked by Bruffee to an affinity for the symbol: "to narrate is to transform remembered experience into symbol [. . .]. To symbolize is to effect significant mental development" (52). Zuckerman's frequent invocations of the symbolic, then, can be read as evidence of his modernity, and of his modernist impulses as a narrator. Indeed, these impulses are further confirmed by the status he affords to the imagination, a concept that—recalling a modernist ideology that finds perhaps its clearest expression in the art of Wallace Stevens—replaces an emphasis on empirical truth with the priority of the mind of the subject. We see this clearly in Zuckerman's frequent refelctions on writing:

> Faunia alone knew how Coleman Silk had come about being himself. How do I know she knew? I don't. I couldn't know that either. I can't know. Now that they're dead, nobody can know. For better or worse, I can only do what everyone does

who thinks that they know. I imagine. I am forced to imagine. It happens to be what I do for a living. It is my job. Now it's all I do. (213)

A striking feature of this passage, nevertheless, is the way the celebration of the imagination we find in canonical modernism here suffers an anxiety of instrumentalization, with Zuckerman "forced to imagine" for a "living" and a "job." And this anxiety is further heightened by the challenge Zuckerman eventually registers to his modernist imagination, with its inherited tendency toward representing "the form and content of 'inner truth' by symbolic projection" (Bruffee, *Elegiac* 68). In *Postmodernism*, Fredric Jameson argues that modernist artworks (his example is Van Gogh's painting of peasant shoes) invite hermeneutical readings that posit the symbol "as a clue or a symptom of some vaster reality which replaces it as its ultimate truth" (8). Against this modern symbol Jameson places the postmodern image (Warhol's *Diamond Dust Shoes*) that offers "no way to complete the hermeneutic gesture and restore to these oddments that whole larger living context" (8). The version of Coleman Silk that is introduced into the narrative by Ernestine's revelations places Zuckerman's hermeneutic gestures into relief, and this Coleman seems to correspond more closely to Jameson's depiction of the postmodern subject, no longer alienated like the modern Zuckerman but instead fragmented: "the subject has lost its capacity actively to extend its pro-tensions and re-tensions across the temporal manifold and to organize its past and future into coherent experience" (25). Thus, while throughout most of *The Human Stain* Zuckerman's brand of skeptical modernity contrasts with and contextualizes Coleman's tragic quest to control reality, both are challenged at the conclusion of the novel by Zuckerman's perception of the "uncohesive" nature of Coleman's life, the event-like quality of his decisions, unconnected to a clear and underlying self persisting through time. This third representational framework, the postmodern one, understands any kind of coherence as an imposition, with all action fragmented, irreducible neither to a monadic or expressive notion of the self, nor to a realism weighted with classically tragic pathos.[10]

Shostak has located this clash of representational frameworks at the heart of Roth's innovation throughout his career; in her words, "Roth discloses the underpinnings of the primary modes of contemporary fictional representation" (*Philip* 188). Normally, he does so from one novel to another, so that "his testing of representational possibilities has seemed to suggest that the ontogeny of Roth's career has recapitulated the phylogeny of the novel, as, for example, in the development from *Letting Go* (realism) to *The Ghost Writer* (modernism) to *The Counterlife* (postmodernism)" (187). If we read *The Human Stain* as part of Roth's attempt to take his later fiction beyond the postmodern concerns of texts such as *The Counterlife*, what becomes most significant about the novel, with this in mind, is that it does not finally arbitrate between the alternative representations of Coleman's life and decisions that it puts forward. Rather, the novel provides evidence for each of these representations, alongside reasons to doubt that evidence. The decision as to what to affirm and believe is left to the reader, and this is where we can reconnect to a discussion of Derrida's work, because the powerful representational play of Roth's novel presents the reader with a situation that

Derrida defines as "a determinate oscillation between possibilities," or, in shorthand, "undecidability":

> I want to recall that undecidability is always a *determinate* oscillation between possibilities (for example, of meaning, but also of acts). These possibilities are themselves highly *determined* in strictly *defined* situations (for example, discursive—syntactical or rhetorical—but also political, ethical, etc.) They are *pragmatically* determined. (*Limited* 148)

In early works such as *Dissemination*, Derrida stressed undecidability in meaning, focusing primarily on discursive and rhetorical situations. The claim that undecidability is the positive condition of the moment of decision comes later, and this quotation from *Limited Inc.* can be seen as a hinge between the early and late Derrida in this regard. Yet Derrida's separation of possibilities "of meaning" from those "of acts," a separation implied within the first parenthesis of the block quote, is in fact partly misleading: decisions on meaning are themselves acts, while acts also have meanings, meanings which are "political, ethical, etc." Yet these acts of meaning can never be understood simply as instantiations of a pure agency; they take place in contexts, and Derrida's notion of "pragmatic" determination reinscribes the contexts in which such acts take place, contexts understood in terms of relations of force: "I say 'undecidability' rather than 'indeterminacy' because I am interested more in relations of force, in differences of force, in everything that allows, precisely, determinations in given situations to be stabilized through a decision of writing" (148).

In *The Human Stain*, we can see Zuckerman's "decision of writing" working to stabilize a set of interpretative possibilities into his text, a set of possibilities "pragmatically determined" by the late- or post-postmodern literary and historical context in which he writes. Derrida makes clear at the beginning of *Of Grammatology* that frameworks of interpretation take their place in rough relation to historical epochs, and with this in mind, "tragic," "modern," and "postmodern" can name both relatively stable frameworks in particular periods and interpretive possibilities in all periods, possibilities that present themselves as viable and undecidable alternatives in the representational matrix of the American novel of the 1990s. This non-closure of interpretive possibilities is signified in *The Human Stain* by Zuckerman's own allusion to the text we are reading, when he tells Les Farley at the finale that he is writing a novel called *The Human Stain*, a novel that, as we know through reading it, suggests that the task of representing its hero's undecidable decision necessarily involves further "decisions of writing" inseparable from that undecidability. The violence of the hero's decision, the cut or wound it makes in the world, repeats itself in any attempt by the other to tell his story, and in any reactivation of the text by the reader.[11]

While producing *The Human Stain* will represent the endpoint of his narrative, Zuckerman also offers at certain moments an explanation of the origin of his task. One such moment occurs at Coleman's graveside, when "standing in the falling darkness beside the uneven earth mound roughly heaped over Coleman's coffin, I was completely seized by his story, by its end and by its beginning, and, then and there, I began this book"

(337). Here the other haunts the self, and the story attains an active and even aggressive dimension vis-à-vis its narrator, who is passively "seized" by it before he appears to have a choice. Another origin story for Zuckerman's task as writer is the dance he and Coleman share early on in their friendship, which occurs on the night when Coleman first opens up to Zuckerman: "Indeed, the dance that sealed our friendship was also what made his disaster my subject. And made his disguise my subject. And made the proper presentation of his secret my problem to solve" (45). The proper presentation of that secret, a secret which Coleman himself never reveals to Zuckerman, involves the narrator's initial decision to believe in the "foolish illusion" that the forms and themes of tragedy can offer closure, and also a further decision to present the story reflexively in a way that eventually places that belief in question.

As such, the maintenance of the secret in *The Human Stain* trumps any notion of truth as unconcealment. Indeed, in a scene in which Zuckerman imagines another dance, this time between Coleman and Faunia, he inserts into Faunia's interior monologue a critique of such a notion of truth: "He's lost his wife, he's lost his job, publically humiliated as a racist professor, and what's a racist professor? It's not that you've just become one. The story is that you've been discovered, so it's been your whole life" (228). Here, Faunia excoriates the complacency of those who think that discovering a secret means revealing it, that, to cite Derrida's words on Abraham again, a "transmitted" secret simply amounts to "a history, a story." Faunia resists this kind of closure, just as Zuckerman does in his words about Mark Silk at Coleman's funeral, and just as an anonymous academic does in the novel's chorus scene:

> Closure. There's one. My students cannot stay in that place where thinking must occur. Closure! They fix on the conventionalized narrative, with its beginning, middle, and end—every experience, no matter how ambiguous, no matter how knotty or mysterious, must lend itself to this normalizing, conventionalizing, anchorman cliché. Any kid who says "closure" I flunk. They want closure, there's their closure. (147)

Rather than closure, the narrative of *The Human Stain* suggests how "the decision of the other in me"—in this novel, Coleman's decision to pass resonating through Zuckerman's observer's voice—always maintains the openness of an interpretive context. The decision to write, in observer-hero narrative, brings one up against the writing of the other's decision, and this decision, just as in the story of Abraham and Isaac, is what finally maintains its secrecy. In *Limited Inc.*, Derrida claims that "the value of truth (and all those values associated with it) is never contested or destroyed in my writings, but only reinscribed in more powerful, larger, more stratified contexts" (146). Philip Roth likewise seeks truth while demonstrating a very contemporary awareness of how truth is inscribed within "powerful, larger, more stratified contexts," contexts that highlight the undecidability, and inescapable complexity, of the hero's decision.

Scholarship to date on American fiction in the 1990s suggests the centrality of Roth's work—and particularly the "American trilogy" to which *The Human Stain* belongs—to any definition of that literary decade.[12] That Roth turned to the observer-hero narrative form at this point has of course a logic internal to his career: the more squarely postmodern Zuckerman of Roth's novels of the 1980s, obsessed with questions of fictionality, selfhood, and performance, gives way in the trilogy to a more realistically presented chronicler of the lives of others. However, as I have argued throughout this chapter, Zuckerman's self-conscious difficulties with adequately narrating the life of another, with representing that life within existing paradigms, should be taken as an index of concerns broader than simply those of Roth as an artist. As I will demonstrate in the three chapters to come, while Roth's novel closes out the twentieth century on this note of representational uncertainty, his concerns are likewise reflected in a series of important American novels from earlier in the century's final decade.

Testimony and Truth: Paul Auster's *Leviathan*

It would be an enormous project, a book that would take me years to finish. But that was the point somehow. As long as I was devoting myself to Dimaggio, I would be keeping him alive. I would give him my life, so to speak, and in exchange he would give my life back to me. (225)

Prologue

When, at the finale of Roth's novel, Nathan Zuckerman tells Les Farley that he is working on a book called *The Human Stain*, we are reminded for the concluding and most striking time that the text we hold in our hands constitutes, within the world of the novel itself, a form of testimony. Not simply an exercise in storytelling, image-making, or discursive reflection, the novel Zuckerman is writing depends upon his act of witnessing, his promise to speak the truth of what he has seen and heard. Despite its official status as a fictional work, something similar can be said about the novel by Roth that also bears the name *The Human Stain*, and this feature makes it far from unique: every fictional text, in its dimension as speech act, implicitly testifies to a kind of truth, and entreats the reader to believe—or to suspend disbelief—in the truth of the events narrated and the perspectives offered. This remains the case even if the narrative voice is disembodied, or the story told is unequivocally fantastic, or the presentation disregards conventional realism in favor of experimental narrative forms.[1]

Yet the testimonial promise is perhaps most apparent in those modes of first-person narration in which a dramatized narrator answers for the text we read, assuming control and responsibility for the form it takes and all the statements—true, false, or ambiguous—that it contains. And within the boundaries of this first-person mode, that fiction and testimony cross paths is even clearer in the genre I have identified as observer-hero narrative. Here, the narrator answers not only for his own experience but also for the experience of a predominant other. This other cannot now answer for himself, often because he is dead when his story is told, but more simply because he is precisely not the narrator of that story. Testimony, within this genre, becomes immediately more far-reaching and more complex, tied up with questions beyond those of self-knowledge and the detailing of one's own truth. To testify in this more extensive manner, it becomes necessary to speak on behalf of another, to bear witness for his/her actions and experiences: in short, to perform the kind of attestation that, as Jacques Derrida liked to remind us, is impossible.

One of Derrida's favorite sayings, to which he returned repeatedly in his late texts, is taken from the poet Paul Celan, and is deceptively simple in form: "*Niemand / zeugt für den / Zeugen*," which can be translated as "no one / bears witness for the / witness." This statement testifies to two things, depending on the understanding of "for": first, the impossibility of putting oneself *in the place of* the witness, of telling his/her story exactly as he/she would tell it; and second, the impossibility of testifying *on behalf of* the witness, of vouching for the truth of his/her testimony when that testimony puts forward an experience confined to him/her. Both readings emphasize the isolation of the witness, his/her singularity and solitude as the sole bearer of a professed truth. Celan's refrain chimes with one of Derrida's own maxims, already cited in the preceding chapter: *tout autre est tout autre*, every other is wholly other. Moreover, as Celan implies and Derrida will make explicit, this other for whom I cannot bear witness need not be another person but can also be oneself, because the self that testifies is never the same as the self that witnessed the event being testified to. This is not simply because a witness is always temporally distant from the event for which he/she bears witness, but also because the event has altered the witness in such a way that a rupture in selfhood, however minimal, has occurred. Maurice Blanchot's short narrative "The Instant of my Death," which Derrida reads at length in his *Demeure: Fiction and Testimony*, draws attention to this feature of testimony. The story of a young soldier who narrowly escapes execution, Blanchot's narrative invokes a separation between the "I" who narrates and the "he" who is narrated, even though both are ostensibly figures for Blanchot himself, and the incident described in the story repeats an incident from his own life. "In his place, I will not try to analyze" (*Demeure* 5), remarks Blanchot's narrator, and the story he tells professes a formidable rift between the younger man's experience and older man's testimony.

In his commentary on the story, Derrida draws out some of the paradoxes that the absolute and irreducible singularity of the witness produces in the character of testimony. The first paradox derives from a situation in which testimony must assert its status as truth, and yet testimony cannot by definition equate to objectively provable truth: "if testimony thereby became proof, information, certainty, or archive, it would lose its function as testimony. In order to remain testimony it must therefore allow itself to be haunted" (29). What testimony is haunted by, then, is precisely "the *possibility* of fiction, perjury, and lie. Were this possibility to be eliminated, no testimony would be possible any longer; it could no longer have the meaning of testimony" (27). This haunting of testimony by the possibility of fiction puts in question, according to Derrida, the distinction between *Dichtung* and *Wahrheit*, fictional speech and truth. This distinction lies at the foundation of our systems of politics and law, and the structure of testimony allows us to see that it is a distinction that depends on a promise, on an appeal to faith rather than knowledge. The second paradox derives from this promise: the witness must on the one hand be the only person who can testify to what he/she has experienced, but on the other hand he/she must promise that anyone in the same place would testify to the same thing: "In saying: I swear to tell the truth, where I have been the only one to see or hear and where I am the only one who can attest to it, this is true to the extent that anyone who *in my place*, at that instant, would have seen or heard or touched the same thing and could repeat exemplarily, universally, the truth of my testimony" (41).

For Derrida, it is the notion of the instant that is crucial here, because (in a third paradox) the instant that makes testimony possible as an "instance"—"The singular must be universalizable; this is the testimonial condition" (41)—is also betrayed by testimony's introduction of temporalization, division, and universalization, all of which deny the instant its singularity and secrecy. Nonetheless, secrecy adheres as a trace in every testimony, because "even where it makes manifest and public" (30), testimony resists complete submission to forms of knowledge and remains tied to the witness's unrepeatable experience. We are witnessing here another iteration of Abraham's singularity as it is explored in *The Gift of Death*; in addition, *Demeure* offers further evidence for why in that earlier text Derrida sees the figure of Abraham as standing at "the origin of this fund without which what we call literature would probably never have managed to emerge as such and under that name" (*Gift* 121). In *Demeure*, it is Blanchot's story that exemplifies the relation between literature and testimony, with the singular instant of Blanchot's experience rendered readable and translatable through a literary text: "This is testimonial exemplarity. Because this singularity is universalizable, it is able to give rise—for example, in Blanchot—to a work that depends without depending on this very event, a readable and translatable work" (94).

In playing on the ambiguity of the term "witness"—referring as it does both to the one who experiences an event and to the one who later testifies to that experience (often in a court of law)—Derrida produces an epistemologically and ontologically inflected understanding of testimony. In a critique of Derrida's approach, however, Andrea Frisch contends that this difference between witnessing an event and bearing witness was not operative in pre-modern versions of testimony, suggesting a historical specificity to Derrida's conception. *Pace* Derrida, Frisch argues that in medieval testimony "the *witness* was not conceived as a first person" (48), but was rather a second-person participant in a dialogic and intersubjective process. As such, it was indeed possible to "bear witness for the witness" in the sense of vouching for his/her character, because witnessing was understood in ethical terms, rather than in the epistemic terms that Derrida invokes through his elaboration and deconstruction of Cartesianism. Frisch therefore suggests that theoretical conceptions of testimony might better be modeled on the dialogism of Bakhtin or on the ethical philosophy of Levinas, rather than on Derrida's singular and solitary epistemic witness.

It is this questioning of the relationship between dialogue and solitude, along with the positioning of testimony at the nexus of epistemology, ontology, and ethics, that leads me in this second chapter to another American novel of the 1990s, Paul Auster's

Leviathan. As we shall see in what follows, *Leviathan* provides us with a different kind of testimonial case—as well as an altered slant on observer-hero narrative as mode of literary inquiry—to that which we witnessed in the opening chapter of this study.

I Testimony, solitude, and politics

In *The Human Stain*, it is the absence of testimonial evidence—Coleman's refusal to speak of his decision to pass before death robs him of the chance to do so—that motivates the speculations of Roth's narrator toward the novel's end. Implicit in Zuckerman's imaginings, so copious and far-reaching in their speculative audacity, is an initial assumption that the truth has been kept secret by the only one who could have explained the decisions and actions that seem, on the surface, so inexplicable. Yet Zuckerman comes to wonder whether the incoherence, or "uncohesiveness," that he discovers might be more fundamental, and whether Coleman's silence might be more than a simple refusal to own up. Moreover, if Derrida and Blanchot are right in their understanding of testimonial epistemology, then any explanation by the one who decides would be just as treacherous as an explanation attempted from the "outside" by others. *Leviathan* tests this very proposition, by foregrounding less the observer's task of imagining the actions and decisions of the hero, and placing more emphasis on the importance of analyzing and evaluating the testimony the hero does offer to explain those actions and decisions. In Auster's novel there are no shortage of narrative explanations provided for the key decisive moments in the life of the protagonist; the task of the novel's observer-narrator becomes to weigh the testimony offered and to suggest his own synthesizing and corrective account. This written counter-testimony is what the reader is given direct access to in the book we read, and it is we who must assess whether such an account attests, in much the same way as Derrida claims all testimony does, to an inescapable link to "fiction, simulacra, dissimulation, lie, and perjury" (*Demeure* 29).

Of all the American writers considered in this study, Paul Auster is the one most evidently steeped in the philosophical frameworks I employ in my reading of 1990s fiction. As Tom Theobald's recent study *Existentialism and Baseball* reminds us, Auster has long been indebted to the influence of French thinkers such as Sartre, Camus, Blanchot, and Merleau-Ponty; earlier criticism on Auster's *oeuvre* would argue for the relevance of Bataille and Lacan as well. To this list it is tempting to add the name of Derrida, while acknowledging Auster's protestations to the contrary.[2] Auster began his writing career as a translator of French poetry, and in interviews and essays has consistently expressed an abiding concern with topics native to the European philosophical tradition. His novels, which generally concentrate on detailing the existential course of individual lives rather than describing what he has termed "the sociological moment" ("Memory's" 118), are full of rumination on moments of decision and transitional moments, and the role they play in existence.

Auster's avoidance of overt sociological concerns in his work not only places emphasis on the plight of the solitary individual, however; it has the corollary effect of locating the world of his characters in something like the timeless and fragmented postmodernity that Fredric Jameson describes. Auster's landscapes tend to be characterized by sterility, from the apocalyptic wasteland of *In The Country of Last Things* (1987), to the strange model of a city in *The Music of Chance* (1990), to the desert setting of *The Book of Illusions* (2002). Even the more conventional urban spaces he depicts often leave characters in a disorientated state, for instance in *City of Glass* (1985), where the protagonist Quinn is engaged in a parody of cognitive mapping when he follows Peter Stillman around the city in a pattern that may or may not be significant. Most notably, the monolithic state apparatus—an oppressive force in the modernist Kafka, and, in a more corporate guise, in the postmodernist Pynchon—has in Auster's work become virtually invisible within a capitalist world of risk and chance that his characters accept as the inescapable context for their existence.[3] For many of these characters, the only imperative that remains is the avoidance of atomized anonymity through the telling of their particular story.

Auster's *oeuvre* has thus had, from the beginning, a strong relationship to forms of testimony.[4] His first prose work of length, *The Invention of Solitude* (1982), is an experimental memoir often read as "Auster's chosen and invented mythology, as the first cause of all his subsequent works" (Barone 14). Concerns and incidents that appear in this two-part work occur again and again, transmuted in various ways, in his series of novels: the father–son relationship, the mentally ill sister, the experience of poverty, the inheritance of a large financial sum, the failed first marriage, the sudden death or shocking murder, the fall from a height, the imperative to write. "In essence," Derrida remarks, "a testimony is always autobiographical" (*Demeure* 43); yet just as in the case of Roth, Auster complicates the correspondences between life, testimony, and fiction in myriad ways. Most significantly for my purposes here, and with the Derrida-Frisch debate concerning testimony in mind, Auster's interpretation of the notion of solitude—a "complex term" that is "not just a synonym for loneliness or isolation" (*Red Notebook* 142)—can be understood to confound traditional notions of first-person autobiographical self-expression. Because "we learn our solitude from others," testimony to that solitude must emerge, according to Auster, in a dialogic context rather than a predominately lyric one—or better, in an undecidable oscillation between the two (144). Testifying to solitude therefore involves an invocation of the other, or others. Commenting on the second part of *The Invention of Solitude*, for instance, Auster has remarked, "On the one hand, it's a work about being alone; on the other hand, it's about community. That book has dozens of authors, and I wanted them all to speak through me. In the final analysis, 'The Book of Memory' is a collective work" (144).[5]

Auster's commitment to a dialogic context for exploring solitude in his fiction is evident in his interest in formally intricate modes of narration. Responding to a query about his use of first and third person, Auster averred that "there's a vast range between those two categories, and it's possible to bring the boundaries of first-person and third-person so close to each other that they touch, even overlap" (145). We see this overlap throughout Auster's body of work. The most frequent narrative mode in his series of novels (16 at the time of writing) is the male first person, but this is always complicated by the pressure of other perspectives and other voices. In *Moon Palace* (1989), for instance, M. S. Fogg's narrative reverts for long periods to that of his friend and mentor Thomas Effing; similarly, the predominately first-person narration of David Zimmer in *The Book of Illusions* gives way at one point to a lengthy scene-by-scene description of the films of Hector Mann and an extensive account of his life, all written squarely in the third person. Equally, predominately third-person Auster texts are rarely straightforwardly so. Toward the end of *City Of Glass* (1985), a previously unannounced first-person narrator appears, while in *Travels in a Scriptorium* (2006), the descriptive reportage of the life and memories of Mr. Blank is complicated by the conversational voice of a writer that intrudes at various points.

Despite this experimental variety in Auster's fiction, though, conventional notions of both solitude and testimony are challenged most forcefully in the narrative form of *The Invention of Solitude*. In "The Book of Memory," Auster writes a third-person account of a character named A, whose life experiences tally with Auster's own. Discussing the similar form of Blanchot's narrative, Derrida remarks that "[t]his passage to a 'he,' in the third person, the young man, of course signifies the discretion of the literary process, the ellipsis of someone who is not going to put himself forward and expose himself indiscreetly" (*Demeure* 53). In the same way, Auster's use of testimony is not about indiscreet exposure; rather, he has suggested that *The Invention of Solitude* is intended as "a meditation about certain questions, using myself as the central character" (*Red Notebook* 106). The other part of the work, "Portrait of an Invisible Man," also involves a complication of narrative mode: it is a first-person text in which Auster attempts to imagine the interior subjectivity of his recently deceased father. The text revolves around epistemological questions, whether and how it is possible to know and write the life of another. As such, "Portrait of an Invisible Man" takes the form of an exemplary observer-hero narrative, with the added complication of its autobiographical and testimonial truth content with respect to Auster's own life.

Leviathan, published a decade after *The Invention of Solitude*, repeats in fictional form many of the concerns and incidents that shape Auster's autobiographical text.[6] But whereas *The Invention of Solitude* was mostly concerned with solitude in the context of privacy and of the family, *Leviathan*—as suggested by its title from Hobbes, its epigraph from Emerson ("Every actual State is corrupt"), and its allusions to Thoreau, John Brown, and Rip Van Winkle—adds a notably public and political dimension. Described by one critic as "Auster's most overtly political work" (Martin 177), *Leviathan* is narrated from a point in mid-1990 and set mostly during the years of the Reagan presidency. The novel's hero figure is Benjamin Sachs, who begins the story as a writer of political essays and novels but ends it as a terrorist blown to smithereens by one of his own homemade bombs. This rather stark occupational and existential transition in Sachs's life is placed against the background of political change in the United States: "in the new American order of the 1980s," the reader is told, "his position became increasingly marginalized" (*Leviathan* 104). Importantly, however, the change in Sachs is not simply explained away as an inevitable consequence of wider sociopolitical transition. Rather, the very question of transition, and the possible connections between the transitions of an individual life and those of the wider social sphere, lies at the center of the story as it is narrated by Peter Aaron, a novelist and a friend of the dead hero.

As in *The Human Stain*, the five chapters of *Leviathan* provide a tragic frame through which the narrator interprets the action of the story. Once again, however, tragedy itself provides just one interpretive possibility, and is openly placed next to other explanations. Among these are the explanations offered by the hero himself for the decisions and transitions that mark his life. In attempting to universalize the singularity of his decisive experience through explanation, Benjamin Sachs in *Leviathan*, unlike Coleman Silk in *The Human Stain*, fulfills what Derrida calls "the testimonial condition" (*Demeure* 41). At the heart of *Leviathan*, as a consequence, is an all-consuming and many-faceted interest in understanding the moment of decision. In introducing the first book of critical essays on Auster, Dennis Barone notes that "[a]ctions have their consequence even if motive is impenetrable, and this is a fact Auster explores in each of his works" (12). But Auster also never fails to explore the mystery of motive itself in considerable depth, and in *Leviathan* he carries out a two-pronged analysis of the moment of decision, examining, in scrupulous detail, both etiology and consequence.

II Truth, art, and knowledge

The novel's opening lines tell of a recent incident, of a man killed suddenly and instantly:

> Six days ago, a man blew himself up by the side of a road in northern Wisconsin. There were no witnesses, but it appears he was sitting on the grass next to his parked car when the bomb he was building accidentally went off. According to the forensic reports that have just been published, the man was killed instantly. His body burst into dozens of small pieces, and fragments of his corpse were found as far as fifty feet away from the site of the explosion. As of today (July 4, 1990), no one seems to have any idea who the dead man was. (1)

The passage reads like a newspaper report (albeit an unusually graphic one), and the tone it initiates continues right the way down the opening page, so that the long first paragraph is almost as forensic as the reports it alludes to. Even so, the crucial problem of witnessing intrudes as early as the second line. "There were no witnesses," we are told, although we are then given a sizeable amount of information, obtained through precise technical procedures designed to retrospectively reduce the mystery of an event in the absence of witnesses to it. As the quoted passage ends, however, it becomes clear that there is also another kind of witnessing in question here. The present time is signalled by a date which, while having obvious political resonance in an American context, is not the date of the death itself, but the date that marks the beginning of the written testimony we are reading. It turns out that the person presenting us with the above information will become the primary witness for the dead man's life. The narrator is a novelist, Peter Aaron, who is undertaking to write the life story of his friend, fellow novelist, and latecomer to political terrorism, Benjamin Sachs.

The urgent necessity of this specific act of writing is immediately proclaimed by Aaron. He is, he tells us, in a race with the police and the FBI: "The story I have to tell is rather complicated, and unless I finish it before they come up with their answer, the words I'm about to write will mean nothing" (2). His complicated story must be told quickly, it must be revised in a hurry, and the physical text must "be ready for them when the moment comes. [. . .] And not just when I've had enough time to finish this—but at any moment, at any moment beginning now" (2). The punctual effect of this "now," as an originally divided marker of elusive presence, reminds the reader of the intricate relation of writing to time, a theme that will be reiterated throughout the novel (it is also an initial reminder of the novel's artifice, of course). Aaron clarifies further that haste is necessary because at stake is nothing less than the maintenance of the truth of the case: "Once the secret is out, all sorts of lies are going to be told, ugly distortions will circulate in the newspapers and magazines, and within a matter of days a man's reputation will be destroyed" (2). Revealing the truth has, claims Aaron, nothing to do with his own feelings about or judgment of Sachs, but is simply a duty he must carry out: "It's not that I want to defend what he did, but since he's no longer in a position to defend himself, the least I can do is explain who he was and give the true story of how he happened to be on that road in northern Wisconsin" (2). However incomplete and provisional its final form (and we are eventually told by Aaron that he gets only three-quarters of the way through his second draft before the FBI return), the book we hold in our hands will be a true account of Sachs's story, will testify to the truth behind the life and death of Aaron's late friend.

This relatively straightforward notion of delivering truth through testimony soon comes up against obstacles, however. In his role as witness, Aaron promises to "only speak about the things I know, the things I have seen with my own eyes and heard with my own ears" (22). Yet this equation of what Aaron has seen and heard with what he knows is put in serious doubt by the story he tells, a story in which any simple knowledge of truth comes under question from a variety of angles. From the first, unlike Zuckerman in *The Human Stain*, Aaron is fully upfront with the reader about how little he has comprehended Sachs's life. He admits that he has personally witnessed only a small amount of what goes on in the story he tells, meaning that there can be "nothing definitive" about his account: "I want to tell the truth about him, to set down these memories as honestly as I can, but I can't dismiss the possibility that I'm wrong, that the truth is quite different from what I imagine it to be" (22). His memories are based, inevitably, on his own observations, but he will not mislead the reader as to their validity: "These kinds of partial observations are subject to any number of errors and misreadings" (29–30). Given his lack of access to primary facts, in order to piece together his own testimony Aaron must rely on the testimonial accounts of others, preeminently Sachs himself, but also other characters including Maria Turner, Fanny

Sachs, and Lillian Stern. And it is here that more pressing problems arise, because not only are many of these accounts mutually conflicting on some basic points, but some are even internally inconsistent. For instance, Maria tells Aaron of the various accounts Lillian has given of how she and Reed Dimaggio broke off their relationship: "That made three different stories, Maria said, a typical example of how Lillian confronted the truth. One of the stories might have been real. It was even possible that all of them were real—but then again, it was just as possible that all of them were false" (165). In this statement, and many others like it, we glimpse the difficulty of a simple distinction between truth and falsity, and, indeed, this distinction is everywhere threatened and under erasure in Aaron's narrative, consistently highlighting what Derrida calls the "essential compossibility" of fiction and testimony (*Demeure* 42).

So while Aaron initially claims to be committed to univocal and referential forms of truth—as we have seen above, his very justification for writing Sachs's story relies upon such a commitment—he comes to acknowledge this essential compossibility of fiction and testimony in several passages. These often describe moments when Aaron's previous certainties are suddenly eroded as new information comes to light. One such passage follows Sachs's revelations about Fanny's mental difficulties and his own abiding fidelity, revelations that throw Aaron completely off-kilter:

> After that lunch, I no longer knew what to believe. Fanny had told me one thing, Sachs had told me another, and as soon as I accepted one story, I would have to reject the other. There wasn't any alternative. They had presented me with two versions of the truth, two separate and distinct realities, and no amount of pushing and shoving could ever bring them together. I understood that, and yet at the same time I realized that both stories had convinced me. [. . .] [I had] a certainty that both Fanny and Ben had been telling the truth. The truth as they saw it, perhaps, but nevertheless the truth. Neither one of them had been out to deceive me; neither one had intentionally lied. In other words, there was no universal truth. Not for them, not for anyone else. There was no one to blame or to defend, and the only justifiable response was compassion. (98)

In accepting both Fanny's and Sachs's testimonies and refusing to choose between them, Aaron moves away from a notion of truth as correspondence to external reality. Instead, as the passage moves from the ground of ontology—"two separate and distinct realities"—to epistemology—"the truth as they saw it perhaps, but nevertheless the truth"—to ethics—"neither one had intentionally lied"—Aaron also begins to favor an aesthetic mode of interpretation, reading his friends' testimonial truth-claims for their internal cogency, performative coherence, and emotive hold: "I realized that both stories had convinced me." In other words, Aaron begins to apply methods of judgment more familiar from reading narrative fiction than from assessing objective reality. Thus, when Maria argues that all of the stories Lillian tells "might have been real," Aaron recognizes that she is not suggesting they are all objectively accurate, but rather that objective accuracy, even if such a thing proves possible, should not be the primary criterion for judging these testimonies.

This account offered by Aaron of the effect on him of his friends' testimonies highlights the dialogic dimension to testimony, the way it relies upon speech acts and on appeals to intersubjective belief. *Leviathan* complicates this situation further, however, by asking what happens when testimony is displaced from the realm of present speech into the realms of writing and of art. This question is asked repeatedly through the novel, in an extended comparison between the thought and practice of three artist figures: Sachs, Aaron, and Maria Turner. Each adopts a distinct position on the relationship between art and life. On the connections between language and reality, for instance, Sachs seems to represent a realist position and Aaron a modernist one: "Words and things matched up for him, whereas for me they are constantly breaking apart, flying off in a hundred different directions" (49). Yet this is far from the full story, because Sachs's faith in the relationship between language and reality has less to do with George Eliot's famous notion of realism as "the humble and faithful study of reality" than with Sachs's talent for seeing literary patterns in the random events of real life: "he was able to read the world as though it were a work of the imagination, turning documented events into literary symbols, tropes that pointed to some dark, complex pattern embedded in the real" (24). Sachs also views history in much the same way, regularly making unexpected connections, "yoking together the most far-flung people and events" (24).

Sachs's literary understanding of history and reality is given expression in his debut novel, *The New Colossus*. Rather than the "conventional first novel" that Aaron had been expecting—"one of those thinly veiled attempts to fictionalize the story of his own life" (36)—*The New Colossus* is a precocious mix of fact, fiction, and intertextuality that, as Linda Fleck has pointed out, in its outline resembles a parallel version of E. L. Doctorow's *Ragtime* (Fleck 263). According to the chronology offered by Aaron, *The New Colossus* appears to have been published in 1973, two years before Doctorow's novel and in a similar post-1960s, early postmodern moment.[7] Like Doctorow's novel, though, it is not directly about that moment—"*The New Colossus* had nothing to do with the sixties, nothing to do with Vietnam or the antiwar movement"—but is instead a historical novel, "a meticulously researched book set in America between 1876 and 1890 and based on documented, verifiable facts" (37). Of the episodes in the book, and their cumulative effect, Aaron observes: "All of them are true, each is grounded in the real, and yet Sachs fits them together in such a way that they become steadily more fantastic, almost as if he were delineating a nightmare or a hallucination" (39). While respecting this creative impulse, Aaron nonetheless reads Sachs's book as an act of testimony, with Sachs as witness against the crimes he perceives his country to have committed: "in spite of the fact that he wasn't writing about himself, I understood how deeply personal the book must have been for him. The dominant emotion was anger, a full-blown, lacerating anger that surged up on nearly every page: anger against America, anger against political hypocrisy, anger as a weapon to destroy national myths" (40).

Sachs's novel confirms, then, that testimonial truth offers a site of collision for epistemology and ethics, as Aaron's reaction to Ben and Fanny Sachs's conflicting stories, and Frisch's reaction to Derrida, likewise suggest. And the existence of the novel equally highlights an irreducibly aesthetic dimension to testimony, something also indicated by the final movement of Sachs's life, when he repudiates writing for the direct engagement of political bombing as "The Phantom of Liberty." Although his decisive career change ostensibly sees Sachs choosing ethics and politics over aesthetics, his choice of mini-replicas of the Statue of Liberty as targets, alongside his habit of releasing elegant and gnomic statements to the press, demonstrate that he has not left a commitment to the priority of artistic forms of coherence completely behind. Fleck describes Sachs as "the consummate metaphorical man," one who constantly draws connections and looks for unifying principles, but she points out that he ends the novel as "a heap of fragments most postmodern" (262). In this contradiction between what Sachs says and what he does, the relationship between testimony and truth suffers further complication. As we shall see, this complication reaches its height in Sachs's reaction to the novel's central event, his fall from a New York fire escape.

Against Sachs's commitment to metaphor and connection, the novel positions Maria Turner's prioritization of metonymy and contingency. A performance artist who carries out strange and varied projects, Maria engages in a complex experiment relating will to chance through self-restriction. Maria is in fundamental agreement with Sachs on the co-implication of literature and life, and its repercussions for the notion of truth; as she tells Aaron, "[Sachs] understood that all my pieces were stories, and even if they were true stories, they were also invented. Or even if they were invented, they were also true" (127–8). At the same time, she offers a very different aesthetic model to that of Sachs, and her commitment to contingency leads Aaron to refers to her as "the reigning spirit of chance, [the] goddess of the unpredictable" (102). Nevertheless, when Maria stumbles upon an anonymous black address book lying on the ground, the narrator suggests that she decides to interpret its discovery in terms of fate rather than chance: "Chance had led her to it, but now that it was hers, she saw it as an instrument of fate" (67). This incident, and the interpretative decision that it provokes in Maria, will eventually lead unavoidably to catastrophe, according to Aaron: "At least two lives were lost, and even though it took years for that to happen, the connection between the past and the present is inescapable" (65).

Aaron's own narrative, the text we read, provides an oscillating engagement with both these approaches to the interrelation of art and life. Far less consistent in his commitment to either connection or contingency than either Sachs or Maria, Aaron can juxtapose statements such as the one just quoted, which suggests an "inescapable" connection between past, present, and future, with other remarks that argue for a view of the world governed by indeterminacy and chance. It is this latter stance he takes in the argument concerning Sachs's fall, and it is also how he explains to the reader the beginnings of his relationships with Maria and Iris. However, in explaining the nature of his own testimony, Aaron reverts to a model of connection: "Each one of us is connected to Sachs's death in some way, and it won't be possible for me to tell his story without telling each of our stories at the same time. Everything is connected to everything else, every story overlaps with every other story" (51).

As Mark Osteen has pointed out, the black address book that Maria finds, which symbolizes how "a single life—even one that remains mysterious or unfathomable in itself—throws out tentacles of connection," thereby becomes in the novel "a phantom version of Aaron's own book" (Osteen 88). Accordingly, the structure of *Leviathan* supplies the reader with connections that make the main story really a network of inseparable stories. While Aaron does not deny his central role in this network—"As much as Sachs himself, I'm the place where everything begins" (*Leviathan* 51)—any suggestion that he might offer a solid centre is undermined by his reference to another story that is being told as he tells his, the one the FBI is piecing together: "In other words, the whole time I'm here in Vermont writing this story, they'll be busy writing their own story. It will be my story, and once they've finished it, they'll know as much about me as I do myself" (7). The final clause of this early quotation, which might initially seem little more than a throwaway remark, in fact announces what will become a central concern of this observer-hero narrative: the complexity of relations between testimony, story-telling, and knowledge of self and other.

If by writing Aaron's story the authorities really *will* know as much about him as he does himself, then this claim can be interpreted in two overlapping ways. On one reading, it means that there is nothing Aaron can keep from those who write his story, no secret knowledge he can protect. This suggests that truly secret self-knowledge is a strict impossibility, that what another discovers about us cannot be trumped by any knowledge we have singular access to. Here Derrida is again helpful, in particular his contention that "the experience of a secret is, however contradictory this may seem, a testimonial experience" (*Demeure* 32). The contradiction lies in the conventional assumption that the secret belongs to the private sphere, whereas testimony is a public phenomenon. In deconstructing this distinction, Derrida goes against the intuitive understanding of both concepts: on the one hand, he highlights the irreducible singularity implied in testimony (though he does not equate this singularity with privacy), and on the other hand he names the secret as "that on the basis of which the public realm and the realm of the political can be and remain open" ("Remarks" 80). But to link the secret to testimony in this manner draws attention to the way both escape knowledge and refuse reference to a stable reality (for example, the self) that might be spoken of or fully represented within the commonality of language. In other words—and as the case of Abraham again exemplifies—the secret is a question of testimony *rather than* a question of knowledge, with all the implications for theories of truth and reference that this insight implies.

The other reading of Aaron's remark can be seen to follow from this insight. It is the more radical suggestion that there is no knowledge that precedes testimony, that testimony itself produces knowledge—not in the guise of referential truth, but as a mode of performative coherence similar to that of fiction. On this reading, Aaron can be understood to suggest that rather than testimony stemming from access to prior knowledge, it in fact becomes knowledge in being written, in taking the form of a story.[8] Thus we can see that the impossibility of knowing the *other*, which is the central insight of *The Human Stain*, is merely the starting point in *Leviathan*, which is further concerned with the vexing impossibility of *self*-knowledge outside of or prior to narrative conventions.

III Tragic, modern, and postmodern

While the moment of full revelation is withheld until the culminating act of *The Human Stain*, as befits the novel's Sophoclean inheritance, the crucial scene in *Leviathan* occurs in its third and middle chapter-act, a long section in which Aaron and Sachs dispute the meaning of the latter's fall from a New York fire escape on the night of July 4, 1986. This debate between the two principals is the novel's test case for understanding the relation of testimony to truth, as well as the moment when the text's opposing principles of connection and contingency meet most starkly. It entails, on Sachs's part, a series of decisions, regarding the meaning of past events and the orientation of future actions. It involves a decision to impute agency where there may have been only accident, a decision to interpret the past as a willed sequence rather than as a case of inexplicable chance writ large, and a decision to use this "unassailable conclusion" (121) as a stimulus for irrevocably changing his life.

The chapter begins with an invocation of the political situation in 1980s America: "The era of Ronald Reagan began" (104). According to Aaron, the character of that decade, its "climate of selfishness and intolerance, of moronic, chest-pounding Americanism," cast Sachs in the role of outsider, increasingly marginalizing him and lessening the audience for his offbeat political essays and journalism.[9] Although Sachs "pretended not to care," Aaron declares that "he was gradually losing faith in himself" (104). This was also the period in which the proposed film of *The New Colossus* was dropped from consideration, and it is this blow that the narrator believes began to tip Sachs over the edge. Yet immediately after stating these concerns about Sachs's well-being at the time, Aaron finds himself admitting that "[a]ll this is speculation," and that there is in fact evidence to the contrary, an increase in Sachs's productivity that suggests that "far from having lost his direction, he was in fact barreling ahead at full tilt" (105). The conflict between belief and evidence manifest in Aaron's claims here marks the beginning of what eventually constitutes a long debate, with contributions from both observer and hero, on issues of human causality, change and self-knowledge, focused on the correct description and interpretation of Sachs's fall. That this section of the text (105–23), which takes us exactly up to the novel's halfway point, is the pivot for understanding everything else that happens in the story seems undeniable. And yet to decide in this way is already to pre-empt one of the core questions in the debate, the question of whether everything is connected and takes part in a larger meaning, or whether there is an irreducible aleatory element to life that robs events of all coherence and sense.

Aaron immediately foregrounds this question in attempting to support his contention that Sachs was suffering internally in the period before his fall. It is a crucial passage that demands to be quoted in full:

> If I question this optimistic portrait of Sachs during those years, it's only because
> I know what happened later. Immense changes occurred inside him, and while it's
> simple enough to pinpoint the moment when these changes began, to zero in on
> the night of his accident and blame everything on that freakish occurrence, I no

longer believe that explanation is adequate. Is it possible for someone to change overnight? Can a man fall asleep as one person and then wake up as another? Perhaps, but I wouldn't want to bet on it. It's not that the accident wasn't serious, but there are a thousand different ways in which a person can respond to a brush with death. That Sachs responded in the way he did doesn't mean I think he had any choice in the matter. On the contrary, I look on it as a reflection of his state of mind before the accident ever took place. In other words, even if Sachs seemed to be doing more or less well just then, even if he was only dimly aware of his own distress during the months and years that preceded that night, I am convinced he was in a very bad way. I have no proof to offer in support of this statement— except the proof of hindsight. Most men would have considered themselves lucky to have lived through what happened to Sachs that evening and then shrugged it off. But Sachs didn't, and the fact that he didn't—or, more precisely, the fact that he couldn't—suggests that the accident did not change him so much as make visible what had previously been hidden. If I'm wrong about this, then everything I've written so far is rubbish, a heap of irrelevant musings. Perhaps Ben's life did break in two that night, dividing into a distinct before and after—in which case everything from before can be struck from the record. But if that's true, it would mean that human behavior makes no sense. It would mean that nothing can ever be understood about anything. (105–6)

This passage already highlights many of the themes of the dialogue to come. The authority of hindsight is offered by Aaron as "proof" that his diagnosis of Sachs has validity, just as Sachs will suggest that retrospection has provided him with greater understanding of the reasons behind his fall. Attributed mental states (even unconscious ones) are given greater weight than any outer evidence by Aaron; similarly, Sachs will privilege his own inner awareness and subconscious desires over more obvious interpretations of his actions on the night of the fall. Aaron underlines the importance of the issue of choice (or lack of it) for understanding Sachs's reaction, a concern Sachs will likewise see as central, though in a different way. Finally, and significantly, the question of coherence asserts itself strongly in Aaron's account. For him, Sachs's psychology and behavior on and after the night in question simply must display continuity with his mental state before the fall. His own entire testimony to this point, Aaron believes, essentially depends for its validity upon the possibility of a continuous and coherent narrative of Sachs's life and self. If this coherence does not exist, if "Ben's life did break in two that night," then there can be no access to the singularity of that experience (which, just as in Blanchot, will be the "unexperienced experience" of death [*Demeure* 47]), and Aaron's testimony "can be struck from the record." Such testimony would lack the function of knowledge that Aaron had earlier claimed for testimony in general, and the narrative we are reading would be no more than a tissue of half-truths and speculations.

In seeing the fall as simply a contingent accident—a "freakish occurrence"—and arguing that Sachs's decisive reaction to it should be understood through connection with his mental state prior to the fall, Aaron promotes what in the preceding chapter

I called the modern understanding of the self. Sachs's response to the fall "make[s] visible what had previously been hidden," and this hidden element gives access to the coherence of the whole, which, as in Kenneth Bruffee's account of elegiac romance, is psychological in nature. At work here is a hermeneutics derived from Freud, positing an unconscious which Sachs cannot control, but which can be uncovered, analyzed, and potentially reconciled through accurate diagnosis and understanding.[10] But just as in *The Human Stain*, where an inexplicable event—the decisive division of a life into a before and after—offers itself as the origin of the modern psychological interpretation (and of the tragic one, as we shall see pertains to *Leviathan* too), this inexplicable event is also what returns to disrupt interpretation, haunting it with the possibility of incoherence, reiterating its "eventness" in a manner most postmodern.

Indeed, the predilection "for events rather than new worlds," a predilection that for Jameson characterizes postmodern hermeneutics (*Postmodernism* ix), is underscored by the single literary allusion Aaron makes in the quoted passage. In rhetorically asking whether a man can "fall asleep as one person and then wake up as another," the narrator is summoning the ghost of a venerable American creation, a reference that is confirmed a few pages later when Sachs opens his eyes in the hospital to a nurse, and "heard her announce to someone that Rip Van Winkle had finally woken up" (118). Rip, of course, is the original American to fall asleep only to wake up in a "new world," one substantially altered during his absence. Nonetheless, the parallels between this mythic figure and Sachs prove less telling than the differences. Whereas Rip Van Winkle suffers initial doubt and uncertainty, wondering "whether he was himself or another man" (Irving 29), Benjamin Sachs claims to experience from the beginning "a feeling of absolute certainty" regarding the meaning of his fall (*Leviathan* 116). Whereas Rip eventually ascertains that it is the world and not himself that is "new," and thus regains his sense of identity as his story concludes, Sachs's finds that all the significant events have happened within him, and that he can never return to his old self. Finally, in response to his new surroundings, Rip refuses the draw of the broader political world, eventually settles back into something resembling his old way of life, and ends his adventures peaceful and content in post-Revolution America. Sachs, by contrast, spends the remainder of the novel, and of his life, travelling restlessly all over the United States, attempting to create a series of political "events" to shake up a complacent world that refuses to accept the renewal he feels is essential.

Consequently, while the narrative arc of "Rip Van Winkle" offers the comforting suggestion that human beings remain the same over time, that character remains fundamentally unaltered by vast swathes of time, political shifts, and bewildering experiences, *Leviathan* offers nothing like this consolation. Much of this is down to the narrative method: whereas Irving's story is told in the authoritative and reassuring register of the folktale, the overt reliance on testimony in Auster's novel undermines the authority that would resolve the mystery of the novel's crucial moment of transition. The promise of such authority is invoked, however, during Sachs's ten-day silence upon waking from his fall. Just as Zuckerman initially wants to believe that Coleman Silk's first-person account might clarify the mystery of his decision, so Aaron initially understands Sachs's silence to be the contingent prelude to a full explanation:

"Something had happened, something more than the physical injuries caused by the accident, and until Sachs was able to speak, or until he decided he wanted to speak, Fanny would never know what it was" (111). Sachs will later deny that his prolonged silence is the result of a conscious decision—"it just happened that way" (118)—but he claims nevertheless to have used this period of reflection to explore his experience and divine the true meaning of his fall: "Something extraordinary had taken place, and before it lost its force within him, he needed to devote his unstinting attention to it. Hence his silence. It was not a refusal so much as a method, a way of holding onto the horror of that night long enough to make sense of it" (119).

When he eventually does speak, Sachs has an unexpectedly complex story to tell, certainly one more elaborate than the straightforward testimony Maria Turner offers during his silence. While her account of his fall does stress contingency, there is nothing incoherent about it: in a random act of misfortune, a woman tripped and fell into Maria from behind, dislodging Sachs from her arms as she held him on the banister of the fire escape. Sachs, in stark contrast, understands the situation in a wholly different manner, readily embracing a reading of events in which he is the agent of his own downfall:

> He had no intention of forgiving himself, he told me. His guilt was a foregone conclusion, and the less time he wasted on it the better. "At any other moment in my life," he said, "I probably would have looked for excuses. Accidents happen after all. [. . .] But the fact was that my accident wasn't caused by bad luck. I wasn't just a victim, I was an accomplice, an active partner in everything that was happening to me, and I can't ignore that, I have to take some responsibility for the role I played. [. . .] Looking back on that scene from my hospital bed, I finally understood that everything was different from how I had imagined it. I had gotten it backwards, I had been looking at it upsidedown. The point of my crazy antics wasn't to get Maria Turner to put her arms around me, it was to risk my life." (120)

In the previous chapter, we saw Zuckerman imagine scenarios in which Coleman Silk denies the relevance of the lessons of tragedy for understanding the consequences of his decision to reject his racial inheritance. Here, on the contrary, Benjamin Sachs does not hesitate to attribute blame and responsibility to himself. Exploiting a hindsight that he claims reveals the true nature of his experience, he decides, in effect, to interpret his fall not as an *event* but as a *decision*, an interpretation that imputes to Sachs an unconscious but willed confrontation with his fate and a tragic drive to self-destruction.

In *Shakespearean Tragedy*, A. C. Bradley claimed that at the core of tragedy lies a "painful mystery" that resists analysis (29). When he asks himself "Why did I do it? Why was I so eager to court that risk?" Sachs confronts this kind of painful mystery, reflecting that "a tremendous chasm would open up inside me" which reveals nothing but "impenetrable" reasons for his wish "to kill myself" (*Leviathan* 121). Thus Sachs's fall, which Aaron sees as nothing but a "freakish occurrence," is viewed by Sachs in uncompromisingly moral terms, with his guilt "a foregone conclusion." This reaction—which Aaron characteristically puts down to long-term and increasing psychological distress, with the events of the night virtually irrelevant ("The business with Maria struck me as trivial, of no genuine importance, a trite comedy of manners not worth talking about" [117])—comes to Sachs as a revelation that is nothing less than metaphysical in import: "In Sachs's mind, however, there was a direct connection. The one thing had caused the other, which meant that he didn't see the fall as an accident or a piece of bad luck so much as some grotesque form of punishment. [. . .] A quick, ludicrous embrace had become the moral equivalent of death" (117). For Sachs, therefore, the real source of his reaction is not explicable psychologically, but metaphysically: the fall is a moment of truth that offers a profound insight into moral causality and the tragic nature of the bad faith in which he had been living. Rejecting his work as a writer, he ends their debate by telling Aaron, "I want to end the life I've been living up to now. I want everything to change. If I don't manage to do that, I'm going to be in deep trouble. My whole life has been a waste, a dismal string of petty failures. [. . .] The days of being a shadow are over. I've got to step into the real world now and do something" (122).

Peter Aaron may consider the inescapable moral guilt and responsibility implied by this tragic reading too weighty and deep to be borne by the modern subject, while Benjamin Sachs may feel that a psychological explanation reductively cheapens the painful moral insight he has gained. But both Aaron's modern explanation and Sachs's tragic one share an identical feature: they both depend on the retrospective maintenance of coherence, and, as Raymond Williams puts it in *Modern Tragedy*, "on the capacity to connect the event with some more general body of facts, so that it is not a mere accident but is capable of bearing a general meaning" (46–7). While Aaron is willing to see the fall as an accident, he is committed to seeing Sachs's reaction as non-accidental; Sachs, by contrast, sees no accident in either fall or reaction beyond the accident of man's metaphysical fate, an accident that possesses tragic meaning. But in the postmodern reading that Aaron explicitly rejects in the long passage quoted earlier, and that Sachs implicitly rejects in his account, such patterns of causation are not so easy to locate. As Aaron recognizes, the threat inherent in the reading of Sachs's reaction as an uncaused, pure event is that "human behavior makes no sense. [. . .] that nothing can ever be understood about anything." Moreover, the distinction between accident and non-accident cannot survive this reading, rendering the logic of narrative itself incoherent. Rather than submit to this conclusion—reminiscent of Zuckerman's ontological insight into Coleman as an "uncohesive person"—the narrator and hero of *Leviathan* prefer to keep their debate on epistemological territory, arguing about the nature of testimony and how one can tell the difference between true and false accounts of experience. With both parties claiming "the proof of hindsight," the debate becomes about the plausibility of the story one can tell to account for a decision:

"I was drunk, and I knew exactly what I was doing. It's just that I didn't know I knew it."

"That's double-talk. Pure sophistry."

"I didn't know that I knew, and the drinks gave me the courage to act. They helped me do the thing I didn't know I wanted to do."

"You told me you fell because you were too afraid to touch Maria's leg. Now you change your story and tell me that you fell on purpose. You can't have it both ways. It's got to be one or the other."

"It's both. The one thing led to the other, and they can't be separated. I'm not saying I understand it, I'm just telling you how it was, what I know to be true." (121)

IV Writing, recording, and storytelling

Following this lengthy exchange between the two principals, the remainder of *Leviathan* deliberately stretches the plausibility of storytelling, featuring a series of bizarre and far-fetched plot twists that eventually culminate in Sachs's self-destruction by the Wisconsin roadside. Providing a determinate interpretation of this manic plot, connecting it to "some more general body of facts," would mean demonstrating allegiance to one of the readings presented by Sachs and Aaron in their debate, or indeed to the reading they both reject. The reader can choose to see what happens in the final hundred or so pages of the novel as the playing out of the logic of Sachs's strange situation and choices, as the unavoidable outcome of a tragic fate, or as a continued series of random events, plausible or implausible. All that is certain, in terms of the text's schema, is that the story continues to be offered to us in uncertainty, as a palimpsest of testimonies, with the narrator Aaron's direct access to key events receding further and further as the novel goes on.

Indeed, by the time he sits down to write the text we read, to attempt "to give the true story" of Sachs's life and death (2), Aaron has been firmly established as an unreliable narrator. Unreliable not because he deliberately hides things from the reader, but because he has shown himself, partly by his own admission, not to be well placed to tell the story. Not only is he lacking direct experience of almost all the events of the novel's second half, but by the end of chapter three the fallibility of Aaron's interpretive abilities has gained full thematic status, when he proves himself a poor reader of the clues presented to him by Sachs's behavior in the period following the fall. Part of the problem is that he continues to insist on a symptomatic reading, searching for an underlying connective truth: "I could have learned to live with this quieter and more subdued Sachs, but the outward signs were too discouraging, and I couldn't shake the feeling that they were symptoms of some larger distress" (123). These outward signs include Sachs's new look, with a shaved head and shaved beard, which Aaron interprets as an indicator of melancholy defiance: "Unless I've seriously misunderstood him, I think that's why Sachs changed his appearance. He wanted to display his wounds, to announce to the world that these scars were what defined him now" (125). But this interpretation will have to be revised again when new information comes to light, as it does in the sequence that best exposes Aaron's fallibility as an interpreter. In a parody of the detective novel genre Auster exploited so fruitfully in his *New York Trilogy*, Aaron follows Sachs around New York one day, and becomes increasingly dispirited by his friend's elusive and seemingly depressive behavior. Only later does he discover that Sachs has by this time turned to Maria, "the embodiment of his catastrophe" (126), and that she is recording his movements on this particular day for one of her projects. Unwittingly, Aaron has become part of the project too, and rather than carrying out a surveillance mission, he has been turned into the subject of one, just as he later imagines himself becoming part of the story the FBI are constructing. At the very moment he thinks he is decoding a set of events, in other words, Aaron is the object of a game, with the events staged in a manner that eludes his knowledge.

"Knowing what I know now," Aaron admits of this incident, "I can see how little I really understood. I was drawing conclusions from what amounted to partial evidence, basing my response on a cluster of random, observable facts that told only a small piece of the story" (126). But the sense that Aaron *now* knows the truth, that as an observer-narrator he can finally decode and synthesize all the information that has been presented, is always in question owing to his indebtedness to the testimonies of his various sources—Sachs, Fanny, Maria, Lillian Stern. In describing how he discovered the truth of the game-playing relationship between Sachs and Maria, for instance, Aaron is careful to give a detailed outline of the source and legitimacy of his knowledge: "As they each told me (in separate conversations at least two months apart), there was never any sex involved. Given what I know about Maria's habits, and given that Sachs's story tallied with hers, I see no point in doubting what she told me" (126). Clearly protesting too much, he reiterates this point a page later: "I'm not just guessing when I say this. Maria held nothing back from me when we talked last year, and the whole story comes straight from her mouth" (127). But in fact the very project that Sachs and Maria are engaged in involves an implicit questioning of the validity of linguistic testimony as the best record of events. When Sachs decides to cut off his hair and beard, not only is he "acting on Maria's advice" rather than sovereignly choosing "to display his wounds" to the world, but the process is mechanically recorded: "She recorded the whole thing with her camera: the before, the after, and all the steps in between" (128). While Aaron resists the change in Sachs's appearance on principle—"I regretted the simple fact of change, of any change in and of itself" (124)—filming the process offers an alternative way of recording change, of inscribing a moment of transition, imbuing it with a presence that seems to offer the possibility of retaining the experience. This is, of course, only the simulacrum of presence, but it is not more of a simulacrum, *Leviathan* suggests, than the retrospective lens of memory which it aims to augment or replace, and which forms the basis of any testimony. And it is not more of a simulacrum than the book itself, which tells a story that turns on a moment of decision that fails to be represented and understood in a determinate manner.

It is against this background that Sachs presents his final testimony to Aaron when, at the beginning of chapter four, he turns up unexpectedly after two years in hiding. As he recounts his story, the reader sees that like the tragic Hamlet—who despite discovering the truth about Claudius early in act three spends much of the rest of the play still in a mode of indecision—Sachs has reacted to his moment of decision with a vexed oscillation between paths of action. In pursuing a path to his final cause, as the Phantom of Liberty, he has taken the longest route imaginable, confronting a seemingly endless series of chance occurrences and moments of choice. Aaron calls

Sachs's account "a long, incredible tale, a saga of journeys and disguises, of lulls and frenzies and last-minute escapes" (231). Indeed, one of the crucial events in the tale, Sachs's killing of Reed Dimaggio in the Vermont woods, appears so incredible that even Sachs acknowledges its implausibility: "He was a convicted felon, and without any witnesses to corroborate his story, no one was going to believe a word he said. It was all too bizarre, too implausible" (154). His only witness becomes Aaron, a novelist who thus comes to recognize not only the "compossibility" of fiction and testimony, but also the outstripping of storytelling by reality. Writing of Sachs's discovery of Reed Dimaggio's identity in conversation with Maria, Aaron remarks:

> My whole adulthood has been spent writing stories, putting imaginary people into unexpected and often unlikely situations, but none of my characters has ever experienced anything as improbable as Sachs did that night at Maria Turner's house. If it still shocks me to report what happened, that is because the real is always ahead of what we can imagine. No matter how wild we think our inventions might be, they can never match the unpredictability of what the real world continually spews forth. This lesson seems inescapable to me now. *Anything can happen.* And one way or another, it always does. (160)

Aaron's recognition here recalls Philip Roth's famous complaint in "Writing American Fiction" that the extremity of American reality "is a kind of embarrassment to one's own meager imagination" (Roth, *Reading* 167). The added twist, of course, is that Auster's passage occurs in a literary text, written by a character who exists only in a fictional world, meaning that the passage asks to be read through the lens of an irony that complicates the testimony.

In the face of testimonial improbability, the writing of observer-hero narrative appears to offer a means by which anxieties concerning the bizarre and implausible nature of change and circumstance can, if not be removed, at least be put on display. Indeed, Sachs himself turns to the genre in his last attempt at writing before undertaking his terrorist career. On his return to New York after the murder, Sachs finds Fanny in bed with another man, and turns once again to Maria, who remarkably happens to know the dead killer Reed Dimaggio. Aaron calls this "the one fact powerful enough to turn an ugly misfortune into a tragedy" (160), and in finally naming this term he provides a legitimation for shaping Sachs's biography, which is also his own story, as a five-act structure, despite his own resistance to the tragic reading that Sachs proposes. But this series of events will also lead Sachs to attempt his own biography of Dimaggio, which he describes to Aaron as follows:

> My first thought was to write something about him. Something similar to what he had written about [Alexander] Berkman—only better, deeper, a genuine examination of his soul. I planned it as an elegy, a memorial in the shape of a book. If I could do this for him, I thought, then maybe I could start to redeem myself, then maybe something good could start to come out of his death. [. . .] It would be an enormous project, a book that would take me years to finish. But that was the

point somehow. As long as I was devoting myself to Dimaggio, I would be keeping him alive. I would give him my life, so to speak, and in exchange he would give my life back to me. (225)

Sachs's explanation here aligns him with the observer-narrator as Bruffee describes him, a man who works through his trauma in telling his tale, and thereby recovers "the coherence of his inner world" (*Elegiac* 52). Dimaggio offers a paradoxical wholeness and emptiness that Sachs can cling to, and his story of the other will become the story of the self, with the decision of the other—in this case, to engage in idealist political action—becoming the decision of the other in me, as happens when Sachs finally repudiates writing for the last time, and begins his life as the Phantom of Liberty. Somewhat ironically, this final decision offers Sachs the artistic vocation he has always sought: Aaron remarks that when Sachs told his tale of the Phantom to Aaron in Vermont, "he talked with the assurance of an artist who knows he has just created his most important work" (231). The overlap between art and life in the novel has here come full circle, and Sachs's artistic and experiential commitment to coherence over contingency reaches its apotheosis in the lengths he goes to ensure that no one is hurt by his deeds: "That was Sachs's greatest fear, and he went to enormous lengths to guard against accidents" (233).

V Literature, the book, and the reader

In *Demeure: Fiction and Testimony* Derrida outlines powerful connections between testimony on the one hand, and "fiction, simulacra, dissimulation, lie, and perjury" on the other. At the same time, however, Derrida's reading of Blanchot's text makes clear that fiction cannot simply be synonymous with lying or perjury, because fiction also invokes the specter of literature: "the possibility of literary fiction haunts so-called truthful, responsible, serious, real testimony as its proper possibility" (*Demeure* 72). Whenever literature is invoked in Derrida's work, it is in the spirit of the "everything to say"; in an interview, Derrida described "the space of literature" as "not only that of an instituted *fiction* but also a *fictive institution* which in principle allows one to say everything" ("This Strange" 36). This principle is what allows literature to maintain a political dimension, although an unstable one: "In the end, the critico-political function of literature, in the West, remains very ambiguous. The freedom to say everything is a very powerful political weapon, but one which might immediately let itself be neutralized as a fiction" (38). In *Leviathan*, Benjamin Sachs's oscillation between writing literature and planting bombs testifies to this ambiguity, although his anxiety that politics might be neutralized by fiction ironically produces a form of protest that does not leave literature behind.

Peter Aaron's testimony, equally, is clearly haunted not only by fiction, but by literature too. In its oscillation between modes of interpretation, and its attempt to record every piece of information about the story of the hero in the search for the truth,

Aaron's narration demonstrates the commitment of literature to "say everything," to include all the events, and all accounts of events, within its borders, even at the expense of a clear and determinate narration. Aaron's text is haunted by the kind of "passionate excess" that both Derrida and Auster have associated with literature, particularly in the sense Aaron's narration gives of the impossibility of establishing truth when there is a surfeit of testimonial accounts of that truth, and of the necessarily messy nature of all truth-telling.[11] Finding a single truth would involve getting "outside the text," and this is something Aaron cannot manage. As one critic comments: "Like Maria Turner, the novel's provocative performance artist who believes in the revelatory power of aleatory techniques and focuses, and like Sachs himself, who takes life's contingencies as cues, Aaron has to accommodate the leakiness, contradiction, and dubious leads that beset his enterprise *within* that enterprise" (Saltzmann 166). But whereas Maria and especially Sachs promote a view of life defined by decision, Aaron's (and Auster's) project to "say everything" seems impelled by a wish not to decide, to maintain the secret by telling that secret without, nonetheless, being able to reveal it.

In Aaron's account, then, the literary novel itself emerges as the primary site of testimony, of testimony not only to a decision made or a transition undergone, but to a life lived at all. This is why Aaron laments the incompletion of Sachs's second novel *Leviathan* as the greatest loss to which his own text testifies:

> Of all the tragedies my poor friend created for himself, leaving the book unfinished becomes the hardest one to bear. I don't mean to say that books are more important than life, but the fact is that everyone dies, everyone disappears in the end, and if Sachs had managed to finish his book, there's a chance it might have outlived him. That's what I've chosen to believe, in any case. (142)

Here, as in Roth's novel, what is finally invoked is a willed belief in the vocation of the writer to testify through imagination to what cannot ever be known or proven. This passionate wish to "say everything" in pursuit of literary truth is what drives Zuckerman onto the ice to confront Les Farley at the finale of *The Human Stain*; when Farley asks if their interview might feature in Zuckerman's writing, the narrator replies, "It's *all* for my book" (357). Peter Aaron is likewise committed to expanding his book to include everything possible, in a manner that could continue indefinitely: "My plan was to go through the manuscript as many times as necessary, to add new material with each successive draft, and to keep at it until I felt there was nothing left to say. Theoretically, the process could have continued for months, perhaps even for years—but only if I was lucky" (243). Up until this conclusion, and against the perspective of Sachs, Aaron has been careful to remain committed to a distinction between literature and life, to see the former as merely a means to support the continuance of the latter. Here, though, he glimpses the potential endlessness of the literary project, and how "lucky" the writer might be who can testify to that endlessness by never finishing his book. It is only the return of an outside authority—in this case, the FBI—that enforces the moment of decision that ends the writing process; yet this decision is also one that begins anew the process of dissemination. Like an event or a decision, a written text will go on to offer itself endlessly to future contexts, as testimony to the mysterious processes of agency and temporality, processes which transcend the control of any origin, any source. This is what Aaron tells the FBI agents, and what, at the beginning and the end of his story, he also tells his reader: "A book is a mysterious object, I said, and once it floats out into the world, anything can happen. All kinds of mischief can be caused, and there's not a damned thing you can do about it. For better or worse, it's completely out of your control" (4).

Narcissism and Explanation: Jeffrey Eugenides's *The Virgin Suicides*

They made us participate in their own madness, because we couldn't help but retrace their steps, rethink their thoughts, and see that none of them led to us. (248)

Prologue

Roth's *The Human Stain* and Auster's *Leviathan* are not only novels of tragedy and testimony. Featuring heroes who die and observers who live on, they are also works of mourning, and it is mourning that brings their narrators most powerfully into confrontation with the narcissistic impulses of the self. "As much as Sachs himself," Peter Aaron admits to his reader, "I'm the place where everything begins"; although Coleman Silk's secret is his own, Nathan Zuckerman contends, it is also "my subject" and "my problem to solve." This emphasis upon the inescapability of the self in telling the other's story reminds us that mourning the other is always both possible, in that it is only the lost other who we could ever mourn, and impossible, in that we can never mourn the other as wholly other. We will only ever be mourning the other as we have taken him/her into ourselves, and thus we are always mourning, narcissistically, a part of ourselves. At the same time, however, that part of ourselves, invaded by the other, no longer belongs entirely to us. This undecidability at the heart of mourning is nicely captured by David Farrell Krell through the metaphor of incorporation: "the bereaved object may come to invade my body and my behavior phantasmically; I may *incorporate* the deceased in such a totalizing way that one might almost say that the dead one has incorporated *me*" (15). Observer-hero narrative similarly captures this undecidability, with the hero's story incorporated into the narrative perspective of the observer at the same time as the observer feels himself to be merely an adjunct to the story of the hero. When the narrators of *The Human Stain* and *Leviathan* produce their intra-diegetic texts of mourning at the finale of their narratives, therefore, this does not signal an escape from narcissism so much as an admission of its unshakeable hold upon the self.

The canonical figure for the problem of narcissism is the mirror, and in an essay on Francis Ponge's "Fable," Jacques Derrida reads the poem as an allegory of self-reflection, constructed so as to evoke "the desire for the other—and to break a mirror" ("Psyche" 324). Yet Ponge's poem merely confirms for Derrida what Narcissus discovers when he plunges his hands into the pool of water to embrace his own reflection: that regardless of our desire for otherness, "everything we say or do or cry, however outstretched toward the other we may be, remains *within us*" (321). Narcissism would therefore seem to offer an insuperable barrier to encounter with the other; and, indeed, this interpretation of the concept has dominated in the Western tradition. As Pleshette DeArmitt has noted, "From Ovid's *Metamorphoses* to Freud's 'On Narcissism: An Introduction' and beyond, the myth of Narcissus and the concept of narcissism have been interpreted as describing a mortifying self-closure that either cuts itself off from the other as other, or fully incorporates all alterity into the structures of the same" (85). Against this prevailing view, Derrida argues that narcissism in fact names a necessary and positive condition for encountering the other, whether in mourning or elsewhere: "without a movement of narcissistic reappropriation, the relation to the other would be absolutely destroyed, it would be destroyed in advance" ("There Is No" 199). Viewing narcissism in this more affirmative light allows us to recognize that "there is not narcissism and non-narcissism; there are narcissisms that are more or less comprehensive, generous, open, extended." The distinctions are of degree rather than kind: "What is called non-narcissism, is in general but the economy of a more welcoming, hospitable narcissism, one that is much more open to the experience of the other as other" (199). The work of mourning is therefore an ongoing tension between self and other, rather than a negation of self by other or other by self, and the relationship between narcissism and mourning provides another paradigmatic figure for the basic structural economy that Derrida's texts of the 1990s foreground again and again in different registers, in discussions of the gift, secrecy, testimony, or forgiveness. As Derrida recognizes in *Specters of Marx*, it can even be said that "the very concept of narcissism [and its] aporias are [. . .] the explicit theme of deconstruction" (98).

It would be a mistake, nevertheless, to view narcissism in mourning as deriving only from the self. Narcissism can also be imagined to characterize the other, a position observer-hero narrative often supports in its depiction of a hero who maintains a haughty separateness unto the point of death. And the stakes are heightened on all sides when the death that must be mourned comes about through the act of suicide: no decision of the other is more stark than this one, none more devastating in its secrecy and in its intimations of a narcissism that is absolute. Indeed, suicide—an act that elicits explanations from the biochemical to the environmental to the other's judgment upon those left behind—puts the very notion of decision itself in question, heralding a crisis in our traditional conceptions of agency. The self-violence of the act combines with a kind of second-order violence in the realm of epistemology; as Derrida puts it, "That a decision cannot become an object or a theme for knowledge is the very site of violence" ("Nietzsche" 229).

But to put things wholly in this way—to invoke an absolute separation between self and other in the act of suicide—would be to affirm the very notion of narcissism as self-enclosure that Derrida wishes to deny. Appropriately, then, the vision of suicide that emerges from Derrida's work offers something of a challenge to prevailing conceptions.[1] His interview addressing the September 11 attacks (titled "Autoimmunity: Real and Symbolic Suicides") is a case in point: here Derrida makes it clear that, rather than view self-killing as a contingent event that ends the life of a subject, he is interested most of all in a kind of originary suicide in the subject, whose self-relation is from the outset exposed to an otherness that violates any conception of a self-enclosed narcissism. Borrowing a metaphor from biology, Derrida terms this originary suicide "autoimmunity," and in *Rogues* he maintains that autoimmunity "consists not only in committing suicide but in compromising *sui-* or *self*-referentiality, the *self* or *sui* of suicide itself" (45). Autoimmunity, then, "threatens always to rob suicide itself of its meaning," because it understands the self as constituted by the other from the beginning, and thus lacking the "supposed integrity" that is often ascribed to it (45). The subject's actions and decisions are thereby framed in a way that compromises any account of suicide as the narcissistic action of a sovereign self.[2]

As a consequence, in trying to tell the story of a suicidal decision and to offer a narrative of mourning that opens up the possibility of explanation, we face this contamination of self by other, and other by self. Observer-hero narratives make this intercontamination manifest: in telling the story of the other's decision, the narrator also tells the story of the self as contaminated by that violent decision of the other. The American novel of the 1990s that most powerfully explores this nexus of narcissism, suicide, mourning and intercontamination is Jeffrey Eugenides's *The Virgin Suicides*, and this is also a text that frames a concern with historical transition more clearly than either of the two novels I have dealt with so far. Moreover, Eugenides's debut novel adds a further layer of complexity to the observer-hero dynamics discussed thus far in *American Fiction in Transition*: in this novel, self and other are not originarily singular, but plural in conception. As such, the dual acts of explaining and mourning the suicidal decision take on resonances quite peculiar to the province of literature.

I Indeterminacy

A tantalizing foretaste of the novel's plot, tone, imagery and method of narration are offered by the striking opening paragraph of *The Virgin Suicides*, which describes the direct aftermath of the suicide of the fifth and final Lisbon girl:

> On the morning the last Lisbon daughter took her turn at suicide—it was Mary this time, and sleeping pills, like Therese—the two paramedics arrived at the house knowing exactly where the knife drawer was, and the gas oven, and the beam in the basement from which it was possible to tie a rope. They got out of the EMS truck, as usual moving much too slowly in our opinion, and the fat one said

under his breath, "This ain't TV, folks, this is how fast we go." He was carrying the heavy respirator and cardiac unit past the bushes that had grown monstrous and over the erupting lawn, tame and immaculate thirteen months earlier when the trouble began. (3)

Immediately the reader is presented with a curious mix of the shocking, the matter of fact, the ominous and the humorous. In the opening clause the relatively casual phrase "took her turn at" (as if this were a game or a ride) contrasts starkly with the portentous resonance of "last Lisbon daughter" and the candid formality of "suicide." The descriptions of the implements of suicide in the remainder of the first sentence are equally stark, yet these implements remain dissociated by the syntax from the actions for which they are used, permitting a slow dawning of effect upon the reader. The knowing quip about TV by "the fat one" in sentence two adds a touch of black comedy. In the third sentence, the decomposition of the house and garden, which in the novel will parallel both the decay of the Lisbon family and of wider society, is described as "monstrous" and "erupting" while being euphemistically indexed to the "trouble" that began over a year earlier. But what is perhaps most peculiar of all in this opening is the sense that we have been here before. Suicide is an event normally considered in terms of singularity and shock, yet the emphasis here is on repetition and ritual. Although it is Mary taking her turn "this time," there seems to be ominously little inaugurality to her action. Here is an event that has occurred so many times it appears to have become standardized, developing a set of norms that the paramedics have become "exactly" familiar with, permitting the narrator to remark that everything in the unfolding scenario is progressing "as usual."

There is something unusual, nevertheless, about the source of our information in this opening, a strangeness initially indicated by the phrase "in our opinion." The narrative perspective here, and throughout *The Virgin Suicides*, is first-person plural, offering the reader the unusual sensation of gaining insight into the plural consciousness and collective memory of a group of teenage boys who have since become men. As the novel progresses, some of the group gain names, but it is never clear how many males are involved in the "we," and no individual speaker is ever identified—there is not a single "I" in the text outside of reported speech. At the same time, the consistency of register, tone and implied addressee often make it difficult to think of the narrator as anything other than an individual speaker; and still the novel, which also leaves it ambiguous as to how the testimony of the men comes to be presented, is asking the reader to make just such an imaginative leap.[3] In this way, *The Virgin Suicides* provides a challenge to conventional modes of reading and methods of literary interpretation, especially methods that rely upon an untheorized notion of narrative voice.

In a reflection on the continuing power of the metaphor of voice in critical readings of literary texts, Andrew Gibson contends that "the narratological conception of voice has been an instance of a peculiarly powerful assertion of the 'fixed point' or center within narrative theory" (641). This centering of an unexamined and idealist conception of voice has bolstered the idea of literary narration as the expression of a unitary consciousness and self-identity, maintaining a residual humanism that ignores the importance of writing and technicity in the production and assimilation of literary texts. Implicitly assumed to issue from a human narrator who the reader "hears" speaking, the notion of narrative "voice" has, according to Gibson, generally "held the specters of difference and non-presence at bay" (642), precluding the analysis of some powerful literary effects. In *The Virgin Suicides* these effects have been deliberately brought to the fore; the voice of the novel, Eugenides told one interviewer, "was the first thing I had" ("Jeffrey"). Eugenides's second novel *Middlesex*, which won the 2003 Pulitzer Prize, likewise features an unusual voice: it is narrated by a hermaphrodite, who shifts identity from female to male in the course of the narrative. In another interview, the author acknowledged his predilection for "impossible voices"; comparing the possibilities of address offered by literature to those of traditional religious texts, Eugenides remarked that "only in novels and in literature can you come up with such voices" ("The Novel").

In an important article on *The Virgin Suicides*, Debra Shostak discusses aspects of the novel's narrative voice, claiming that its plural quality initially "promises to offer a more reliable point of view than one might expect from a single voice" ("A story" 809). This point of view would, in its evocation of communality, "seem to have social legitimacy," but Shostak goes on to outline the many ways in which, "rather than merging the multiplicity of conflicting interpretations through an implied coincidence of viewpoints, the 'we' exacerbates the indeterminacy in the text" (809). Shostak focuses on the issue of desire, and on how the novel's construction of an objectifying male gaze contributes to the indeterminacy she theorizes. We could note in addition that this indeterminacy inescapably infects the critical language used to discuss *The Virgin Suicides*. The novel's combination of a singular sensibility and a plural grammar complicates conventional norms of narrative analysis: for instance, should we say "narrator" or "narrators," and should we refer to "boys" or "men"? Likewise, reader expectations also become altered: when the narrator(s) tell us that "Cecilia writes of her sisters and herself as a single entity" (*Virgin* 42), this otherwise strange behavior has become less surprising because this is exactly what the narrator(s) have been doing too. This intermixing of plurality and singularity also impacts greatly on the indeterminacy the novel suggests between myth and reality, an indeterminacy that is the subject of Francisco Collado-Rodríguez's essay on the novel. When the girls are collectivized they often come to stand for a female principle to weigh against the male principle of the narrative voice (Collado 36), and this evokes magical or mythic overtones to the girls' existence, a reading frequently encouraged by the way the men retrospectively describe their relationship with the Lisbon sisters:

> We knew that the girls were our twins, that we all existed in space like animals with identical skins, and that they knew everything about us though we couldn't fathom them at all. We knew, finally, that the girls were really women in disguise, that they understood love and even death, and that our job was merely to create the noise that seemed to fascinate them. (*Virgin* 43–4)[4]

Over the course of *The Virgin Suicides*, the knowledge the men claim at this early juncture concerning the Lisbon girls will be steadily undermined, and the basic unreliability in the narrative point of view is exacerbated throughout the novel by the indeterminate presentation of events and small details. For instance, visual particulars do not give themselves up freely. When we are told early in the text that in response to seeing a "Good Humor truck" pass his house, Mr. Lisbon "smiled, or winced—we couldn't tell which" (59), it seems the boys may simply be unable to grasp a particular facial expression. But in the same sequence, Mr. Lisbon himself suffers a series of uncertain visual moments while walking through his house ("I thought I saw somebody, but when I looked, there was nothing there" [60]), which culminate in his seeing the ghost of Cecilia, before Bonnie removes the sheet to reveal herself. While these events might be explicable on their own as effects of Mr. Lisbon's melancholy imagination, this kind of uncertainty later becomes endemic for the narrator(s) too, as when the boys are unable to tell whether Mrs. Lisbon is wearing a veil while mourning her daughters' deaths (240), or when a sighting of the Lisbon girls at the window on the night of the mass suicide offers only obscurity: "Mary blew us a kiss, or wiped her mouth. [. . .] And they were gone" (205). Visual memories likewise suffer contradiction by other evidence, as when a photograph gives the lie to the collective memory that the Lisbon shutters had been closed during the October following Cecilia's death (89), or when Mrs. Pitzenberger claims to see Cecilia with a suitcase before her fall, only for no suitcase to be found (47).

Likewise, words overheard in the novel are often of doubtful status. For instance, when the girls rally around to prevent the elm tree outside the Lisbon house from being cut down, the boys report a conversation between the men from the parks department and the sisters, during which Therese claims, "There's no scientific evidence that removal limits infestation," and Bonnie, Mary and Lux back her up. Immediately afterwards, however, the boys comment as follows: "Actually, none of this might have been spoken. We've pieced it together through partial accounts, and can attest only to the general substance" (181). The uncertainty this invests in the sequence is typical of how information is presented by the narrator(s) who, at least until the finale, observe the lives of the Lisbon girls at a distinct remove, a remove that, as with Peter Aaron in *Leviathan*, puts the content of many of their assertions into serious question.

Alongside sights and sounds, similar indeterminacy surrounds "the smell we could never identify" (165), a strange olfactory mixture of life and death that issues from the Lisbon house and that the boys insist on analyzing in obsessive detail. In conjunction with the first-person-plural narrative voice the two texts share, this smell underscores the importance for Eugenides's novel of William Faulkner's short story "A Rose for Emily." Many of the images and themes of that famous story—the formerly grand but decaying house, the distant figure in the window, the voyeurism of a small neighborhood, the shift across generations, the onset of modernity—also characterize *The Virgin Suicides*. Shostak offers an insightful analysis of Eugenides's relationship to Faulkner, and of how the younger writer's fascination with point of view relates to the techniques of his modernist precursor. While the fact that "meaning shifts when the vantage point shifts" is a basic lesson of Faulkner's texts with their multiple narrators (Shostak, "A story" 813), *The Virgin Suicides* locates shifts of perspective within the same narrative voice, in part by foregrounding the narrators as "both readers and storytellers" (809).

The result is that the novel actively conveys "the power of an interpretive framework to produce meaning" (812), turning it into an "allegory of reading" (809).

In Shostak's view, such an overwhelming focus on perspective and interpretation also makes Eugenides's novel into a treatment of "the epistemological problem of historiography" (812). Yet Shostak's insistence that there can exist a mode of historical writing that would allow the Lisbon girls to escape the clutches of mythology and become full subjects—and that the girls do in fact assert their historicity and subjectivity in their mass suicide at the novel's end (Shostak 824-6)—embraces a reading of the suicides that merely participates in the series of failed explanations that we will see the novel itself critique. I would prefer, instead, to theorize what Shostak refers to as the narrators' "circulation among emplotments, narrative modes, and interpretive models" (813) within the broader terms offered by *American Fiction in Transition*; namely, as the symptom of a contemporary crisis in locating the correct framework for representing moments of decision and models of transition. According to Shostak, the reader, who "must recognize the narcissism and singularity of [the narrators'] visions as well as the gaps between them," can finally remain exempt from the interpretive play of the text (827). I would contend, by contrast, that all that we as readers can recognize in the observer-hero structure of *The Virgin Suicides* is our own implication in the narcissistic and autoimmune relation of self and other, and in the undecidability that results from such a relation.

II Implication

The Virgin Suicides mostly details the observer-narrators' memories of the year of their teens, during the 1970s, in which the Lisbon sisters took their own lives. The present action of the novel, in so much as there is any, follows the attempt by the narrators, now middle-aged men in the 1990s, to interpret and explain the sisters' mysterious deaths via the collection, assimilation and discussion of a series of "exhibits"—official reports, testimonies from family and neighbors, and items from the girls' lives. The men recount a narrative of loving obsession and bewilderment at sudden, shocking loss. Yet the task they face in answering the endlessly reverberating central questions—What caused the Lisbon sisters to bring their lives to such a violent end? Why did this catastrophe happen?—is complicated by the status of the girls' moment(s) of decision. "It is only," Derrida argues, "the *implication* of the decision that is irreducible" ("Nietzsche" 229). This "of" is a classic Derridean double genitive, making "*implication*" refer equally to that which occurs after and as a result of the decision, and to the idea that the decision can be no more than implied by (or inferred from) the occurrence of an event which is also, seemingly, an act. In *The Virgin Suicides*, the girls' suicides constitute a single event, in as much as they "fracture the consciousness of an entire community into a before and after," as one reviewer of the novel puts it (Kakutani). But the suicides are also a chain of events, a sequence that is causally connected in a complex and forbidding way. Suicidal events in turn imply acts, which in turn imply decisions, and it is this relationship between the event of the suicides, the suicidal acts, and the implied moment or moments of decision which lie behind them, that is central to the epistemological and narrative drives of the text.

The beginning of the suicidal chain is Cecilia's first attempt on her life, recounted immediately following the opening paragraph. The youngest Lisbon sister opens her wrists in the bathtub, but is found and revived before her injuries become fatal. When the treating doctor comments that she is too young to know how bad life gets, she responds, "Obviously, Doctor, you've never been a thirteen-year-old girl" (7). If nothing else, this retort implies a level of intentional agency on Cecilia's part in the act she commits. This is complicated, however, by a second remark, when in reply to the psychologist Dr. Hornicker's inquiry as to why she had tried to kill herself, she tells him, "It was a mistake" (21). These are the only two quotations attributed to Cecilia regarding her first suicide attempt. Her actual death comes at the climax of the novel's opening chapter, and her jump from the roof onto the garden fence, although not witnessed by the narrators, is described in a paragraph of lyrical intensity: at the moment Cecilia is impaled by a spike "through her inexplicable heart" (31), the boys, downstairs at her birthday party, hear "the sound of a watermelon breaking open" (30). In the midst of their account of the event comes the following observation:

> A human body falls fast. The main thing was just that: the fact of a person taking on completely physical properties, falling at the speed of a rock. It didn't matter whether her brain continued to flash on the way down, or if she regretted what she'd done, or if she had time to focus on the fence spikes shooting toward her. Her mind no longer existed in any way that mattered. (30)

This statement, in emphasizing the physical and material actualities of the fall rather than its subjective reality for Cecilia herself, disavows a standard literary technique of entering a character's mind at a point of high drama. The suggestion is not only that this would be false from a realistic or epistemological perspective but, more strikingly, that the ontological questions normally asked can in fact be put to one side. The processes of the mind are immaterial to the reality of the fall itself. Once the decisive act has been committed, what follows is merely a physical necessity, with the acting consciousness now an irrelevancy. In other words, the fall itself will tell us nothing about the reasons for the fall, aside from the implication that it was deliberate.

But even this implication cannot become a certainty. In *Leviathan*, Benjamin Sachs recovers from his fall and constructs an explanation that claims it both as a deliberate act on his part, and as symptomatic of a larger metaphysical and ethical fall rather than simply a physical one. Cecilia does not recover, and her "inexplicable heart" therefore remains closed to observers. And so various interpretive schemas are applied in the gap left by the indeterminate quality of her death, schemas that combine epistemological and ethical assumptions in a number of different ways.

One example is the interpretation offered by the Catholic Church, as represented in the novel by Father Moody:

> Officially, Cecilia's death was listed in church records as an "accident," as were the other girls' a year later. When we asked Father Moody about this, he said, "We didn't want to quibble. How do you know she didn't slip?" When we brought up the sleeping pills, and the noose, and the rest of it, he said, "Suicide, as a mortal sin, is a matter of intent. It's very difficult to know what was in those girls' hearts. What they were really trying to do." (37–8)

Not only, then, can we not infer the reasons for Cecilia's death from the physical facts of her fall, or from her state of mind during it, but according to Father Moody her prior decision to die cannot be inferred with any certainty either. And according to Derrida, if it could be inferred with certainty, it would not properly qualify as a decision. "The decision, *if there is one*," Derrida remarks, "must interrupt causality, be revolutionary, and so on. I say, 'if there is one,' not because I doubt that there is one, but because, simply, I don't know if there is one. A decision, if there is such a thing, is never determinable in terms of knowledge. One cannot determine a decision" ("Nietzsche" 229). For Derrida, then, not alone can we not explain the reasons behind a decision, but we can never be certain that a decision has genuinely taken place. Derrida's own argument here likewise twins epistemology with ethics: for there to be a "free" decision—for genuine human agency to exist—there must be something beyond calculation and determination; *a posteriori*, it will always appear as if the decision was made in accordance with "a cause, a calculation, a rule" ("Force" 25), and thus was not free in this way after all, and thus not a decision. Yet the circularity of this argument does not discount for Derrida the occurrence of decisions. It merely moves them out of the zone of explication through knowledge, and places them in the sphere of implication in radical secrecy.

This radical secrecy applies equally to the decision of the observing boys to narrate the story of the Lisbon girls. This decision, which can only be an implied one, appears to occur outside the play of rational forces with which human beings place themselves as the central agents in their own stories. The narrators of *The Virgin Suicides* are under no illusions about free will, and the oscillation in the novel between a rational epistemology and a yearning for the passivity of fate is perhaps best summed up by a sentence late in the text, when the boys are waiting for the signal from the Lisbon sisters to come to their home during the night to help them escape: "None of us remembers thinking anything, or deciding anything, because at that moment our minds had ceased to work, filling us with the only peace we've ever known" (204–5). Their submission to the workings of something larger than themselves is where we should look for a Derridean "passive decision, condition of the event" on the boys' part. Entered by the other, impelled to account for the decision of the other, their narrative attempts to account for the occurrence of something truly shocking, a genuine event.

In *The Virgin Suicides*, this resistance of the implied moment(s) of decision to identification, representation, and explanation adds a second-order violence to the already violent cut of the event of suicide itself. And a further order of violence is added to this, when the vacuum created by the disappearance of the Lisbon girls invites a violence of interpretation that is brought to bear by those inside and outside the suburban community in which they lived. The novel cites numerous causal explanations of the sisters' act(s) and interpretations of their decision(s); it also presents various allegorizations of the act/event of their collective suicide. The boys set about undermining each of these readings with irony and counter-evidence, while at the same time continuously circling around and constantly returning to the fact of the girls' deaths, attempting to place these deaths in the context of the lives they ended.

III Explanation

Following the death of Cecilia in chapter one, much of the rest of *The Virgin Suicides* is taken up with recounting explanations for her suicide, and eventually for those of her sisters too. After Cecilia's first attempt, rumors had circulated throughout the neighborhood, and according to the narrators, "Everyone had a theory as to why she had tried to kill herself" (17). Of these, "The most popular theory at the time held Dominic Palazzolo to blame" (19). Apparently the youngest Lisbon girl had been in love with a local boy, who himself had heroically jumped off a roof out of love for another girl; his subsequent move to New Mexico with his family is taken to have sparked Cecilia's first attempt. Amy Schraff's story (20) and the psychiatrist's interpretative report (21), which blames Cecilia's repressed libidinal energy, seem to bear this explanation out. But Cecilia's diary, opened and examined after her successful suicide attempt, puts this earlier explanation in question. There is only one entry about Dominic, which reads: "Palazzalo jumped off the roof today over that rich bitch, Porter. How stupid can you be?" (32). Indeed, rather than offer solid clues, the diary provides evidence just as contradictory as the statements by Cecilia herself following her first attempt: "The diary is an unusual document of adolescence in that it rarely depicts the emergence of an unformed ego. The standard insecurities, laments, crushes, and daydreams are nowhere in evidence. Instead, Cecilia writes of her sisters and herself as a single entity" (42). This strange over-identification initially seems telling, but when Cecilia goes to kill herself the second time while the party is progressing below, her act appears unpredicted by her sisters: "Even at this point, the other girls didn't act as though they knew what was about to happen" (46–7). Again, any knowledge on their part of Cecilia's intentions can only be inferred, and the surface evidence is inconsistent.

The mystery of Cecilia's suicide only deepens as the novel develops, despite the various attempts by characters to reduce that mystery through definitive explanation. In the main, what the reader is presented with in the reactions to the youngest Lisbon girl's death are clear examples of observers ignoring evidence in order to treat a singular event within their already-formed interpretive structures. The narrators work to expose the shallowness of these preconceptions by highlighting contradiction, often in a humorous manner. Mr. Buell's early explanation is a case in point: "'It was like anything else in this sad society,' he told us. 'They didn't have a relationship with God.' When we reminded him about the laminated picture of the Virgin Mary [which Cecilia held between her hands as she slit her wrists], he said, 'Jesus is the one she should have had a picture of'" (18). Mrs. Buell's opinion, in contrast to her husband, is that "the parents were to blame" (17). This is a view that, based on the evidence the boys present, seems plausible, although Mrs. Buell's authority to make the remark is immediately undercut by a petty argument with Mrs. Scheer about a simple incident following the suicide attempt, foregrounding her own unreliability and the unreliability of memory in general. The point throughout *The Virgin Suicides* is that people read what they want to read into the event of the suicides. The comical reactions to the diary make this clear: "Cecilia's diary begins a year and a half before her suicide. Many people felt the illuminated pages constituted a hieroglyphics of unreadable despair, though the pictures looked cheerful for the most part" (41).

The reductive reaction to Cecilia's death, and to those of the other girls that follow it, is encapsulated in the newspaper reportage of Linda Perl, the journalist assigned to cover the story as it develops. Ms. Perl, named no doubt ironically for her wisdom, produces written accounts that are emblematic of "the many 'human interest' pieces that had begun to proliferate at the time" (96), moving easily from the particulars of a case towards a series of generalizations. As a result, "the searchlight of Ms. Perl's prose also tends to wash out the girls' features" (177), and information that contradicts her explanation of events is excised from the picture. This is typical of how the press and wider culture react to the suicides, covering over the mystery of the event with effortless explanation: "The newspapers, later writing about what they termed a 'suicide pact,' treated the girls as automatons, creatures so barely alive that their deaths came as little change" (176). It is in these passages that the narrative voice is most cutting, the irony least warm. When the Lisbon girls finally kill themselves, Ms. Perl is one of the first to recuperate their actions into a narrative: "Ms. Perl (who later published a book with a chapter dedicated to the Lisbon girls) described their spirits sinking further and further in an inevitable progression." The boys are disdainful of her reading—"We knew better" (200)—and consistently place their private and particular knowledge against Ms. Perl's totalizing explanations: "Scouring the neighborhood in her blue Pontiac, she cobbled together reminiscences into airtight conclusions, far less truthful than our own, which is full of holes" (222).[5]

The boys' hole-ridden narrative account also takes in scientific explanations of the girls' suicides. The main representative of the scientific point of view in the novel is Dr. Hornicker, who is initially presented as a voice of authority when he writes in his report on Cecilia's first attempt, "Despite the severity of her wounds, I do not think the patient truly meant to end her life. Her act was a cry for help" (21). However, this opinion is rather discredited by the gruesome suicide Cecilia carries out only weeks later, and Hornicker's theories are consistently undermined throughout the text in a similar manner to the spokespersons of other explanatory frameworks. Later he will explain Lux Lisbon's promiscuity as "a commonplace reaction to emotional need"—"'Adolescents tend to seek love where they can find it,' he wrote in one of the many articles he hoped to publish" (87–8)—but then alters this position in his diagnosis of Post-Traumatic Stress Disorder, a theory that "convinced many people because it simplified things." This theory also has the added bonus of turning Cecilia's death into a kind of medical metaphor:

> Her suicide, from this perspective, was seen as a kind of disease infecting those close at hand. In the bathtub, cooking in the broth of her own blood, Cecilia had released an airborne virus which the other girls, even in coming to save her, had contracted. No one cared how Cecilia had caught the virus in the first place. Transmission became explanation. (157)

Later again, however, Hornicker distances himself from this analysis and switches from a psychological diagnosis to a chemical one: "At a hastily called Lions Club meeting, Dr. Hornicker, the guest speaker, brought up the possibility of a chemical link, citing a new study of 'platelet serotonin receptor indices in suicidal children'" (220). After the other girls die, he tests Mary in line with this diagnosis, finding "no evidence of a psychiatric illness such as schizophrenia or manic-depression," and declaring himself satisfied that "we had her serotonin up, and she looked good" (232). Mary, of course, kills herself soon after. Switching his views based on the latest fashionable research and with the aim of self-promotion, Hornicker is far from an authoritative character in the text. Thus, the loaded gun metaphor he resorts to in his final report (and which Kenneth Womack and Amy Mallory-Kani make much of in their article on the novel, giving Hornicker's opinions serious credence) should be read not as the definitive medical statement of an expert on the suicides, but rather as the last resort of a bemused physician whose every other conclusion has failed.

As if to reiterate this point, on the same page as Hornicker's concluding explanation, a Darwinian diagnosis from a less "expert" source is equally mocked: "Mr. Eugene, who told us that scientists were on the verge of finding the 'bad genes' that caused cancer, depression, and other diseases, offered his hope that they would soon 'be able to find the gene for suicide, too'" (247). Mr. Eugene's is just one of a number of summary judgments that emerge as the novel moves towards its conclusion; others include the political and historical analyses offered by Mr. Conley and Mr. Hedlie:

> Mr. Conley adjusted the tweed necktie he wore even while cutting the grass and said, "Capitalism has resulted in material well-being but spiritual bankruptcy." He went on to deliver a living room lecture about human needs and the ravages of competition, and even though he was the only Communist we knew, his ideas differed from everyone else's only in degree. Something sick at the heart of the country had infected the girls. [. . .] Mr. Hedlie mentioned that *fin-de-siècle* Vienna witnessed a similar outbreak of suicides on the part of the young, and put the whole thing down to the misfortune of living in a dying empire. (231)

The opinions of Mr. Conley and Mr. Hedlie are presented ironically by the narrative voice here, in part through the recording of small quirky details about their character and persons. And yet there is a sense in which the explanations they give do not differ significantly from the kind of readings offered by contemporary literary critics. Much of the extant scholarship on *The Virgin Suicides* unintentionally bears this out, acquiescing in a similar mode of explanatory emphasis as do characters within the novel itself. Thus Womack and Mallory-Kani, for example, carry out a self-proclaimed "adaptationist reading" of the novel, arguing that the Lisbon suicides should be understood in evolutionary terms, with the girls carrying out "a maladaptive, fitness-reducing decision by choosing to commit suicide, thereby removing themselves from the spatiotemporal continuum" (171). Christian Long sees the cause less in Darwinian terms than in terms of the ecology of postwar suburban life: "Cecelia, Lux, Bonnie, Mary, and Therese remove themselves from suburbia as a warning against the environmental and ecological wages of suburban sprawl" (362). According to Collado-Rodríguez, who offers an eco-critical reading tinged with archetypal categories, "the end of the novel eventually favors the mythical understanding of the girls as priestesses of Mother Earth who offer themselves as scapegoats in a fertility rite meant to bring about the regeneration of life" (36). And for Clare Hayes-Brady, who reads Eugenides's novel and Sofia Coppola's film adaptation through the lens of voyeurism and narcissism, "the girls' suicides are a hopeless response to the suppression of their identities," and the strictures put on the sisters' development by the watching boys mean that "the girls are forced into a position where suicide is the only escape, the single human act left to them" (213).

These readings attempt to divine not only the cause of the Lisbon girls' suicides, but also the meaning of their story, with cause and meaning made to connect in each critic's account. In this way, the deficiency of meaning at the heart of the novel is addressed, and a kind of closure is achieved. This is the kind of closure that suicide characteristically resists; viewed from a narratological perspective, suicide can even function as "a metaphor for resistance to narrative closure" (Wolfe 121). In "Frames of Female Suicide," Margaret Higonnet argues for a specific link between the challenge suicide poses to narrative and the unrepresentability of woman within socially sanctioned narrative modes. By fragmenting the "natural" course of life, suicide eludes the conventional meanings of the social order, creating "a rift in meaning" that calls for competing narratives: "Proliferating narratives respond to the need to make sense of this kind of death. Within the confines of admissible types of cause, each model of analysis seeks to explain the origins of suicide through a sequence that leads up to a shocking terminal point" (Higonnet 229–30). The production of such narratives in the reading of the fragmented life "turns the spectator into an active participant in the production of meaning" (230), and narratives of suicide eventually come to function as "sites of social reconstruction" (241). But this is not the end of the process, because such narratives ask to be read and re-read, issuing an endless challenge to the tools of literary analysis: "because narratives are interpreted according to social models of plausibility and value, the fundamental tools of comparative critical analysis—such as character, tone, and above all genre—are called into question by the undecidability of suicide, especially female suicide" (241).

We are returned again here to the connected issues of gender and genre—discussed in the introduction to this study—alongside an additional questioning of the genre of literary criticism itself. With this in mind, the structure of observer-hero narrative, which we can interrogate on the one hand for its (in)capacity to articulate the meaning of female suicide, on the other hand can be seen to retain a flexibility in thematizing the problems not only of reading and writing, but of critical distance itself. Shostak, the author of the best essay to date on *The Virgin Suicides*, underestimates the importance of the observer-hero structure in this respect. Shostak notes that *The Virgin Suicides* demands "readers who are sensitized to the ideological premises that may underlie the male gaze at the female" ("A story" 810), and with this in mind she argues that the "central interpretive and ethical problem" in Eugenides's novel "concerns how a reader should judge the representation of the others who are the sole focus of the narrators' inquiry" (809). Nonetheless, Shostak seeks an answer to the story's deficiency of meaning by prioritizing "the reinsertion of the girls's uncontextualized voices" (826), thereby aiming to view the Lisbon sisters as autonomous historical beings with an "implied or embedded viewpoint" (814). She appears to suggest, therefore, that we can have the narrative without the observer, that the reader should by rights allow the girls an independent narrative of their own.

The problem is that this perspective simply displaces the problem of critical distance from the observing boys to the observing reader, and fails to deal with the novel's real claim—that *any* form of explanation is framed by narcissism, that narcissism cannot be transcended by explanation. Shostak argues that "Eugenides offers the reader a chance to do what the narrators fail to do" (824), and this is no doubt true to the extent that the reader can recognize, at a higher level, the narcissism of the boys. But this is not the same as transcending one's own narcissism in the direction of a historical other undistorted by the subjective lens of the self. We can see this problem reassert itself in Shostak's own account when it comes to explaining the girls' behavior on the night of the suicide. Shostak's view is that the sisters kill themselves "to force the boys, by virtue of their curiosity, to witness the deaths such objectifying constructions provoke" (824). But rather than fulfill Shostak's stated ethical aim, "to allow the girls to fall from myth into history" (826), this explanation of their violent action simply re-emphasizes their mythic status as sacrificial scapegoats (however willing) to the patriarchal gaze. On this interpretation, it is either the case that the girls function as the ultimate narcissists, existing in a closed loop of self-reflection that rejects anything like a social realm—Shostak posits that "the Lisbon suicides might [. . .] represent claims against social obligations" (824)—or their action must be interpreted as tragic: of Lux Lisbon, Shostak writes that "proof of her status as subject lies in that at last, like her sisters, she exerts her will over her own fate" (824). Or, finally, it may be that "the suicides escape the coherence of ritual in an assertion of inexplicable chaos" (824). This is what I have been calling, throughout *American Fiction in Transition*, the postmodern interpretation of the event, one that rejects coherence for a world ruled by events rather than decisions.

IV Allegory

While Shostak's essay frames both the tragic and the postmodern reading of Eugenides's novel, the narrative explanations offered within the novel by doctors, journalists, neighbors, and local people—as well as the critical explanations offered by other scholars writing about the novel—all signify a modern need to understand extreme events through totalizing modes of understanding. The constantly revised medical diagnoses of Dr. Hornicker; the reductive journalistic accounts of Ms. Perl; the anti-capitalist tirades of Mr. Conley; Mr. Buell's lament at the modern loss of religion; Mr. Hedlie's evocation of the determinism of the current historical moment; Mrs. Buell's suggestion of parental neglect—all of these totalizing explanations founder on counter-evidence offered by the observing boys, and an undercutting irony, often gentle and humorous but sometimes sharp and aggravated, pervades the narrative tone throughout.

Nevertheless, in their own attempt to understand the deaths, and to "coalesce our intuitions and theories into a story we could live with" (241), the narrators do consider consenting to these modern understandings: "For a while we tried to accept the general explanations, which qualified the Lisbon girls' pain as merely historic, springing from the same source as other teenage suicides, every death part of a trend" (238). Yet they find that these ready-made interpretations merely heighten the stark resistance of the event to diagnostic comprehension, and in their capacity as a kind of Greek chorus, the boys evoke their own tragic perspectives, as when Joe Hill Conley senses "an ancient pain arising from Mrs. Lisbon, the sum of her people's griefs" (120), or when, after Cecilia's death, the girls are described as "like Aeneas, who [. . .] had gone down to the underworld, seen the dead, and returned, weeping on the inside" (66). "In the end," the boys conclude, "the tortures tearing the Lisbon girls pointed to a simple reasoned refusal to accept the world as it was handed down to them, so full of flaws" (245). Once again, this tragic refusal does not seem to submit to further explanation; any attempt to represent truth directly comes up against the "painful mystery" likewise evoked by the cases of Coleman Silk and Benjamin Sachs. One character articulates this explanatory impossibility as follows: "'All wisdom ends in paradox,' said Mr. Buell, just before we left him on our last interview, and we felt he was telling us to forget about the girls, to leave them in the hands of God" (247).

"[W]hile everyone agreed the suicides came as predictably as seasons or old age," the narrators summarize, "we could never agree on an explanation for them" (220). In the absence of definitive explanation, the ritual and allegorical quality of the suicides begins to dominate the response of those left behind. Eventually the Lisbon suicides come to function for their community as an emblem of a deeper social and historical malaise: "It had to do with the way the mail wasn't delivered on time, and how potholes never got fixed, or the thievery at City Hall, or the race riots, or the 801 fires set around the city on Devil's night. The Lisbon girls became a symbol of what was wrong with the country, the pain it inflicted on even its most innocent citizens" (231). The Day of Grieving established in the local school to mark Cecilia's death reflects this turn to the allegorical and symbolic. In attempting to acknowledge the difficult singularity of

Cecilia's act, the community ends up effacing it: "The result was that the tragedy was diffused and universalized. As Kevin Tiggs put it, 'It seemed like we were supposed to feel sorry for everything that ever happened, ever'" (104). This revisionist turn to allegory comes at the expense of attempts to explain and understand the girls' deaths in causal terms. Rather than continue to seek reasons, people eventually prefer to see the suicides as a kind of uncaused event, stemming not from a tragic past or a modern present, but rather appearing to return as a proleptic symptom from the future:

> Everyone we spoke to dated the demise of our neighborhood from the suicides of the Lisbon girls. Though at first people blamed them, gradually a sea change took place, so that the girls were seen not as a scapegoats but as seers. More and more, people forgot about the individual reasons why the girls may have killed themselves, the stress disorders and insufficient neurotransmitters, and instead put the deaths down to the girls' foresight in predicting decadence. (243–4)

Much scholarship on the novel likewise treats the girls' lives and deaths as fundamentally allegorical, with critics differing on the nature of the allegory. Alongside his interpretation of the sisters as representing Mother Earth, Collado-Rodríguez reads with an eye to the novel's magical realism, emphasizing the role of the fish flies as a metaphor for Biblical plague (35). Long, who explicitly criticizes the "tree = Lisbon Girls rubric" under which much of the novel's criticism operates, nonetheless argues for a definitive allegorical interpretation: "The proper metonymic relationship thus rests in the built environment [. . .] in which the Lisbon girls are nature painfully absenting itself from the suburbs" (360). For Hayes-Brady, "Virginity in both novel and film is ultimately symbolic" (209n1), while for Womack and Mallori-Kani, as we shall see below, the death of the girls is an allegory for the tribulations of American history itself. For all these critics, the Lisbon girls function in the end as they do for the coroner in *The Virgin Suicides*, "like something behind glass. Like an exhibit" (221). I would contend, however, that just as in *The Human Stain*, the refusal of allegorical equivalence or totality in *The Virgin Suicides* is not only an important part of the novel's ethical message, but is also a key aspect of its attempt to map a genuine temporality.

V Transition

Of the three novels discussed to this point in *American Fiction in Transition*, *The Virgin Suicides* is the one that most explicitly addresses the problem of historical transition. The setting of the action is the early 1970s, a period of American history that witnessed what the subtitle of one recent book about the decade calls "The Great Shift in American Culture, Society, and Politics" (Schulman). Noting this setting, and taking into account various allusions interspersed throughout the narrative, critics have offered historicizing analyses of the novel's form and content through the lens of events from that decade. At its best—as in Christian Long's discussion of the spread of Dutch Elm disease in the 1970s, and the shift in American suburban planning and energy policy that arose in response to the disease and the concomitant oil crisis (Long 357–9)—such criticism illuminates the novel and its context, and provides added resonance to many of Eugenides's chosen details, such as "the harsh sunlight" that penetrates the suburban streets after the Lisbons have died and their elm tree has been cut down (*Virgin* 244). At its worst, however, such historicizing gestures traverse the indeterminacies of the novel in favor of an historical referent, ignoring the way *The Virgin Suicides* engages in the theoretical reframing of historical transition itself.

Womack and Mallory-Kani's article is a case in point, with the authors making a strident attempt to ally key events in the Lisbon narrative with important moments in the historical Watergate crisis. Whereas Long places the story of *The Virgin Suicides* in 1975 (358), Womack and Mallory-Kani argue that it begins in June 1972, locating Cecilia's first suicide attempt specifically on Tuesday, June 13 of that year.[6] Their pinpointing of this date for the suicide attempt draws on the first photo the boys offer for inspection, which is dated June 13 but which in fact "shows the Lisbon house shortly before Cecilia's suicide attempt" (*Virgin* 5). Ignoring this ambiguity, Womack and Mallory-Kani go on to argue that Eugenides "takes great pains [. . .] to ensure that key events in the death throes of the Nixon administration coincide with evolutionary moments in the lives of his characters" (165). Many of the statements they make in the passage that follows this statement are factually incorrect: not only the date of Cecilia's initial suicide attempt, but the coincidence of the Lisbon party with the Woodward-Bernstein story linking Howard Hawks to the White House, and the reference to Mrs. Lisbon's "own Saturday Night Massacre of sorts," which actually occurs on a Friday night (165). In addition, the authors insist on an exact overlap of the time scheme of the historical Watergate controversy with the duration of the story in *The Virgin Suicides*, when the periods in question are actually more than two years versus 13 months respectively (165–6; see *Virgin* 3). Furthermore, if we are to use textual evidence to try to date precisely the action in the novel, June 1973 seems a more likely beginning point than June 1972. This is because Eugenides's narrators refer to the opening game of the baseball World Series as taking place on October 13 in the year of the Lisbon suicides, a correspondence of event and date that occurred historically in 1973 but not in any of the other candidate years, 1972, 1974, or 1975 (*Virgin* 89).

Nonetheless, even to attempt to date the action of the novel in this way is, I would argue, to go against the grain of the text's attitude toward history and historical transition. In a gesture to more mythic temporalities, the narrators clearly favor seasonal rituals over day-and-date historical occurrences as the background to their story: we hear of the yearly raking and burning of leaves, the onset of "June, fish-fly season" (4), the annual school prom and society balls. Moreover, "extensive layoffs at the automotive plant" (93) in Detroit can hardly be pinpointed to a single date or even year, instead gesturing toward a larger narrative of decline; meanwhile, a cemetery strike referred to throughout the novel appears to be based on an historical event that took place in Detroit not in the 1970s but in 1966.[7] Indeed, despite the impression Womack and Mallory-Kani give of close historical correspondence, there are in fact no year-dates mentioned in Eugenides's novel, and almost no reference to historical events happening outside the frame of the narrators' lived world. At issue here is not simply a case of accurate or inaccurate scholarship: what I am suggesting is that interpreting incidents in any novel by locating one-to-one correspondences with the historical world requires that any imaginative distance the novel invokes between created and actual world be downplayed or ignored by the critic. Labeling this kind of criticism "allegorical interpretation," Derek Attridge has noted that it is "frequently spurred by a lack of specificity or some other peculiarity in a work's temporal and geographical locatedness" ("Against" 40). Attridge argues that instead of striving to re-introduce this occluded specificity, critics should avoid the jump to allegory and attempt a more literal reading of the words of the text. In the specific case of *The Virgin Suicides*, one feature of the text's refusal of direct historical correspondence is that it helps to support the dialectic of myth and reality which is consistently evoked in the depiction of the Lisbon girls. Eugenides has suggested that "what fiction can do that non-fiction can't [. . .] is chart out the territory beyond realism to a certain extent" ("He's Not"), and the novel offers plenty of evidence for this aesthetic position, while resisting all interpretations that would minimize the gap between text and world.

A still more important feature of the novel's resistance to exact historical correspondence is that *The Virgin Suicides* questions explanatory stories of historical transition by drawing attention to the historical situatedness of explanation itself. Dr. Hornicker's shifting medical opinions, for instance, telescope a series of changing diagnostic fashions into the confusions of a single physician at a single transitional moment. And, by analogy, what the novel does in maintaining distance from the 1970s context even as it evokes its particularities, is to question objective models of historical transition assumed by historians looking back with hindsight. By emphasizing the narrators' subjective phenomenological experience of the period, and by not allowing them to revise that subjectivity out of their own retrospective narration, *The Virgin Suicides* refuses a point of view on historical change shorn of a necessary appropriative narcissism. The Lisbon girls gain allegorical status for the inhabitants of their suburbs precisely because they become the lens through which transition is measured. No longer viewed as "scapegoats," the Lisbon girls become "seers"; and yet the "seeing" here is not done by them but by their neighbors, in a narcissistic projection of historical experience onto a departed other. "[T]he girls' foresight in predicting decadence" is in fact the men's hindsight in projecting decadence, and yet that feeling of decadence is itself a function of the other's violent impact upon the self. "The passive decision, condition of the event, is always in me, structurally, an other event, a rending decision as the decision of the other": Derrida's words from *The Politics of Friendship* (68) never apply so clearly as here, where the openness of the self to the violent other results in the making of history itself, but history always viewed from a perspective that cannot finally be transcended.

"So much has been written about the girls in the newspapers," Eugenides's narrators conclude, "so much has been said over back-yard fences, or related over years in psychiatrists' offices, that we are certain only of the insufficiency of explanations" (247). In the face of such insufficiency, the men offer their hole-ridden account—the novel itself—as a form that shies away from simple answers and allows for the remembrance and expression of genuine singularity. The text's ethics of narration suggest a privileging of testimony without judgment, a mode of storytelling in which all forms of implication, explanation and allegorization are subtly undermined. Yet when we reach the final page of *The Virgin Suicides*, this reading is itself suddenly placed in question. To this point the power and skill of the novel has resided in its mix of wry ironizing and searching speculation with an affecting nostalgia. But real hurt and bitterness explode powerfully in the concluding paragraph, with the narrators offering their own explanation of the girl's action:

> But this is all a chasing after the wind. The essence of the suicides consisted not of sadness or mystery but simple selfishness. The girls took into their own hands decisions better left to God. They became too powerful to live among us, too self-concerned, too visionary, too blind. What lingered after them was not life, which always overcomes natural death, but the most trivial list of mundane facts: a clock ticking on a wall, a room dim at noon, and the outrageousness of a human being thinking only of herself. (248)

The abrupt alteration of tone in this passage from everything that has come before it is as blunt and shocking as any descriptions of the suicides themselves could be. Unexpectedly, the men break their reverie to impute to the Lisbon girls' actions a single cause: selfishness. Words like "powerful," "visionary," and "outrageousness" heighten the stakes of the claim, and offer it the feeling of definitive statement. The "trivial list of mundane facts" given by the narrators continue the novel's theme of precise material details resisting symbolic or allegorical meaning. Now, however, "the outrageousness of a human being thinking only of herself" has been added to this list of brute "facts," and the narrators' previous indeterminacy of presentation and the story's deficiency of meaning are transcended in favor of summary judgment.

It is hard to resist the seductive logic and emotional power of this concluding outburst, the persuasive passion finally revealed by the only real authority in the novel, the narrative voice. Yet if *The Virgin Suicides* has taught us anything to this point, it is skepticism of simple answers. We have been trained to resist swift conclusions, single motivations, linear causalities. Unsurprisingly, then, the closing lines of the novel hint at a deeper, more nuanced reading:

> They made us participate in their own madness, because we couldn't help but retrace their steps, rethink their thoughts, and see that none of them led to us. We couldn't imagine the emptiness of a creature who put a razor to her wrists and opened her veins, the emptiness and the calm. And we had to smear our muzzles in their last traces, of mud marks on the floor, trunks kicked out from under them, we had to breathe forever the air of the rooms in which they killed themselves. It didn't matter in the end how old they had been, or that they were girls, but only that we had loved them, and that they hadn't heard us calling, still do not hear us, up there in the tree house, with our thinning hair and soft bellies, calling them out of those rooms where they went to be alone for all time, alone in suicide, which is deeper than death, and where we will never find the pieces to put them back together. (248–9)

In this conclusion, the repetition of "we" and "us," alongside the emphasis on the inability to "imagine" the other's "emptiness" and the insistence that the only thing that finally matters is "that we had loved them," should remind the reader that narcissism has not finally been transcended in the search for truth. Indeed, in explaining the decision of the other through the imputation of an absolute narcissism to the other, it is the narcissism of the self that here resounds. The "emptiness" of the other is finally filled in with a "selfishness" that is the only imaginable reaction to the fact that the events of the text are not about "us," but that "we" must deal with their consequences. We must mourn the other whose death offers us the beginning and end of our story, but which removes us from the center of that story. Eugenides's observer-hero narrative powerfully registers Derrida's insight that "there is not narcissism and non-narcissism; there are narcissisms that are more or less comprehensive, generous, open, extended" ("There Is No" 199). It does so, finally, through a narrative of mourning in which the self can never leave itself, or the other, behind.

4

History, Time, and Justice: E. L. Doctorow's *The Waterworks*

I report, that is my profession, I report, as a loud noise testifies to a gun. I have given voice to the events of my life and times, and from my first timid type-inch of apprentice writing until the present moment I have taken the vow to do it well and truly. (56)

Prologue

To penetrate the secrecy of the hero's decisions; to bear witness in his or her place; to mourn the hero as wholly other to the self: these are, as we have seen, impossible acts. Yet the struggle to accomplish them is a necessary part of any effort to do justice to the decisive life of the hero. Each of the novels by Roth, Auster, and Eugenides I have discussed involves just such an effort by the observer to do justice: to the hero's presence and actions, to the transition he or she has wrought on the observer's experience of the world, and to the observer's now altered sense of how that world can and should be represented in language. Moreover, in the sequence presented in *American Fiction in Transition*, each successive novel has seen the observer gesture increasingly outward from the hero's effect upon narrative and discourse to his or her ability to shape history itself. In the postmodern present this ability is far from always evident, and *The Human Stain* makes this plain. While Nathan Zuckerman posits, as one interpretive possibility, the tragic power of history to determine the life of an individual, he offers little sense of Coleman Silk's reciprocal ability to determine history. Peter Aaron in *Leviathan* invokes the specter of historical agency more clearly, describing Benjamin Sachs's decision to leave writing behind in favor of political action. Yet Sachs's acts of civil disobedience ultimately have their symbolism compromised and even negated by those acts' re-incorporation into the postmodern culture industry. In *The Virgin*

Suicides, the Lisbon sisters are portrayed initially as victims of history but subsequently as seers into history and prophets of American decline. The connection between their deaths and wider social transformation remains allegorical, however, serving only to undermine a retrospective image of historical transition rather than offer the key to understanding that transition and locating its cause.

In spite of gestures toward historical agency and historical transition, therefore, in none of these observer-hero narratives of the 1990s is the hero conceived of as a truly historical actor. But what if a hero were capable of bringing about transition, of embodying the kind of historical agency that postmodernism denies? How would an observer do justice to such a hero? How would his or her decisions be framed and represented? And would our conception of history have to change? In this concluding chapter of my study, I address these questions through the consideration of a novel by E. L. Doctorow, the writer Fredric Jameson once dubbed "the epic poet of the disappearance of the American radical past" (*Postmodernism* 24). Jameson cites Doctorow's early fiction as exemplifying postmodernism, but I consider the latter's 1994 novel *The Waterworks* as engaged in a transition beyond postmodern temporality through the attempt to do justice to alternative conceptions of history and time. The novel does so, however, from a position of historical distance: unlike the other texts I have considered, *The Waterworks* is not set during the postmodern era but a century prior, with the events it describes taking place in New York City in 1871. With regard to the genre at the heart of this book, too, *The Waterworks* provides a contrasting case study: while Doctorow's observer-narrator McIlvaine substantively resembles Zuckerman, Aaron, and the men who narrate *The Virgin Suicides*, identifying the hero of the novel is not quite such a straightforward task. Narrating from a viewpoint about 30 years after the events of his story, McIlvaine describes the decisive actions of a number of male characters, oscillating in focus between them. And it is through this narrative oscillation between heroes, and the competing conceptions of temporality associated with each, that the novel addresses its larger themes of history and justice.

For Jacques Derrida, time and justice are deeply bound up with one another, and this is one way in which, as we saw in the introduction to this study, he distinguishes dialectical thought from what he calls undecidability. For Derrida, the dialectical method, in presuming to know how history moves and to describe historical transition from a position beyond it, cannot capture the necessary "experience and experiment of the undecidable" that constitutes temporality in the first place (*Limited* 116). A philosophy of history of this kind denies the possibility of "decision in the order of ethical-political responsibility" (116), and thereby denies the possibility of just decisions, which do not occur beyond temporality but from within time and on account of time.[1] "Justice is thus essentially a matter of temporal finitude," Martin Hägglund writes, summarizing Derrida's position here, "since it is ultimately because of temporal finitude that one has to make decisions" (41). Emerging from decisions made in time, justice does not therefore name, for Derrida, the possibility of a utopian realm of eternal egalitarianism—a possibility figured in the Kingdom of God, or in a different way in the postmodern End of History—but rather arises only in relation to singular cases within time and across history.

But just as there is no eternal justice, there is also no present justice, no decision that can ever be said to be wholly and manifestly just. Derrida distinguishes justice from law on this point: "one cannot speak *directly* about justice, thematize and objectivize justice, say 'this is just' and even less 'I am just,' without immediately betraying justice, if not law" ("Force" 10). One can say that an act is lawful, because the law describes the set of behaviors that are permissible (or prohibited) at a particular historical moment. Yet if the law offers a prescription for actions in general, the question of justice arises only in relation to unpredictable events and acts that cannot wholly be subsumed under the generality of law. Derrida explains this as follows: "Law is the element of calculation, and it is just that there be law, but justice is incalculable, it requires us to calculate with the incalculable; and aporetic experiences are the experiences, as improbable as they are necessary, of justice, that is to say of moments in which the decision between just and unjust is never insured be a rule" (16).[2]

The irreducible and ongoing need for just decisions has the further effect of persistently exposing the violence inscribed in the founding of the law as a social and historical force. Derrida writes of the "originary violence that must have established this authority," arguing that "in its initial moment, it is neither legal nor illegal—or, others would quickly say, neither just nor unjust" ("Force" 6). Rather than see the law as emerging historically through democratic agreement concerning standards of behavior within the community or *polis*, Derrida insists on an initial moment of institution that violently brings a constative use of language—describing what we agree to be reality— into conflict with a performative use of language, which brings a new reality into being. Derrida explores the signing of the American Declaration of Independence from this point of view, pointing out that in reading this key document, "One cannot decide— and this is the interesting thing, the force and 'coup de force' of such a declarative act— whether independence is stated or produced by this utterance" ("Declarations" 49). And this uncertainty is not, Derrida makes clear, a question of a contingent lack of knowledge, "of an obscurity or of a difficulty of interpretation"; it is instead absolutely necessary to the founding force of the document: "this undecidability between [. . .] a performative structure and a constative structure, is *required* to produce the sought- after effect" (49).[3]

When we say that an event such as the signing of the Declaration of Independence is "historic" or "makes history," therefore, we do not conceive it simply as an event within an already unfolding history, a history whose law we can divine, but precisely as a decisive interruption of this kind of history. A new and undecidable temporality of history emerges in the event of the Declaration, one in which agency clearly has a performative role to play. This interruption of history embeds itself, however, not as a present moment but only as a trace. Events of historical agency, such as the institution of a law or the founding of a nation, therefore depend upon what Derrida calls a "*simulacrum of the instant*" (51). This simulacrum or trace of the instant is never fully overcome or eradicated; it can always be returned to and revived through close attention to time and to language. The instant thus resists sublation by the dialectical process, by the law of history; and the same is true of any decision that would claim the status of justice:

> That is why the ordeal of the undecidable that I just said must be gone through by any decision worthy of the name is never past or passed, it is not a surmounted or sublated moment of the decision. The undecidable remains caught, lodged, at least as a ghost—but an essential ghost—in every decision, in every event of decision. Its ghostliness deconstructs from within any assurance of presence. ("Force" 24–5)

For Derrida, then, "the time is out of joint," as he writes in *Specters of Marx*, citing Hamlet's reaction to seeing his father's ghost in Shakespeare's play. In opposition to Hamlet's anguished declaration that he was "born to set it right," however, Derrida argues that time can never be set right, and that this out-of-joint quality of temporality is a necessary condition for justice to emerge at all. "Justice as the experience of absolute alterity is unpresentable," Derrida writes, "but it is the chance of the event and the condition of history" ("Force" 27). In this final chapter of *American Fiction in Transition*, I explore justice as the chance of the event and the condition of history in E. L. Doctorow's observer-hero narrative, *The Waterworks*.

I The poetic hero

The opening lines of *The Waterworks* immediately suggest that the time is indeed out of joint. "People wouldn't take what Martin Pemberton said as literal truth, he was much too melodramatic or too tormented to speak plainly," the narrator informs us. "So when he went around muttering that his father was still alive, those of us who heard him, and remembered his father, felt he was speaking of the persistence of evil in general" (1). Echoes of the melodramatic and tormented Hamlet abound here, but whereas Shakespeare's audience is offered visual and aural evidence of the "persistence of evil" in Hamlet's Denmark through the arrival of his father's ghost, here the audience for Pemberton's claims only have his words to go on. And the referential status of these words can easily be misunderstood, as McIlvaine tells us twice more in quick succession: "I interpreted what he said as metaphor, a poetic way of characterizing the wretched city that neither of us loved, but neither of us could leave" (6); "To a certain extent both [Miss Tisdale] and Dr. Grimshaw assumed, as I did, that Martin could not have meant the statement to be taken literally" (7). But Martin Pemberton does mean what he says to be taken literally, although whether he is literally correct in his claim that his father is still alive will not be quite so clear. Words are slippery here, meaning ambiguous; it is not simply time that is out of joint at the opening of *The Waterworks*, but language too.

The difficulty language has in keeping reality in joint is not simply a problem to be overcome, however; it provides, McIlvaine tells us, access to a realm of truth beyond the everyday: "In misunderstanding him, I found a greater truth, though I would not realize it until everything was over and done. It was one of those intuitive moments of revelation that suspend themselves in our minds until we come around to them by the ordinary means of knowing" (9). This access to "intuitive moments of revelation," to temporalities beyond "the ordinary means of knowing," is one of the repeated motifs of the book, leading one critic to describe *The Waterworks* as a "gnostic drama of spiritual forces" (Diemert 362). McIlvaine, notwithstanding his self-proclaimed identity as an "old lapsed Scotch Presbyterian" (*Waterworks* 241), is acutely sensitive to dreams, to premonitions, to "the faintest shadow on my own reasoning" (17). He is obsessed, as we shall see, by chronology, consistently jumping backward and forward in his narration in order to gesture to the resolution of mysteries while still professing faithfulness to his experience of events as they unfold. When reporting an overheard conversation early in the novel, for instance, McIlvaine comments, "All this would become clear to me by and by. At that moment I felt only that sudden sensitivity to the unknown that makes it a . . . specific unknown . . . as if we discern in the darkness only the dim risen quality that draws us towards it. Nothing more" (23).[4] Combined with the gothic texture of these lines, this final standalone phrase points to another literary influence on *The Waterworks*. In an essay, Edgar Lawrence Doctorow has described his namesake Edgar Allan Poe— author of the famous refrain "Nevermore"—as "a mythic presence in the American literary consciousness" (*Creationists* 11). In interview, Doctorow has confirmed that *The Waterworks* constitutes his homage to Poe ("Left Out" 31).[5]

Renowned for their gothic sensibility and doubling motifs, Poe's tales offer some of the earliest examples of observer-hero narrative in the American literary tradition. "The Fall of the House of Usher" (1839), in which a nameless narrator becomes absorbed by the life and habits of his melancholy friend Roderick Usher, is perhaps the most obvious precursor to this opening movement of *The Waterworks*, and to the fall of the House of Pemberton in the novel as a whole. Poe's later "tales of ratiocination," which feature an unnamed narrator describing the actions of the detective Dupin, will become equally relevant when we are introduced by McIlvaine to the policeman Edmond Donne.[6] And "The Man in the Crowd" (1841), which again features a nameless narrator, this time following a mysterious man through a crowded city, anticipates Doctorow's framing of the relationship between the individual and the industrial urban space of democratic modernity. Although McIlvaine is more fully developed and worldly than a typical Poe narrator—in this sense he more closely resembles the bourgeois lawyer who narrates Melville's "Bartleby, the Scrivener"—the initial description given of Martin Pemberton links him quite closely to the historical figure of Poe. Not only is this protagonist a freelance by profession, like his predecessor, but we are told that women "imagined him as something of a poet, though he was if anything a critic, a critic of his life and times" (1). Pemberton's inhabitance of the Poe-tic realm of hero is confirmed by his impact on the observer's own sense of self. McIlvaine remembers him "seeming to live at some level so beyond you that you felt your own self fading in his presence, you felt your hollowness or fraudulence as a person" (2).

If the novel's participation in the observer-hero genre is established by its first chapter, however, a surprise is in store in the opening lines of Chapter 2: "This would have been sometime in April of 1871. I saw Martin Pemberton only once after that, and then he was gone" (7). Pemberton's disappearance, linked to his search for his father Augustus, will provide the engine of the plot, as McIlvaine conducts his own search for the missing freelance. Absence only accentuates the connection between observer and hero, something McIlvaine discovers when he visits Pemberton's empty rented room: "I saw the burden of an educated mind. I also saw that someone loved him . . . I realized that I had come here without admitting to myself that I was magnetized by this wretch of a freelance" (16). And it is not only McIlvaine who comes under the spell of Martin Pemberton, whether present or absent, dead or alive. As he searches for information about the disappearance, McIlvaine conducts a series of interviews with Pemberton's friends and family, including his fiancée Emily Tisdale, his stepmother Sarah Pemberton, the family pastor Charles Grimshaw, and the artist Harry Wheelwright. All are traumatized by Pemberton's disappearance, and Emily Tisdale echoes McIlvaine's sentiments in her profession of attachment: "He inhabits me . . . and there's nothing I can do about it. This I suppose is love. [. . .] I have always been chained to Martin. Through all his tempests . . . his struggles . . . here or not here" (161). But it is Wheelwright who registers most clearly in narrative terms the hero's impact upon those who are fated—like the boys in *The Virgin Suicides*—to have their own life story framed by their interaction with a powerful other. When interrogated concerning his friend's disappearance, Wheelwright's response is recorded as follows: "He stared at the floor and a low moan escaped from him. He said: 'When I write my memoirs I myself will be the subject of them. I do not intend to go down as a mere chronicler of the Pemberton family. I absolutely will not. My paintings will hang in museums. My own fate is another story, not this one. Not this one'" (98). And in case the reader misses the point, the same sentiments are repeated by Wheelwright a few pages later: "I will never tell of these things in my memoirs. When I write my memoirs I will be the subject of the narrative. [. . .] My own fate will be another story . . . not this one" (105).

II The prosaic observer

Like Wheelwright, McIlvaine has found his own story incorporated into that of another; yet unlike Pemberton's artist friend, McIlvaine also has access to a form of narrative that is irreducible to individual memoir and "makes the collective story of all of us" (9): the newspaper. Pemberton's disappearance occurs during McIlvaine's tenure as city editor of the New York *Telegram*, and McIlvaine's involvement with "the cheapest commonest realm, the realm of newsprint" (8) ensures that his hero's story is framed in terms less romantic than prosaic, against a background of everyday distraction: "But even as our search for Martin Pemberton continued . . . [. . .] We had jobs, duties . . . We met our responsibilities . . . which always appeared to us as . . . diverse" (142). In emphasizing "a sense of the life around this matter" (59), McIlvaine shifts his narrative from the concentrated world of pre-modern quest romance to the diffuse world of quotidian modernity, and this emphasis is matched by his professed commitment to the outlook most associated with that transition, that of realism. McIlvaine employs local detail in his story "to impress upon you what a realist I am" (60), and insists that "the world I am spreading out for you here in the flat light of reality is the newsprint world" (61). He also maintains that despite the "intuitive moments of revelation" that haunt his experience, there is nothing spectral or supernatural about the reality in which he lives: "To me, a ghost is as tired and worn-out a fancy as the Romish conceit of my friend Grimshaw. I abhor all such banalities. [. . .] This is not a ghost tale" (61).

Realist though he is, McIlvaine nonetheless acknowledges that the historical emergence of newspapers has heralded the replacement of one kind of realism by another. "In a village, people don't need the newspaper," he tells us. "Newspapers arise only when things begin to happen that people cannot see and hear for themselves" (83). Newspapers thus offer a historical supplement to first-person perception, an early harbinger of the process Jameson will dub cognitive mapping. Such mapping has become necessary because the experience of the modern city is of "some kind of day-to-day crawl through chaos, where there is no hierarchy to your thoughts, but a raucous equality to them" (119). Michael Wutz has explored Doctorow's novel as staging "the building crisis in information processing and knowledge production following a booming postbellum economy" (157), and in *The Waterworks* a range of competing discourses—religion, law, modern science—have begun to operate primarily as modes for categorizing knowledge and archiving experience.[7] McIlvaine puts journalism alongside these, overtly positioning the newspaper as a bulwark against the vacuum of meaning that encroaches in modernity: "if journalism were a philosophy rather than a trade, it would say that there is no order in the universe, no discernible meaning without . . . the daily paper" (12). But this modern meaning can no longer be linear, can no longer take the form of a single narrative. The seven parallel columns that make up McIlvaine's daily broadsheet are therefore, in his rather grand description, "projections of the multiple souls of a man . . . and no meaning was possible from any one column without the sense of all of them in . . . simultaneous descent" (111).

Notwithstanding the challenge of mapping this urban reality in non-linear form, McIlvaine has never before felt that his beloved newspaper would fall short of its task. The impression of New York that the veteran journalist holds dear is of a city riotous but without real mystery, "a city of souls whose excitements have always been reportable" (60–1). Yet the inherent limitations of journalistic reportage soon become a key theme of McIlvaine's narrative. These limitations can be institutional, as when McIlvaine attempts to publish an exclusive on the Tweed Ring (the disintegration of which provides the novel's historical background), only to be shot down by the *Telegram*'s editorial board owing to the implications for advertising and personal connections. McIlvaine resigns in protest, but this confrontation with the corrupt forces of urban modernity is merely the precursor to a larger story. Evidence gradually emerges that Augustus Pemberton, Martin's father, has indeed faked his own death, and a number of other New York businessmen have similarly disappeared along with their entire fortunes. As McIlvaine waits and waits to run his exclusive on this macabre set of events, and then never does, he offers his reluctance as the recognition of a more profound limitation to journalistic norms, "a premonition that, even completed, the story was not . . . reportorially possible . . . that there are limits to the use of words in a newspaper" (200–1).

Deciding against a newspaper exclusive, then, McIlvaine begins to consider "telling the whole story within the pages of a book" (229). On one level this book is, of course, *The Waterworks* itself, but unlike in the cases of Roth's *The Human Stain* or Auster's *Leviathan*, Doctorow does not present the text we read as the work of McIlvaine the writer as well as narrator-observer. Instead, the novel is presented as an oral document, with McIlvaine retrospectively telling his tale to an unnamed addressee. This is sometimes indicated rhetorically, as when McIlvaine admonishes his listener (and by extension the reader of his story) as follows: "You may think you are living in modern times, here and now, but that is the necessary illusion of every age. We did not conduct ourselves as if we were preparatory to your time" (9). The oral character of the narration is more persistently indicated, however, by the continual use of ellipses in the text. These ellipses have elicited many and varied interpretations by reviewers and critics,[8] but their effect on the reading process is distinctive, and is summarized by one critic's observation that their inclusion "slows down the pace of an urban detective novel in much the same way as the thick descriptions of jungle landscape slow down *Heart of Darkness*, ensuring that readers take the necessary time to ponder the tale's meaning" (Tokarczyk, *E. L. Doctorow's* 154). The allusion here is not accidental, as Doctorow himself has named Conrad's best-known observer-hero narrative as another precursor to *The Waterworks*: "I always imagined [McIlvaine] was dictating, that the unnamed stenographer—me possibly—became the captive audience. But I decided I didn't need to frame it all up, as Conrad does when an unnamed narrator gives us the scene [. . .] as Marlow begins one of his marathon monologues" (*Conversations* 205).

In *Heart of Darkness*, the tensions, hesitations, silences, and desperate outbursts that litter Marlow's "marathon monologue" testify to the immense effect upon the narrator of the ambivalent hero Kurtz. More revelatory still are proleptic gestures in the narrative, such as the scene in which Marlow tells a lie to the Assistant Manager "simply because I had a notion it somehow would be of help to that Kurtz whom at the time I did not see—you understand. He was just a word for me. I did not see the man in the name any more than you do" (Conrad 29). In *The Waterworks*, the tensions and hesitations figured in McIlvaine's ellipses are accompanied by similar moments of prolepsis, and as in Conrad's novel those moments are linked to the anticipation of a powerful other. This other will not turn out to be the poetic hero Martin Pemberton, however. Having initially positioned Pemberton as the Hamlet of the piece, McIlvaine will in fact discover that "my freelance, finally, was only a reporter bringing the news, like the messenger in Elizabethan dramas . . . the carrier of essential information, all eyes upon him delivering the dire news . . . but for all his gallant duty, only a messenger" (136). Displacing the poetic hero, two competing modern figures will emerge through the middle section of McIlvaine's story. It is these two figures—representing law and science, and ostensibly moral hero and evil villain—whose challenge to the narrator's methods of representation turns *The Waterworks* firmly in the direction of an inquiry into the relationship between history, time, and justice.

III Modern times

After a lengthy investigation, Martin Pemberton is finally discovered nearly dead from starvation in the basement of the Home for Little Wanderers, an orphanage on the northern edge of the city. He is returned to the Tisdale residence to recuperate, and after a long silence (one that recalls Benjamin Sachs in *Leviathan*), he tells his macabre story. Children are taken from the New York streets to the orphanage, where their bodily matter is extracted and transported to an unknown location. There it is put to work by the mysterious Dr. Wrede Sartorius, whose experiments on the voluntarily disappeared businessmen—including Pemberton's father Augustus—seem designed to uncover the secrets of immortality. While this arrangement clearly exploits the anonymous street children that litter the city—"I define modern civilization as the social failure to keep all children named," McIlvaine tells us archly (79)—it is a plan in which all the most powerful elements of society appear to have involved themselves: "Men had turned their fortunes over to Sartorius . . . betrayed their families. Politicians conspired in his behalf. The opportunistic Simmons had moved from Augustus Pemberton's employ to his. He'd converted these men of the world, these . . . realists, into acolytes. He was a holy man, he commanded belief" (169).[9]

The powerful charisma of Conrad's Kurtz resonates in this description of Sartorius, and as with the "holy man" of *Heart of Darkness*, the doctor's actual appearance in *The Waterworks* is prefigured by intrusions upon McIlvaine's chronological telling, by the acknowledgment of time and narrative out of joint. Sartorius first impinges upon the narrator's consciousness as "a moment's belated awareness of the shadow cast by the name as it was uttered by Sarah Pemberton" (90): in other words, as a trace imprinted unconsciously, signifying only in retrospect. McIlvaine will, from this point onward, continually allude to Sartorius only to retreat again, each time acknowledging the strain the figure of the doctor imposes upon his narrative method: "I withhold here the circumstances of our first sight of Sartorius. I want to keep to the chronology of things but at the same time to make their pattern sensible, which means disrupting the chronology" (119). When Sartorius is finally described in detail by McIlvaine, this is likewise relayed in an anxious manner: "I had not seen him, at this point, you understand, but I hold his image in my mind and I will assign it to him here, out of the chronology of things . . . to suggest the force of him . . . as if we were able to derive him from the disaster he had brought about" (170). And even when he comes around to introducing Sartorius in this manner, McIlvaine worries that conveying the doctor's effect may be beyond the reach of his language: "I don't know if I can portray the effect of an overriding mentality . . . This man I had never seen seemed to characterize the room where Martin lay" (169).

Yet in spite of this talk of "force" and "overriding mentality," Sartorius turns out to be, unlike Conrad's Kurtz, far from an imposing personality in the flesh. "The doctor himself I find difficult to represent to you," Martin Pemberton tells his listeners. "He doesn't expend his energies on the formation of a . . . social self. He is quiet, almost ascetic in his habits, courteous, unprepossessing" (176). In his own observer-hero narrative, embedded like a play within the play of McIlvaine's larger story, Pemberton insists not only on Sartorius's dearth of personal magnetism, but also on his lack of malevolence, declaring that "[t]he doctor is not an immoralist" (172). Instead, Sartorius "thinks with pieces of the world. He sees into its structures. If he has one working principle, I think, it is to connect himself to the amoral energies human life in society generates . . . irrespective of its beliefs" (190). The force that the doctor possesses, then, his ability to "command belief," stems not from a charismatic personality but from his connection to larger historical forces: "It's as if . . . there's an alignment of historical energies magnetized on him which . . . for all I know, is probably all . . . that makes him visible" (176). Thus, when Pemberton insists of Sartorius's laboratory that "whatever the agency of man could do was done there" (191), the conception of agency inscribed in these words is far from the liberal notion of man acting through individual choice within a historical context. What is inscribed is something closer to the unexpected trace of radical historical alterity, of an agency with the power to alter history itself.

For Derrida, doing justice to history as "the experience and experiment of the undecidable" (*Limited* 116) requires that we "maintain two contradictory affirmations at the same time. On the one hand we affirm the existence of ruptures in history, and on the other we affirm that these ruptures produce gaps or faults in which the most hidden and forgotten archives can emerge and constantly recur and work through history" ("Deconstruction" 163). The figure of Sartorius inhabits both sides of this binary, both a rupture and a forgotten archive. Placed retrospectively by the author Doctorow into the buzzing modernity of postbellum New York, Sartorius is a rupturing imposition from the future, something Michael Wutz confirms in his discussion of the doctor as representing Doctorow's imagined synthesis of divergent streams of scientific thought during the period: "Sartorius's steam-driven apparatus measuring cerebral electricity, in fact, ingeniously unites the two predominant paradigms of late nineteenth-century science—thermodynamics and electromagnetic field theory" (169). Alongside this rupturing futurity, however, Sartorius represents the historical unfolding of scientific possibility, unchecked by moral or justificatory concerns, as a city official notes to McIlvaine near the conclusion of the novel: "He was a brilliant practitioner. He kept going! That is the point—he kept going . . . through, beyond . . . sanity, whatever that is. Or morality, whatever that is. But in a perfect line with everything he'd done before" (224). All the labored narrative contortion on McIlvaine's part—to register Sartorius's effect on chronology at the same time as maintaining chronology—thus serves to support the assessment of the doctor offered by this city official: "I will say this to you: He was a man ahead of his time" (224). Sartorius is literally ahead of his time, an imposition from the future onto the imagined past, but one who opens an archive of possibility, an alternative course for history to take.

Sartorius therefore emerges simultaneously from within history and outside of it, wreaking havoc upon its ordered progression. He recalls Derrida's description of the *arrivant*, the other that arrives to disrupt the historically entrenched homogeneity of the self and same:

> He surprises the host—who is not yet a host or an inviting power—enough to call into question, to the point of annihilating or rendering indeterminate,

all the distinctive signs of a prior identity, beginning with the very border that delineated a legitimate home and assured lineage, names and language, families and genealogies. (*Aporias* 34)

It is precisely assured lineages, families, genealogies and the border between the living and the dead that will be put in doubt by the arrival of Sartorius. In discovering the ability to keep his older clients artificially alive through transfusion from the young, he disrupts the accepted historical progress of generational succession. The older generation are not allowed to die—they carry on in a near-vegetative and undead state—while the younger generation grow old prematurely; Martin Pemberton sees "first one, then another, of the orphan children begin to age, like leaves turning yellow" (191).[10] McIlvaine recognizes that the "historical energies" magnetized on Sartorius therefore represent "not only a concordance of wealth, and government, and science but a profound ... derangement of the natural order of fathers and sons" (231). Sartorius's model of time disrupts historical chronology, natural succession and moral causality; it simultaneously brings into being a new archive, the transition to a new opening of history. As Pemberton notes of his time spent with Sartorius (in an image whose connotations I will return to): "It was like coming ashore on the freshened winds of a newfound land" (191).

The figure who emerges in *The Waterworks* to counteract the temporal and historical breach occasioned by the event of Sartorius is the municipal police detective Edmond Donne. Sought out by McIlvaine as the one honest officer in the city, Donne soon takes over the investigation and becomes the source of direction and activity, provoking McIlvaine to remark, "I felt as if I was giving up . . . my diction . . . for his" (91). Donne embodies in one man the role McIvaine had earlier claimed for the newspaper, possessing as he does an unusual talent for cognitive mapping—"he held the whole city in his mind as if it were a village" (82)—and for non-linear thinking: "he was like a walking newspaper who could carry the stories simultaneously in their parallel descents" (112). As well as his spatial omniscience, Donne stands for the principal of temporal integrity, for the priority of the always already over the event of the new. With Donne as hero, *The Waterworks* becomes aligned with the conventions (and to some extent the diction) of the detective story, and Donne resembles Poe's detective Dupin, whose approach to a case is to employ rationality to uncover and explain what has already occurred.

To the observer-narrator, the actions of the detective-hero may seem to constitute the emergence of the new—McIlvaine wonders at "the question I will never be able to resolve to my satisfaction . . . the conjunctions of which Edmund Donne was capable" (153)—but in Donne's own understanding there is nothing new, only things waiting to be brought to light. McIlvaine recalls that when he first approached Donne about the case, the policeman reacted with a lack of surprise, "with a look of recognition in his eye, as if he might have been waiting for this . . . waiting for me to arrive . . . with what he was expecting" (85). Soon after they team up to investigate the case, Donne observes to the narrator, "This is the way it happens—you want evidence of what you already know" (107). When the journalist and the policeman explore a seemingly unrelated case involving the disappearance of street children, Donne sits in a tavern with no apparent purpose, waiting "for what, he didn't know, except, as he would tell me much later, he would know it when he saw it" (115). He does not have to wait long before a child enters and offers important new information in the Pemberton case. Donne's version of time is all about recovering what is already known, allowing time to reveal itself to him until a final "brilliant and culminating insight" leads him to locate Sartorius's laboratory in the city waterworks (201). At the conclusion of the novel, he marries the widowed Sarah Pemberton, and McIlvaine has reason to believe that rather than being a new alliance, this is simply a restitution of an earlier bond, the re-emergence of a latent or forgotten archive.

Regardless of Donne's own penchant to domesticate historical rupture or deny its possibility, his own arrival constitutes a genuine event in McIlvaine's narrative, one that, McIlvaine feels, may even be what brings Sartorius into being: "as I had brought in the protagonist for my quest, he brought with him, like his shadow, his opposite" (91). And Donne as protagonist also brings with him a series of wider social interests, taking the story "into another realm, making it the concern of a particular class of people in our society" (91). This is a class, the liberal and professional bourgeoisie, that has most to gain in an unfolding of time according to the norms of industrial capitalism and the succession of generations. It is therefore the class that Sartorius's intervention into the course and chronology of life (with the support he receives from the new super-rich) does most to harm. Emily Tisdale offers a voice for this class, appealing to Donne in terror at the implications of Martin's revelations: "Can our lives ever be the same? What is to be done, do you know Captain? Is there something for us to do that will . . . restore the proportions of things?" (183–4). What Donne provides is precisely a restoration of the proportions of things, a conception of time as moral causality, a sense of historical agency in which individuals can once again be praised or blamed:

> In this moment I understood, as they must have, that Donne's researches had provided an answer of a kind . . . that where, before, all had been chaos and bewilderment and hurt, now it was clear that something understandable . . . an act . . . had been committed . . . a deliberate act or series of acts . . . by which we could recompose the world, comfortingly, in categories of good and evil. And I felt the first stirrings of some communal perception . . . that the missing son and fiancé might be embarked on something heroic. (135)

By restoring moral equilibrium to the community, Donne allows for a familiar conception of heroism to be reintroduced, whereby Martin Pemberton can readopt his role as Hamlet, and together with the modern detective and trusty journalist can address time out of joint and set it right again, putting to rest the ghosts of his father and of the scientist who has kept the old man undecidably dead and alive. However, the concluding movement of *The Waterworks* does not unambiguously affirm this restitution of temporality and generational chronology. Rather, in detailing the fate of Sartorius at the hands of the society that Donne, Pemberton, and McIlvaine represent, the novel stages its debate about time as a debate about justice.

IV Theories of justice

This debate about justice occurs between McIlvaine, Donne, and the Reverend Grimshaw after the capture and subsequent institutionalization of Sartorius. To McIlvaine's chagrin, when the doctor's laboratory is discovered and Sartorius is arrested, he is not put on trial but placed in an insane asylum through the workings of a public board that does not publish its findings. "I am not interested in sentimentalizing Dr. Wrede Sartorius's career as a personal tragedy," McIlvaine tells the reader (125); instead, he views the doctor's incarceration as an act of historical suppression by what he calls "institutional thought":

> Whatever the institution . . . and however worthy or substantive . . . its mind is not an entirely human mind . . . though it is made up of human minds. If it were really human it would be capable of surprises . . . If it were wholly human it would be motivated by all sorts of noble or ignoble ideas. But the institutional mind has only one mental operation: It abhors truth. (221)

This robotic conception of the institution portrays a self-consistent, persistent, and predictable sameness, a conception of law without justice. McIlvaine sees the challenge provided by the singular case of Sartorius as having been ignored by the institution that judges him. According to the narrator, this is tantamount to disregarding the capacity for surprise that structures every human decision, the singular concern with justice that informs the law and can reform it. It thereby also represents a disregard for truth, linked in the above paragraph to that which is "entirely" or "really" or "wholly" human. Yet it is precisely the question of the human that Sartorius's intervention has put in doubt; when bodies can be kept indeterminately dead or alive, when, as Sartorius directly tells McIlvaine at the conclusion, "all life is contingent" and "we must rid ourselves of our poetic conceits" (234), the notion of the human is no longer a stable ground upon which to build a present conception of justice. Martin Pemberton's summary of Sartorius's philosophy states the case: "Normality obstructed the scientific vision, it suggested a self-assurance of form that life had no right to claim" (192).

As a consequence, and just as Sartorius's visibility is a product of "historical energies magnetized on him," so his public invisibility after his arrest becomes a test case for a broader debate about justice where notions of the human and of history are at stake. The overt debate between McIlvaine, Donne, and Grimshaw sees the convergence of three distinct moral arguments, based on three versions of a higher principle of justice that each appeals to. In countering Donne's initial statement that "I think justice has been done," Grimshaw replies, "How, sir, if the man is left alive to do more murdering evil" (230)? Grimshaw, representing one understanding of Christianity and justice, first takes Sartorius's moral wrong for granted and secondly assumes that it will be borne out and proven by a public trial. But Donne's response puts both the assumptions that inform this view into doubt:

> If you have a trial, he will have to be heard. Any lawyer would see that the
> only hope of a defense would be in taking his testimony. He could argue in his
> perversity that our interruption of his work cost the lives of his patients. And
> our proofs, you know . . . are largely circumstantial. At least his ideas will be
> heard . . . his . . . genius will be on view. I can't think that would be of any benefit
> to a Christian society. (231)

One reading of Donne's statement is that the detective is in implicit agreement with
the rights of Christianity to condemn moral evil, but differs from Grimshaw in his
lack of belief that the processes of a court will succeed in condemning Sartorius
for his crimes. Alternatively, the statement could show that Donne acknowledges
Sartorius to have strong moral claims within the law as it stands, indeed that he has
a claim to legal superiority owing to the crimes that society has perpetrated against
him and his patients. Therefore, rather than risk a trial, "justice has been done" by
identifying him as insane and placing him in the institution that most closely covers
his case (the time-honored link between insanity and genius being used to simplify the
categorization of Sartorius). This notion of justice is not in line with accepted forms of
legal process, as Donne admits: "What we have done may be unconstitutional . . . it is
not due process . . . but it is all the justice you could wish for" (230). Such a conception
of justice is instead summarized neatly and somewhat sardonically by McIlvaine:

> You will not hear from me that Edmund Donne had his limits. Perhaps he felt,
> after all, that the rights of society had been honored [. . .] we had managed to rid
> our city of this . . . horror. We had worked it out. There was a degree of satisfaction
> to be taken. A young man's life had been saved. A family had been restored to itself.
> And in the course of things Donne had found a face to look upon that he had loved
> once before . . . or was newly in discovery of . . . but, in either event, was in hopes
> of seeing every day and night for the rest of his life. (231)[11]

McIlvaine wants a trial for a different reason to Grimshaw: the narrator would
like to see justice debated, lawful process undergone, truth brought out into the open.
He reacts to Donne's claims to justice by appealing that "the rights of the society are
scanted" (231). The reader is left, then, with incompatible claims to justice: Donne
asserts that justice requires unconstitutionality in certain cases, McIlvaine maintains
that such unconstitutionality is a forthright denial of justice, and Grimshaw claims
that moral evil is a priori detectable and overrides all other considerations. In all of
these assessments a communitarian rhetoric prevails: there is no talk of Sartorius's
individual right to a trial, not even by the doctor himself. Indeed, in his interview with
McIlvaine, conducted in the mental asylum, Sartorius resists the narrator's suggestion
that he should be given his "day in court": "That would only be hypocrisy. I respect the
self-interest behind this expedient. It is more in character with the society" (233). And
at the conclusion of the novel, the "rights of society" are in fact strongly reasserted,
something that occurs most obviously through the act of marriage. Two pairs of
principles, Edmund Donne and Sarah Pemberton, and Martin Pemberton and Emily

Tisdale, exchange vows in the final chapter, and this ending provides for a conventional denouement to a social comedy, as well as the reconstitution of a surrogate bond between father and son.

None of this, however, lifts the gloom for McIlvaine. Rather, a feeling of dread pervades these final scenes, one that recalls McIlvaine's comment at the novel's opening: "Can you imagine what it is like to live in a city of thieves, raucous in its dissembling, a city falling into ruin, a society in name only?" (8). Despite the seemingly happy ending, McIlvaine insists that communal bonds have not been reconstituted, that this remains a society in name only. The final chapter of *The Waterworks* is full of hints about the isolation of the individual in New York life, the absence of any larger social unit. "One way or another, these were all single, unrelated men," McIlvaine notes of the principles in his story (239), and further on, he describes Martin Pemberton's aunt as having a tenuous connection to her nephew "in the great tradition of this in-name-only family" (241). And finally, in discussing his art with McIlvaine, Harry Wheelwright confesses that his intent is "to paint human faces unlocated, with nothing behind them . . . alone in the universe . . ." (242). Just like Conrad's Marlow, Doctorow's humans live with "nothing behind" (Conrad 30), with no explicit moral foundation on which to ground a judgment for all. Thus the means-end expediency that Sartorius acknowledges comes to dominate, captured in the rhetorical question the civil representative directs at McIlvaine at the end of their conversation years later: "What we did worked out, didn't it? Civilization was avenged, was it not?" (226).

Recalling his feeling of insufficiency at these society weddings, McIlvaine laments the temporal spirit that animates this form of life: "I can't tell you how deeply I despise our custom of steadfast carrying on . . . in the manner of people of our sort" (243). For him, this plodding onward marks a forgetting, a disrespect of history, demonstrating "[t]he way people, the best people, must go spiraling off in the resolution of things. As if there will be no memory" (243). When Donne remarks to the assembled parties at the Pemberton-Tisdale wedding that "Mr. McIlvaine saw before anyone else that something was . . . amiss" (243), the narrator is appalled by the denigration of the mystery through the use of such a mild term. In every mind but McIlvaine's, the ruptures of Sartorius and his supporters have been addressed, and time has been put back in joint, society reconciled unto itself once again. For the observer–narrator, however, events have left a permanent mark, and the surface reconciliation masks a more ominous reality: "There was a more fathomless threat there than to Christianity . . . that left my eyes blasted to peer into it" (231).[12]

V Religion, Utopia, and the time of transition

If Sartorius and Donne represent two contrasting models of time and history, then McIlvaine's own narrative offers a weighing of other alternatives, both through its content and its form. One such alternative, as some quotations have already indicated, is what we might call religious time. One prominent characterization of this religious time in McIlvaine's narrative is teleological, where history is seen not as rupture or as sameness but as a progressive unfolding toward an ultimate goal. Thus McIlvaine's summary of his discontent at the novel's conclusion:

> I'll grant you, perhaps it is sentimentalism to think a society is capable of being spiritually chastened . . . in some self-educative way . . . of pulling oneself up just one . . . rung . . . toward moral enlightenment. That we would, as a kind of municipal congregation, drop to our knees and gather our children to us. What really happens is that we shunt off our evil, embody it in . . . our defendants and turn away. (229)

The language and imagery here—spiritual chastening, congregation, gathering children, scapegoating—is clearly drawn from a religious register. Despite the dissatisfaction with "worn-thin, shabby, church-poor words" (31) that has led him away from Presbyterianism, McIlvaine's diction is consistently religious in tenor. He compares the waterworks reservoir to "a baptismal font for the gigantic absolution we require as a people" (58); he speaks of police work as a "civil religion" and of "the priestly mind of Edmund Donne" (118); he describes in detail the interior of St James's church in one of the novel's closing passages (245). Nevertheless, not only is McIlvaine skeptical of the tenets and practices of organized religion—as his rather dismissive treatment of Grimshaw throughout *The Waterworks* indicates—but his interaction with Sartorius has a profound effect on any conception he might hold of a transcendent God. At the finale of their interview in the asylum, Sartorius tells McIlvaine that "[o]nly Science can find the diction for answers [. . .] we will find the language, the formulae, or perhaps the numeration . . . to match God." Asked by the narrator whether God himself cannot be relied on for answers, Sartorius responds, "Not as God is now composed" (235).

Sartorius's notebooks are burned following his incarceration, so that the narrator has no access to the scientist's specific vision for re-composing God. Nevertheless, as he surveys St James's church and reflects on Sartorius's final words, McIlvaine's religious sensibility is alienated by a sense of the fragility of the institution that surrounds him: this might be "God as he is presently composed" (245), but science will soon produce an alternative, and the onward march of history will sweep all of this ancient finery away. In response to this insight, and in place of a religious conception of time as teleological, there is another temporal vision articulated by McIlvaine at various points in his narrative, one that suggests not history's fulfillment but its negation. In its religious dimension, one name for this temporality is eschatological, a temporality supported by "the proselytizers abroad in the city—Adventists and Millerites, Shakers and Quakers, Swedenborgians, Perfectionists, and Mormons" (31). But in *The Waterworks* the negation of history more frequently takes another form, that of utopia. In an essay linking Doctorow's novel with Toni Morrison's *Beloved* (1987) as postmodern works, Marianne DeKoven highlights the strand of McIlvaine's prose that lyrically evokes a pre-historical New York, describing this strand as "the persistence of utopianism in modernist form within the reconfigured formal conventionality of postmodernism" (DeKoven 78).

DeKoven focuses on a scene in *The Waterworks* that recalls perhaps the most canonical of all American observer-hero narratives, *The Great Gatsby*. In the famous conclusion to Fitzgerald's novel, Manhattan Island "flowers" as "a fresh, green breast of the new world" (Fitzgerald 189) for those Dutch sailors setting their eyes upon it for the first time. In Doctorow's novel, this reaction is reversed: "I envisaged the first Dutch sailors giving up on the place as a mosquito-infested swamp, and returning in their long boats to their ships . . ." (150). This comment by McIlvaine is the precursor to the narrator's dream of an alternative pastoral utopia at the climax of the same chapter:

> Ever since this day I have dreamt sometimes . . . I, a street rat in my soul, dream even now . . . that if it were possible to lift this littered, paved Manhattan from the earth . . . and all its torn and dripping pipes and conduits and tunnels and tracks and cables—all of it, like a scab from new skin underneath—how seedlings would sprout, and freshets bubble up, and brush and grasses would grow over the rolling hills . . . (157)

The narrator associates this vision of a pre-historic (or post-historic) Manhattan with "the lean, religious Indians of the bounteous earth, [. . .] those savage polytheists of my mind" (157-8). These are nonhistorical beings, with a circular sense of time that rests on "inadequate stories," but their ignorance has become the envy of the weary modern. It is an ignorance connected by McIlvaine to the innocence of children, as he reflects on the "paradisial beginning" of the love between Emily Tisdale and Martin Pemberton: "their young souls urged into wing, their voices from dawn to dusk in this garden as constant as the birds' . . . and [I] think of the superior state of childhood, when love is lived without knowing it is called that" (50). The corruption of this utopian innocence, in its romantic dimension, is confirmed by the scene in which Martin receives sexual favors from "a young housemaid," and realizes how much like his father he is "as she kneeled before him and he held her head and felt the working muscles of her jaw and the rhythmic pulling of her cheeks" (53). In its religious dimension, innocence corrupted by modern desires is represented, most frequently, by Reverend Grimshaw, for instance in his concern with recent scholarship on the Bible: "his steeple lost in the shadows of factories, Charles Grimshaw was thirsting for historical verification of the words of Scripture" (42). And in its spatial dimension, no better example can be found in the novel for the way "history destroys or distorts potential or attempted utopias" (DeKoven 77) than the "indoor park" at the center of Sartorius's laboratory in the waterworks, "an obverse Eden" that reminds Martin Pemberton of "a Roman bath, had Rome been industrialized" (*Waterworks* 180-1).

As DeKoven rightly notes, then, utopia in Doctorow's novel "can only be imagined outside, and in explicit negation of, history" (89). DeKoven's reading is in line with the Jamesonian conception of postmodernism, wherein the figure of utopia represents the last remnant of a possible alternative to late capitalist stasis, albeit that such a utopia cannot be conceived in any temporal relation with present circumstances. For Jameson, as for DeKoven, postmodern literary texts valorize utopia as the necessary contemporary alternative to "an account of agency" or "a coherent historical and practical-political picture of transition" (Jameson, *Archaeologies* 232). In *The Waterworks*, this would mean that McIlvaine's lyrical and antihistorical utopian visions are to be privileged, that when he declares early in the novel, "Where you'll find mankind not shackled in history is Heaven, eventless Heaven" (4), we are to understand such heaven in a normative sense, as an eventless space to be desired. But can such eventlessness be preferred to a historical time that is open to possibility, whether good or bad? Perhaps more importantly, should such an eventless Heaven be preferred?

I would argue that *The Waterworks* answers both these questions in the negative, portraying history, for all its horror and threat, as the only source of justice and transition. This is the case both in a descriptive sense—it is not possible for us to experience "eventless Heaven" while "shackled in history"—and in a normative sense—even if we could, we should not desire to experience such a Heaven, because it would rob us of the possibilities that our timebounded modernity provides. The difference between the descriptive and normative sense here might also be reinscribed as the difference between an atheist and a radically atheist position, to cite the terms Hägglund provides in his book on Derrida. For Hägglund, "Atheism has traditionally limited itself to denying the existence of God and immortality, without questioning the desire for God and immortality" (1). Radical atheism, on the other hand, would not consider mortal life to involve a lack of being that we desire to transcend in the direction of atemporal eternity; rather, "the so-called desire for immortality dissimulates a desire for survival that precedes it and contradicts it from within" (1). On Hägglund's reading, McIlvaine's "eventless Heaven" would be a place where nothing could happen, where time would bring nothing to pass; it would therefore be no different from the state of death. The descriptive sense in which we lack the ability to experience heaven would be trumped on this reading by the normative sense in which we should not desire to do so, even if such a thing were possible.

The descriptive/atheist position in *The Waterworks* could be evidenced by innumerable quotations, as when, for example, Sartorius avers that "[c]ivilization does not fortify the membranous mind, or alter our subjection to the moment, the moment that has no memory [. . .] We live subject to the moment" (208–9), or when McIlvaine notes that "time estranges us from the belief we are all given—the pious and the blasphemous alike—that we are born to live in pleasure or pain, happiness or despair, but always in great moral consequence" (228). The normative/radically atheist position is more complicatedly rendered, but can be found both in McIlvaine's positive descriptions of historical time and in his negative comments about static time. In one lyrical description, for instance, it is disorder rather than utopia that receives affirmation:

> There are moments of our life that are something like breaks or tears in moral consciousness, as caesuras break the chanted line, and the eye sees through the breach to a companion life, a life in all its aspects the same, running along parallel in time, but within a universe even more confounding than our own. It is this other disordered existence . . . that our ministers warn us against . . . that our dreams perceive. (213)

Here the disordered existence that takes place in time, even in the time of dreams, is privileged over the censorious approach to dreams (and to time) found in religion. Elsewhere, it is the chaotic existence that marks modern democratic life that receives a kind of veiled affirmation, as for example in the following observation by McIlvaine: "I'm all for democracy but I'll tell you that I've lived through times in this town that have made me long for the stultifying peace of kings . . . the equanimity that comes of bowing and scraping in the dazzling light of regal authority" (5). Here the static temporality of the "peace of kings" is aligned with strict social hierarchy and "bowing and scraping" inequality; for all the difficulties posed by democracy, then, it offers a temporality that allows the possibility of justice to emerge.[13]

Of the old rich men who inhabit the ghostly municipal carriage that Martin Pemberton has seen moving through the streets of New York, McIlvaine writes: "I saw Sartorius, for all his imperial achievement, as . . . their servant. They, not he, had ridden up Broadway with the news . . . that there was no life, no death, but something that was a concurrence of both" (218). This "something" that not is fully life nor death but a concurrence of both can only be time itself: a genuinely historical time that sees each instant occur as a simulacrum—living, dying and becoming a trace all in one infinitely divisible moment. It is only this historical temporality that calls for decisions in the face of the undecidable, decisions whose difficulty are the requirement and the possibility for justice to exist at all. The dialectic between this historical temporality and the religious time that McIlvaine's narrative also foregrounds is captured most vividly in the two closing paragraphs of *The Waterworks*, worth quoting in full, in which New York is pictured on the Sunday morning of Donne's wedding as McIlvaine walks up Broadway away from the church:

> Of course it was a Sunday, the day of rest. But my illusion was that the city had frozen in time. All our mills and foundries and presses were still . . . our lathes and our boilers . . . our steam engines and pulleys and pumps and forges. Our stores were shut . . . our carriage works and iron works and sewing machine and type writer manufactures . . . our telegraph stations . . . our exchanges . . . our carpentries . . . our electroplaters . . . our stoneyards and lumber yards . . . our abbatoirs and fishmarkets . . . our hosiery mills and garment shops . . . our smithies and stables . . . our manufacturers of tool dies and turbines and steam dredges and railroad cars and horse collars . . . our gunsmiths and silversmiths . . . our stoveworks and tin ware stampers . . . our coopers and clockmakers and ships' chandlers . . . our brickworks . . . our makers of ink and paper mills . . . our book publishers . . . our mowers and harvesters and sowers and reapers . . . all still, unmoving, stricken, as if the entire city of New York would be forever encased and frozen, aglitter and godstunned. (246)

As the voice of our hitherto idiosyncratic narrator suddenly descends into a parody of the modernist list, the impression rendered is indeed of a frozen city, like a two-dimensional painting of a moment of stasis amid the usually frenzied life of the city's constituent parts. The institutions listed here embody both humanity and its abstraction in labor, and the stasis McIlvaine observes leaves those institutions "still" and "aglitter," but also "stricken" and "godstunned." The temptation of stillness and glitter, of a utopian time in which nothing can happen, is clear here; but so too is its rejection as a "stricken" vision. The final portmanteau "godstunned" sums this up, evoking a deity that stuns his subjects not by engendering awe but precisely by demanding subjection, "bowing and scraping in the dazzling light of regal authority" (5).

Yet if hints of the normative, radically atheist position can be detected here in the negative connotations of "stricken" and "godstunned," the entire passage has already been placed in relief by McIlvaine's prolegomena that it is all merely "my illusion." The narrator reiterates this point in the novel's final, single-line paragraph:

> And let me leave you with that illusion . . . though in reality we would soon be driving ourselves up Broadway in the new year of Our Lord, 1872. (246)

The illusion is that the rigidity of these institutions uproots them from the forces of history, protects them from the alterity of time. The illusion is that God can be made to stand for utopia and stasis, when instead God can only be coextensive with history, where humanity are "driving ourselves" rather than being driven. This is Doctorow's 1990s answer to the apparent depletion of agency that heralds the postmodern turn to utopia, its concern for "events rather than new worlds." In this novel the world, whether in 1871, 1872, or 1994, is always new—year to year, day to day, moment to moment.[14]

If there can be said to be an overarching conception of time operating in *The Waterworks*, then, it is best embodied in the formal qualities of McIlvaine's observer-hero narrative. I have emphasized the importance of McIlvaine's obsession with chronology—the paradoxical conjoining of his "abhorrence of suspense" (232) with his insistence that it is "knowing in advance the whole conclusive order . . . which makes narration . . . suspect" (119)—because *The Waterworks* makes plain once again the career-long engagement by Doctorow with the idea that "[t]here is no history except as it is composed" ("False" 160). Something like this sentiment is expressed by McIlvaine about Martin Pemberton's oral recounting of his trauma: "there was nothing as good for him, for anyone, as getting the story told, turning it into an object made of language . . . for everyone to lift and examine" (194). This is exactly what McIlvaine's own oral recounting does, and it is only in the telling that the trauma of transition can be framed and understood.

Getting the story told, turning it into an object made of language, is precisely the concern of observer-hero narratives of the American 1990s. The trauma of transition is at the heart of these texts, and in *The Human Stain* and *Leviathan*, the struggle to narrate the hero's decisive life, and the oscillation between interpretive modes that this struggle entails, allegorizes the problem of understanding historical transition in a postmodern age. In *The Virgin Suicides*, this allegory is made more explicit, but the suicidal action of the Lisbon sisters still retains a strictly symbolic and noncausal relationship to historical change. In *The Waterworks*, finally, Sartorius and Donne emerge as figures of contrasting historical agency and possibility, and McIlvaine's wish to do justice to both produces the tensions in his text, tensions that point toward alternative conceptions of time and models of transition. The oscillation between potential heroes in *The Waterworks* means that justice always resides in the judgment of the singular case, and every reading makes this case anew. American literary writing in the 1990s is in some sense defined and enabled by this awareness—the awareness of an undecidability that is not simply a form of relativism, but rather the necessary opening to future responses, events of reading and writing, that lie beyond the present and beyond the postmodern.

Notes

Introduction

1   In his book on the postmodernism debate and Jameson's contribution to it, Perry Anderson remarks that Jameson's treatment of subjectivity is "perhaps the most famous of all facets of his construction of the postmodern" (56); it is likewise a leading feature of my use of the term throughout this book.

2   Whether Pynchon's novel exemplifies the Jamesonian reading of late capitalism, or prospectively critiques that reading as itself a paranoid reduction, has been a subject of debate for critics. For representative treatments from both camps, see Redfield and Simons.

3   Jameson writes in *Postmodernism* that "Modernist styles thereby become postmodernist codes" (17), just as the subjective alienation characteristic of modernism becomes either schizophrenic fragmentation or a "degraded collective 'objective spirit'" in postmodernism (25). Jameson's totalizing concept of style, elaborated in his first book *Sartre: The Origins of a Style* and returned to many times since, sharply distinguishes his view of language from Derrida's emphasis on dissemination, as explored in works such as *Of Grammatology* and *Dissemination*.

4   The best-known example Jameson offers for this claim about literature's altered state is his reading of Doctorow's postmodern novel *Ragtime* (1975), in which he famously corrects Linda Hutcheon's earlier assessment of the novel. Whereas Hutcheon praises *Ragtime*'s "extended critique of American democratic ideals through the presentation of class conflict rooted in capitalist property and moneyed power" (*Poetics* 61), Jameson argues that "this is what the novel would have meant had it not been a postmodern artifact" (*Postmodernism* 22). What *Ragtime* actually conveys (brilliantly, according to Jameson) is the loss of the historical referent and the short-circuiting of "an older type of social and historical interpretation which it perpetually holds out and withdraws" (23). Doctorow's novel therefore *exemplifies* the cultural logic of late capitalism rather than adopting an oppositional position toward it.

5   For a complementary list of twenty-first-century studies that proclaim the end of postmodernism (and for some dissenting voices), see Woods xv–xvi. John Frow asked the question "What Was Postmodernism?" as early as 1997 (and Michael Rosenthal before him in 1992), while in Steven Connor's grand narrative of the postmodernism debate, outlined in his 2004 introduction to the *Cambridge Companion to Postmodernism*, "autonomy" names the situation that prevailed by the mid-1990s, when "postmodernism became the name for the activity of writing about postmodernism" (4). This was followed by "dissipation" in the new century, when mainstream debate moved elsewhere.

6   This position statement from the opening page of Jameson's text expands Ihab Hassan's earlier assertion that postmodernism marks the emergence of the specific critical problem of *literary* change.

7   Although Bewes does not say this, a challenge to the spatialized conception of the
    postmodern also means a challenge to the Marxian conception. As Perry Anderson
    outlines, Western Marxism—from Lukács to Gramsci to Benjamin to Adorno to
    Sartre to Althusser to Jameson—betrays "a deep historical pessimism" in always
    speaking "not of an alleviated future, but of an implacable present" (76).

8   Dissatisfaction with this critical approach is one important factor behind the ongoing
    historicist turn in the study of postmodern American fiction. Recent work on Don
    DeLillo, for instance, has insisted on reading his fiction as responsive to specific
    historical contexts (such as American foreign policy, or the rituals of the Catholic
    Mass), rather than to an "abstract model of postmodernity" (Hoberek, "Foreign" 108)
    or an "abstractly defined realm of postmodernism" (Hungerford, "Don DeLillo's"
    346). Elsewhere, Amy Hungerford has argued that critics of postwar fiction should
    now prefer the "rigorously historical argument" of a text like Mark McGurl's *The
    Program Era* to "cultural materialist accounts" such as Jameson's ("On the Period,"
    413–14). I have argued for the continued importance of the Jamesonian conception
    of postmodernism from a historicist and institutional perspective in my essay
    "Beginning with Postmodernism."

9   Anderson examines the origins of the term "postmodernism" in his book on Jameson,
    but for an account that links the history of the word more closely to artistic practice,
    see Bertens. Tim Woods remarks that "postmodern" emerged in the 1960s to describe
    the features of a wave of new fiction, "although the concept only gained its dominance
    as a generic term in the 1980s" (64). It is important to recognize in this connection that
    since his initial 1982 Whitney lecture on the topic—which Perry Anderson described
    in 1998 as "a prodigious inaugural gesture that has commanded the field ever since"
    (54)—Jameson has consistently developed his own understanding of "postmodernism."
    On the shifting meaning of the term in Jameson's work after the 1991 publication of
    Postmodernism, see Dunst; on Jameson's late turn to modernism and to a more hopeful
    account of the contemporary dialectic, see Gladstone and Worden.

10 See the introduction and selections in David Duff's anthology *Modern Genre Theory*
    for an excellent historical outline of this field of study.

11 On the transitional importance of the genre in the American context, see also
    William Hedges's claim that Washington Irving "transformed the sketch into a bona
    fide short story" (150) in his observer-hero narrative "The Stout Gentleman," from
    Bracebridge Hall (1922).

12 Bruffee argues that Conrad was in fact the originator of the elegiac romance genre,
    and devotes three of his seven chapters to analyzing the growth of the narrative
    structure in Conrad's early stories through to *Lord Jim*. However, the appearance
    decades previously of *The Blithedale Romance* and particularly *Moby-Dick* (which
    Bruffee admits is an elegiac romance) draws attention to the many elisions involved in
    the construction of Bruffee's historical thesis.

13 There are exceptions to this rule, of course: *Swann's Way* by Marcel Proust and
    Absalom, Absalom! by William Faulkner both offer close variants on the genre of
    observer-hero narrative.

14 Again, Duff's anthology mentioned in note 10 is the best reference text for these
    developments (see esp. pp. 8–11, 15–18). It is no surprise that this tendency by
    Bruffee and Buell to ignore socio-cultural perspectives on genre goes hand-in-
    hand with their downplaying of issues of race and gender. See Section IV of this
    introduction for a further discussion.

15 For wide-ranging discussions of representations of heroism in contemporary
    American culture, see Lisa DeTora's introduction to *Heroes of Film, Comics and
    American Culture* (2009), and chapter 1 of Stephanie Halldorson's *The Hero in
    Contemporary American Fiction* (2007).

16 This cultural work can also be undertaken through exploiting the observer-hero
    structure in other media that depend on narrative. An example from American film
    would be Terrence Malick's *Badlands* (1973), where Martin Sheen's small-town rebel
    takes his girlfriend, played by Sissy Spacek, on a killing spree across the Midwest. The
    romantic clichés through which Spacek's character portrays Sheen in her voiceover—
    the equivalent of the observer's sympathetic presentation of an ambivalent hero in a
    literary text—are ironically juxtaposed with the depiction of his sociopathic behavior,
    in ways that recall early observer-hero narratives such as *Moby-Dick* and *Heart of
    Darkness*.

17 To take the example of Emerson, Robert Richardson's biography reads the former's
    texts as a working out of the kinds of questions asked by Bush: "*Representative Men*
    is Emerson's major effort to reconcile the reality of the unequal distribution of talent
    with a democratic belief in the fundamental equality of all persons" (414). Richardson
    also mentions the influence of Puritanism on Emerson, and a fuller account of the
    emergence of American Romanticism than I can offer here would address the role
    of Puritan conceptions of heroism and interiority as an influence on the character of
    observer-hero narrative in the American context.

18 It is not hard to see this "democratic" aspect of the European political novel in the
    way it strives toward the representation of the social whole, as in Eliot's *Middlemarch*
    or Balzac's *Lost Illusions*. Similarly, to describe the Russian political novel as "tsarist"
    is to articulate something distinctive about a novel such as Dostoevsky's *Crime and
    Punishment*, in which Raskolnikov's experiment in murder is driven by his dreams
    of becoming a proto-Nietzschean superman, beyond good and evil. We should note,
    however, that this account becomes more complicated when we ask the question
    of where authority resides in these traditions of the political novel. The omniscient
    narration of the English and French novel, with power centered in the perspective
    of the author, then begins to look less democratic; whereas the dialogic character of
    Dostoevsky's novels (as famously analyzed by Mikhail Bakhtin) divides the authority
    between author and hero in ways that challenge the tsarist reading.

19 It is true that three of the novelists named here are Jewish-American, while the other
    is Greek-American, so these are not white males in the traditional American sense
    of WASPs. I use the category of white male here, however, to refer to writers whose
    popular reception in American culture after World War II has led to their gender
    and ethnicity now rarely being taken as necessarily central to their concerns. This
    is relatively clear in the cases of Auster, Doctorow and Eugenides, but the reception
    of the work of Philip Roth, who has written on Jewish themes throughout his career
    and who is widely considered a "Great American Novelist," is perhaps an even more
    telling testament to the historical processes of cultural assimilation to whiteness
    (or, alternatively, of the cultural expansion of the category of whiteness). A broad
    account of Jewish assimilation in the postwar era is offered in Karen Brodkin's *How
    Jews Became White Folks*, and in the literary context Morris Dickstein has noted that
    the mainstreaming of Jewish-American writing began "as early as the 1960s, [when]
    influential critics argued that American Jewish writing no longer counted as a distinct
    or viable literary project, for younger Jews had grown so assimilated, so remote from

traditional Jewish life, that only nostalgia kept it going" (3). Against this sociocultural and literary background, Roth's *American Pastoral* (1997) and *The Human Stain* both tell, in their different ways, stories of Jewish assimilation into mainstream American life. Both also record the tensions concomitant with this process, however; in an essay on *The Human Stain* that will be cited again in Chapter 1, Jennifer Glaser argues that both texts can be read as tragic novels of racial passing, where in the case of *American Pastoral* the passing is between Jewishness and whiteness.

20 For a brief summary of the problems posed by Jefferson's "character" for the intellectual history of the early national period, see Hutchison 10.

21 Wiggins's views here epitomize the reading of black masculinity associated with Daniel Patrick Moynihan's controversial report of 1965, *The Negro Family: The Case for National Action*. The discourse of racial liberalism provides a major intellectual context for Gaines's novel; for an analysis of how the Moynihan Report helped to shape this discourse, see Geary.

22 This progress is portrayed as double-edged where Wiggins is concerned: his educated mode of expression leaves him tellingly isolated from his community as the novel's representative of a bourgeois future for African Americans, a future that remains, in the Jim Crow world of the text, frustratingly far away. It also opens him up to white suspicion: in a number of scenes Wiggins reflects on the need to hide his education from the white authority figures he confronts. For instance, when Sheriff Guidry asks why Wiggins, rather than Jefferson's grandmother Emma, is visiting Jefferson in the jail, Wiggins reports the conversation as follows: "'She's old,' I said. 'She doesn't feel that she has the strength to come up there all the time.' 'She doesn't, huh?' Sam Guidry asked me. He emphasized 'doesn't.' I was supposed to have said 'don't.' I was being too smart" (48).

23 Edwards expands as follows: "Scholarly and popular histories alike have privileged charismatic leaders, from Frederick Douglass to Martin Luther King Jr., over the arduous, undocumented efforts of ordinary women, men, and children to remake their social reality; I argue that the uncritical investment in charisma as the motor of history ignores its limits as a model for social movements while showing us just how powerful a *narrative* force it is" (xv). Against this background, literature plays for Edwards an important interrogative role: "African American literature has registered the faultlines in black politics since Reconstruction, contesting how the charismatic scenario has often structured black political desire, the social life of black politics, and black political history as a field of knowledge itself" (xvi).

24 Merivale also notes that Grace's narration thereby offers "an exemplary parable of the problem of writing a text with any useful correspondence to the 'real world' at all" (52). This postmodern reading of Didion's novel as staging a problem of reference feeds into my discussion of novels of the 1990s that consciously stage this problem as one interpretive possibility among many. Returning briefly to the American theme, too, we might observe that the particular ambiguities central to observer-hero narrative become all the more evident when, as in the case of *A Book of Common Prayer*, the hero figure is described by the narrator as a symbolic representative of America itself. Grace's description of Charlotte—"She was immaculate of history, innocent of politics. [...] A not atypical *norteamericana*" (Didion 60-1)—is evaluated very differently by two other early critics of the novel, depending on how they view the development of Grace's character. Samuel Coale remarks that "Didion indicts the American myth, the western faith in self-renewal and ultimate progress" (166-7);

Victor Strandberg, by contrast, claims that the purpose of the story is "to defend America's traditional middle-class ideals" (227) and to bring Grace and Charlotte to Boca Grande "to establish in the highlight of contrast the superiority of their original *norteamericana* ethos" (231–2). The general point to make here is that observer-hero narrative allows for these diverging assessments by staging the narrative problem of judgment rather than resolving it.

25 In his section considering female elegiac romance as a radical variation on the genre, Bruffee also discusses Willa Cather's novella *My Mortal Enemy* and F. Scott Fitzgerald's *The Last Tycoon*, the latter of which has a female narrator. In Buell's article on observer-hero narrative, Cather's *A Lost Lady* is the only example of the genre he cites not written by a white male.

26 Bruffee's call for further analysis of examples is in keeping with Mary Eagleton's astute observation that criticism which wants to identify and affirm sexual difference in writing usually falls back on a weak inductive empiricism: "In short it is never possible to produce the definitive evidence to prove that 'x' is the writing of a woman and 'y' the writing of a man. Most studies that attempt such definitions end by offering qualified suggestions and contending that we need more stylistic analysis to really substantiate any proposition" (259).

27 In *Fredric Jameson: Live Theory*, for instance, Ian Buchanan takes a number of critics—including Catherine Belsey, Simon During, and Brian Massumi—to task for what he claims is their misconstrual of key Jamesonian ideas. Like Derrida's infamous "il n'y a pas d'hors texte," terms such as "totalization" and "allegory" have often proven an effective rallying point for Jameson's critics.

28 The key Marxist category of class remains central to Jameson's analysis here. "Totality," according to Buchanan, "is a codeword in Jameson's work for 'class consciousness' and more allusively Lukács, to whom he attributes the concept" (107). As a consequence, "[w]hen Jameson uses the word 'totality,' or speaks of 'totalizing' procedures, he means precisely this: no class or class fraction can function politically until it has found the means of representing itself to itself" (108). In *Signatures of the Visible*, Jameson calls this process "*figurability*, the need for social reality and everyday life to have developed to the point at which the underlying class structure becomes *representable* in tangible form" (37).

29 In his superb discussion of the origins and meaning of the term "undecidability" in Derrida's lexicon, David Bates notes that the third meaning of undecidability that Derrida outlines here "is absolutely crucial for understanding Derrida's later work on the political" (5), because it links his early work on linguistic undecidability (in *Dissemination*, for instance) to the undecidability of ethical-political action and decision in his later work (Bates's main example is the essay "Force of Law"). Bates shows in addition how the concept of undecidability originates in interwar debates within logic and mathematics, where thinkers such as Gödel, Brouwer, and Wittgenstein emphasized how "[t]he fundamental incompleteness of all logics only highlighted the flexibility and adaptability of a human mind that would never be wholly confined to these logics," and that "the decisive acts that moved thinking forward were in a way strangely foreign to the established and formalized systems of thought that came before them" (13). These incompleteness theorems clearly prefigure Derrida's vision of the decision as a break with prior calculation and dialectical thought. It should also be recognized, nonetheless, that Derrida does not reject the *desire* for totalization—quite the opposite—but rather questions its effects.

As he has remarked in interview, "What I should be tempted to denounce as a lure—
i.e., totalization or gathering up—isn't this what keeps me going?" ("This Strange" 34).

30 The passage from which this phrase is drawn is one of the most famous in Jameson's
oeuvre: "History is what hurts, it is what refuses desire and sets inexorable limits to
individual as well as collective praxis, which its 'ruses' turn into grisly and ironic
reversals of their overt intention. But this history can be apprehended only through
its effects, and never directly as some reified force. This is indeed the ultimate sense
in which History as ground and untranscendable horizon needs no particular
justification; we may be sure that its alienating necessities will not forget us, however
much we might prefer to ignore them" (*Political* 102).

31 Jameson's refusal to grant importance to an ethical or moral discourse in his work
has opened him to criticism from other Marxists as well as thinkers of divergent
persuasions. For instance, Terry Eagleton, in a review of Jameson's *Archaeologies of
the Future*, chides Jameson for setting up a "tattered straw man of ethical thought,
partly to have the pleasure of bowling it over with a materialist flourish." According to
Eagleton, "Whereas Aristotle saw ethics as a sub-branch of politics, Jameson confuses
morality with moralism, a move which then allows him to write it off" (25–6).

32 Furthermore, the very possibility of periodizing in any conventional sense would
be open to question from a strictly Derridean perspective. In his preface to *Of
Grammatology*, Derrida explicitly argues that the propositions he ventures in the
book "demand that reading should free itself, at least in its axis, from the classical
categories of history—not only from the categories of the history of ideas and the
history of literature but also, and perhaps above all, from the categories of the history
of philosophy." And even when Derrida uses the terms "age" or "epoch," he claims to
refer to "a *structural figure* as much as a *historical totality*" (lxxxix).

33 These are subjects I take up in "Beginning with Postmodernism." See also Dames,
"Theory and the Novel," and Ryan, *The Novel After Theory*.

34 Anderson is explicit in claiming an avant-garde role for Jameson himself: "The
theoretical instance the avant-garde form represented has not, however, disappeared.
Rather, its function has migrated. For what else is Jameson's totalization of
postmodernism itself? [. . .] Here, viewed comparatively, is where the critical ambition
and revolutionary *élan* of the classical avant-garde have passed" (117). Anderson's
account of Jameson also serves to imbue the latter with a suitably heroic political
agency, an agency that sees the previously repressive concept of postmodernism
"wrested away by a prodigious display of theoretical intelligence and energy for the
cause of a revolutionary Left" (66).

Chapter 1

1 *Fear and Trembling* offers a good example of a text that can come to participate in
a genre through a process of historical re-contextualization. When this "dialectical
lyric" was first published in Danish in 1843, Johannes di Silentio was listed as its
author; nowadays, in all editions, Søren Kierkegaard is named as author, implicitly
turning di Silentio into the intermediary, albeit minimally dramatized, first-person
observer-narrator of the text.

2 Derrida invokes here Melville's "Bartleby, the Scrivener," another observer-hero narrative in which the hero responds to all requests with a kind of secrecy and silence, repeating the phrase "I would prefer not to." According to Derrida, Abraham's response is of the same kind, opening onto the same "reserve of incompleteness" (*Gift* 75), increasing the pathos of his resolute but inexplicable decision: "He will not decide *not to*, he has decided *to*, but he would prefer *not to*" (76).

3 In the relatively short time since its publication, *The Human Stain* has garnered a very large critical response, in keeping with what Derek Parker Royal terms "a revitalization of Roth studies within academia" ("Introduction" 2). As well as being the subject of essays in various edited collections devoted to Roth, and in a range of academic journals, *The Human Stain* has also featured more prominently than any other novel in the issues of the journal *Philip Roth Studies* published to date, pointing to its increasingly privileged status within the extensive Roth canon.

4 For an account of how early reviewers and critics of *The Human Stain* have generally underplayed Zuckerman's imaginative role in the story's construction, see Royal, "Plotting" (esp. 117n4). In the two novels that preceded *The Human Stain* in Roth's "American trilogy"—*American Pastoral* (1997) and *I Married a Communist* (1998)—Zuckerman also narrates the story, but plays a less dramatized role in the action that unfolds. Indeed, Debra Shostak remarks on the "relative self-abnegation" that marks the two earlier books when compared to Zuckerman's active part in *The Human Stain* (*Philip* 257). This active participation by the observer-narrator in the story he tells will also be a crucial factor in Auster's *Leviathan*, Eugenides's *The Virgin Suicides*, and Doctorow's *The Waterworks*.

5 Further examples are Tim Parrish's claim that "never before had [Roth's] work so clearly portrayed the effect that history has on an individual's possibility for self-creation" (209), and Jennifer Glaser's remark that the novel's "high tragedy" stems from Coleman's inability to change with the times in his "adhering to outmoded standards" (1473).

6 The complexites of Roth's borrowing from the tragic tradition are equally evident in *American Pastoral*. While the chapter titles—"Paradise Remembered," "The Fall," "Paradise Lost"—would seem to suggest that the paradigmatic intertext is Genesis, it is not Swede Levov's Adamic *pursuit* of knowledge but his more Oedipal *avoidance* of it that the novel portrays as central to his downfall.

7 The metafictional aspects of Roth's aesthetic have provoked a large amount of critical debate. Aside from Shostak's book, the most original recent treatment appears in Mark McGurl's *The Program Era*, where McGurl reads the "autopoetic" reflexivity of Roth's fiction through the frame of systems theory (51–6).

8 See, as one example among many, Posnock, "Purity and Danger: On Philip Roth."

9 Zuckerman draws Faunia's difference to Delphine Roux most starkly on this point. For Faunia, sex is a wholly concrete act; she says to Coleman at one point, "Don't fuck it up by thinking it's more than this. You don't, and I won't. It doesn't *have* to be more than this" (228). Delphine, by contrast, recoils at the purely material nature of intercourse; what she wants is "Sex, yes, wonderful sex, but sex with metaphysics" (262).

10 This is why David Lodge offers only a partial sense of how *The Human Stain* unfolds when he claims that in his late trilogy Roth "adopted something like the model of the classic realist novel, in which individual fortunes are traced across a panorama of social change and historical events, the individual and the social illuminating and borrowing significance from each other in the process" (249). To read the novel

only in this way, without paying heed to the complications to tragic realism offered by the observer-hero narrative structure, would be a mistake; in the end, Coleman appears to lack the "essential subjectivity" that, as Shostak remarks, "is fundamental to realistic narrative, which poses the self against conditions, internal and external, to see just how it will cope" (*Philip* 187).

11 In an important article that complements my treatment of *The Human Stain* as a novel of the American 1990s, Jennifer Glaser offers a historicist reading of the novel's engagement with cultural discourses prevalent in the decade. Glaser reads *The Human Stain*, "written during the heyday of identity politics" (1472), as Roth's response to multiculturalism and to the Jewish American's "ambiguous place during the culture wars of the 1980s and 1990s" (1465). In common with other critics, however, Glaser underestimates the importance of the observer-hero structure of the novel, and does not take sufficient account of the epistemological and ontological speculations engaged in by Zuckerman in the final two chapters.

12 Jay Prosser's edited volume on American fiction of the 1990s, to cite one instance, contains a chapter devoted to Roth's American trilogy.

Chapter 2

1   In the origin text of speech–act theory, J. L. Austin's *How to Do Things with Words*, fictional utterances are famously disregarded from consideration as "parasitic" upon standard forms. Derrida's critique of Austin on this point in his essay "Signature Event Context" led to a dispute with John Searle, with Derrida's contributions collected in *Limited Inc*. Subsequent to this debate, perhaps the clearest consideration of the status of fictional speech acts is found in J. Hillis Miller's *Speech Acts in Literature*.

2   Auster claimed in a 1993 interview never to have read Derrida, but to "know who he is and basically what he writes about," professing himself "astonished" that their work could be seen to have anything in common ("Unpublished"). That Auster does share with Derrida a concern with writing, conceptuality, inheritance, responsibility, testimony, solitude, the gift, and the event, indicates that in dismissing any connection Auster perhaps had in mind the reductive version of Derrida characteristic of much American literary criticism. Indeed, Auster was responding directly to a question about Alison Russell's influential early article on *The New York Trilogy*, which employs a received version of Derridean thought that, as Jeffrey Nealon rightly remarks, "seriously distorts" Derrida's texts through a misunderstanding of undecidability (Nealon 108n8). Nealon's own essay, by contrast, is an innovative reading of *City of Glass* that employs concepts drawn from Blanchot. For readings of Auster novels in which Derridean ideas and concepts are effectively employed, see Brault, Segal, and Shiloh.

3   In his novels, essays, and interviews, Auster usually discusses chance solely in terms of metaphysical and narrative concerns, and in their many treatments of the theme of chance in his work critics overwhelmingly follow the author's lead. Rather surprisingly, then, a reading of Auster's work from the point of view of the new economic criticism remains to be written; connections between his fiction and the structures of late capitalism have thus far been limited to critical discussions of *The Music Of Chance* (1990), a novel that treats capitalism directly rather than symptomatically. See Dotan and Oberman.

4 An aspect of this relationship to testimony, which draws Auster even closer to Derrida, Blanchot, and Philip Roth, is his Jewish heritage. On Auster's Jewish contexts, see the essays by Bewes, Josh Cohen, and Fredman.

5 Derrida's own remarks on the notion of solitude are rather mysterious, and perhaps add weight to Frisch's critique of his epistemic emphasis: "Solitude, the other name of the secret to which the simulacrum still bears witness, is neither of consciousness, nor of the subject, nor of *Dasein*. It makes them possible, but what it makes possible does not put an end to the secret" ("Passions" 24). Nonetheless, I would suggest that Auster's "Book of Memory" in *The Invention of Solitude* may be as close an instantiation as exists in English of the imaginary text Derrida once claimed had moved him toward writing in his youth, as follows: "The idea of an internal polylogue, everything that later, in what I hope was a slightly more refined way, was able to lead me to Rousseau [. . .] or to Joyce, was first of all the adolescent dream of keeping a trace of all the voices which were traversing me" ("This Strange" 34–5).

6 See the concluding section of Linda Fleck's article for a "full-blown 'premodern' reading" (265) of correspondences between *The Invention of Solitude* and *Leviathan*. Aliki Varvogli has similarly read *Leviathan* as a rewriting of Auster's earlier observer-hero narrative, *The Locked Room* (1986) (142–4). Apropos this repetition and rewriting, Auster has remarked that all of his books are really "the same book": "The story of my obsessions, I suppose. The saga of the things that haunt me. Like it or not, all my books seem to revolve around the same set of questions, the same human dilemmas" (*Red Notebook* 123).

7 Aaron, writing in 1990, mentions that he first read Sachs's book "fifteen years ago" (36), two months after it had come in paperback, and is told by a publicist at the time that it was published "a couple of years ago" (9). Auster's *Leviathan*, of course, owes its own debt to Doctorow's blend of fact and fiction: for instance, Aaron meets Sachs for the first time when the former stands in as a late replacement for the poet Michael Palmer, presumably the real-life author who published his first volume of poetry, *Blake's Newton*, in 1972. The fact that Sachs's novel acts as a double of one of the most canonical novels of American postmodernism positions Auster's own book, written in a moment of aesthetic transition in the 1990s, as something of a follow-up commentary on that earlier literary moment. Sachs's second novel, to be titled *Leviathan*, never gets written, except of course as the book we hold in our hands.

8 Again, Derrida makes an important distinction between testimony as story, and what he terms "the essence of testimony": the latter "cannot necessarily be reduced to narration, that is, to descriptive, informative relations, to knowledge or to narrative; it is first a present act. When a martyr testifies he does not tell a story, he offers himself" (*Demeure* 38). Commenting on the relation between autobiography and fiction in J. M. Coetzee's work, Derek Attridge also suggests that knowledge arises in testimony: "The text does not *refer* to the truth; it produces it. Confession, that is to say, is not separable from fiction" ("Deconstruction" 114).

9 Aaron characterizes Sachs's political writing as follows: "Sachs was more interested in politics and history than in spiritual questions, but his politics were nevertheless tinged with something I would call a religious quality, as if political engagement were more than a way of confronting problems in the here and now, but a means to personal salvation as well. [. . .] political action for him boiled down to a matter of conscience" (25). Sachs's thinking is regularly linked by Aaron to that of Thoreau, especially the Thoreau of *Civil Disobedience*.

10 Aaron's commitment to modern psychology and psychoanalysis is clear in many
    passages, for example when he discusses the relationship between *The New Colossus*
    and Sachs's youth: "since the book is filled with references to the Statue of Liberty,
    it's hard to ignore the possibility of a connection—as if the childhood experience of
    witnessing his mother's panic somehow lay at the heart of what he wrote as a grown
    man twenty years later" (35).

11 In *Demeure*, Derrida unpacks the word "passion" in his reading of Blanchot's text, and
    describes the haunting of testimony by literature as "perhaps the passion itself, the
    passionate place of literary writing, as the project to say everything" (72). In interview,
    Auster has described each of the novels that make up his *New York Trilogy* as "about
    a kind of passionate excess" (*Red Notebook* 110). Auster is also in agreement with
    Derrida not only on the passionate basis of literature, but on its scope: as he remarked
    to another interviewer, "What's interesting about fiction is that it can encompass
    everything" ("Memory's" 117).

Chapter 3

1 Suicide and its agnates appear on a number of occasions in Derrida's *oeuvre*,
   but in most cases suicide does not receive a full thematic treatment, the kind of
   treatment received on a regular basis by concepts such as the decision, the secret,
   or impossibility. To cite some instances: Derrida briefly discusses suicide in his
   article "*Le Toucher*: Touch / To Touch Him" (141); in his interview with Elizabeth
   Roudinesco, *For What Tomorrow* (150); and in his discussion of "cultures of death"
   in *Aporias*. In all these contexts, however, another concept—respectively, the kiss,
   the death penalty, death in general—forms the main locus of discussion. Derrida's
   apparent reluctance to approach the subject of suicide in a thematic way has been
   noted by critics, and it extends from the theoretical to the personal: Vivian Nun
   Halloran has observed that in his mourning address at the funeral of Sarah Kofman,
   Derrida seemed to go out of his way not to address Kofman's suicide, the date of
   which marked the 150th anniversary of the death of Nietzsche (Halloran, pars 16–17).

2 For a clear-cut discussion of Derrida's understanding of autoimmunity as "a condition
   for *life in general*," see Hägglund 13–15. Hägglund also offers a provocative discussion
   of suicide as an affirmation of life through a necessary affirmation of time (165).

3 The narrators occasionally allude to the oral character of their testimony, which seems
   to be addressed to a judge or jury who are considering a series of "exhibits" presented
   to them by the boys. For instance, after describing a photograph, the narrators then
   counsel: "Please don't touch. We're going to put the picture back in its envelope
   now" (119). This oral quality connects *The Virgin Suicides* to *The Waterworks*, while
   differentiating those novels from *The Human Stain* and *Leviathan*. In all four books,
   nevertheless, the observer's retrospective perspective on the events narrated remains
   the crucial factor.

4 For more analysis of the history and effects of first-person-plural narration, see
   Richardson, *Unnatural* 37–60. *The Virgin Suicides* is briefly discussed on page 52 of
   Richardson's study.

5 In *The Other Heading*, Derrida remarks on the process by which newspapers and the press excise undecidability in favour of airtight conclusions, producing "the form of *judgment that decides* (yes or no) and that is produced in a *representation*" (92).

6 Long's attribution of the events of *The Virgin Suicides* to 1975 seems to be based less on evidence from the novel than on the opening scene of Sofia Coppola's film adaptation, which locates the action in "Michigan, 25 years ago." The official cinematic release of *The Virgin Suicides* in the United States and United Kingdom was May 2000, but the film was initially screened at the Cannes Film Festival in May 1999, which would place the action in 1974. As it happens, this element of vagueness in dating the action of the film (as well as the retrospective relationship to time that Coppola's "years ago" connotes) is truer to the conception of history and historical transition in the novel than are the accounts provided by many of its critics.

7 See the report in the *Owosso Argus-Press*, October 4, 1966 (Anonymous).

Chapter 4

1 Derrida opposes not simply the particular philosophy of history embedded in dialectical thought, but the notion of a philosophy of history *tout court*: "Where there is a philosophy of history there is no longer history, everything may in principle be foreseen, everything is gathered into the gaze of a god or a providence. Now, if there is a historicity, it supposes the limit of a philosophy of history; a philosophy of history that takes historicity into account is a contradiction" (Derrida and Ferraris 64).

2 This is not to say that law and justice are oppositional concepts; rather they represent co-constituting poles. As Derrida notes: "Everything would still be simple if this distinction between justice and *droit* were a true distinction, an opposition whose functioning was logically regulated and permitted mastery. But it turns out that *droit* claims to exercise itself in the name of justice and that justice is required to establish itself in the name of a law that must be 'enforced.' Deconstruction always finds itself between these two poles" ("Force" 22). I will return to the relationship between these two concepts later in this chapter; for a clear explication at the general level, see Hägglund 40–3.

3 In the American context, Derrida points out, the "fabulous event" that is the signing of the Declaration of Independence is "only possible by means of the inadequation of a present with itself" ("Declarations" 50). In the document itself, however, the act is explained through the invocation of a Being that transcends time and precedes the history that produces the event of signing: "[God] founds natural laws, and thus the whole game that tends to present performative utterances *as* constative utterances" (51). We will see this religious perspective represented in *The Waterworks* by Reverend Grimshaw's arguments concerning justice and by McIlvaine's own sense of temporality, discussed in Sections IV and V.

4 McIlvaine's narration contains ellipses throughout, which I record here as they appear in the text. I continue to use square brackets to indicate my own excision of words from a quotation. I will return to the question of McIlvaine's ellipses in Section II.

5   Marshall Bruce Genrty has dubbed *The Waterworks* "Doctorow's Poesque Preface,"
     arguing that "[t]his whole novel may be viewed as an elaboration of the page in
     [Doctorow's] *The Book of Daniel* (1971) about how Poe showed America its ruination"
     (81). Brian Diemert lists references to Poe among allusions to a range of American
     authors in *The Waterworks*, including Hawthorne, Melville, Fitzgerald, and Stowe
     (356, 370n12/13). In a review, Ted Solotaroff summarizes the connections as follows:
     "Hints and glints of Poe are embedded in its twinned interests in mystery and science,
     its detective-story format, its necrological overlay, its protagonist—a brilliant, noir,
     disinherited literary journalist—its man-about-New York ambiance, even a mansion
     named Ravenwood" (137). Gentry adds to this the predominance of "lovely, pale
     women" which the novel shares with the tales and poems of Poe, and in his feminist
     reading Gentry offers a provocative interpretation of McIlvaine as an unreliable
     narrator in the Poe mold: "By the novel's end, I believe, McIlvaine basically becomes
     one more of the novel's elusive villains; like any of a number of Poe narrators, he
     starts out seeming reasonable but eventually reveals his corruption" (73). This reading
     would significantly distinguish Doctorow's narrator from those of Roth, Auster, and
     Eugenides; most reviewers and critics, however, interpret McIlvaine along the lines of
     Roz Kaveney's claim that the narrator is "a model of honesty: a credible witness of the
     incredible, because so mundane and such a prig" (40).
6   Generally considered the first modern detective stories, Poe's tales of ratiocination (as
     he dubbed them in an unsigned review of his own work in 1845) are "The Murders in
     the Rue Morgue" (1841), "The Mystery of Marie Rogêt" (1842), and "The Purloined
     Letter" (1844).
7   This development is figured by the lawman Donne's bureaucratic archival work and
     the scientist Sartorius's extensive notebooks, and its secularizing quality is expressed
     in McIlvaine's comment about Reverend Grimshaw: "I had nothing against the good
     doctor except that he had worn away, as we all do, and his religion no longer had any
     authority . . . other than as organizer of his daily life and conduct and as filing system
     for his perceptions" (43).
8   Among the initial reviews, for instance, Gary Davenport dismisses the ellipses as "a
     pointless and irritating mannerism" (647), whereas Simon Schama praises McIlvaine's
     "mutilated diction" as a metaphor for a torn postbellum society, the correlative
     of Wheelwright "painting the torso of a Civil War veteran, horribly deformed by
     the wounds of battle." Later critics have offered equally varied assessments, from
     Brian Diemert's suggestion that his ellipses show McIlvaine "lacks the confidence to
     state that literature might be capable of a beneficient influence" (367), to Marianne
     DeKoven's reading of them as signifiers of "the unspeakable," "marking the place of an
     absented, discredited, historically defeated, but nonetheless utopian desire" (89).
9   Like Kurtz, Sartorius is a product of Old World Europe, and McIlvaine briefly
     considers the origins of the doctor and his unusual name (124). For further
     speculation on the connotations of Sartorius's name, see Diemert 370n12, Schama,
     and Wutz 239n4.
10 In interview, Doctorow has placed this idea in a 1990s context by comparing the old
     generation feeding off the young in *The Waterworks* to George H. W. Bush's attempt
     to maintain power against the Clinton generation in the 1992 American presidential
     campaign ("E. L. Doctorow" 51).
11 It is important to recognize here, as Michael Wutz has noted, that the ostensible
     presentation of Donne and Sartorius as moral hero and villain of *The Waterworks* is

far from unambiguous. Whereas Donne is guilty of "repeatedly circumventing the law," operating as "a self-incriminating maverick" (Wutz 163), the city official at the finale of the novel admits to McIlvaine that children had never died at Sartorius's hands: "Not from any of his procedures [. . .]. Physically, the children's health was never impaired" (226). Although this seems to contradict Martin Pemberton's evidence that he had seen orphan children age "like leaves turning yellow," the inclusion of the scene with the official indicates that Doctorow wishes to complicate the reader's (and McIlvaine's) judgment of Sartorius by giving him claims to moral superiority, claims his captor Donne seems to recognize in his comments on a possible trial. Most critics assume Sartorius's moral evil and thereby simplify the questions the novel is asking concerning time and justice. DeKoven, for instance, describes the "seemingly benign but in fact lethal orphanage where children are housed in order to die into the unnaturally prolonged lives of plutocrats" (87). Doctorow's depiction of the orphanage is a good deal more equivocal than this statement acknowledges.

12   My reading here contradicts those of critics, such as Michelle Tokarczyk, who view the conclusion to *The Waterworks* as a happy and positive one. Tokarczyk sees McIlvaine siding with Donne in the temporal struggle between the detective and Sartorius: "Sartorius represents a radical disruption of the categories of life and death, although these categories are continually reinscribed by the policeman Edmund Donne, who is described as bringing order to chaos, and by the narrator's own discoveries" (*E. L. Doctorow's* 152–3). And in her initial review of the novel, Tokarczyk summarized the ending as follows: "*The Waterworks* ends optimistically with Sartorius's destruction and commitment to a mental hospital; presumably, at least some of the children have been saved. [. . .] *The Waterworks* offers hope that human perseverance and decency can prevail. Evil is not completely destroyed, but it is mitigated by people's ability to go on with their lives" ("*The Waterworks*" 436). It is precisely this unreflecting "going on" that McIlvaine rails against at the finale of the story.

13   It is worth noting, with regard to the question of justice, that McIlvaine portrays both the scientific and religious worldviews of 1870s New York as equally unconcerned with questions of social justice with respect to the street children of the city: "For certain religious sensibilities such children fulfilled the ineffable aims of God. For the modern folk, Mr. Darwin was cited, and the design was Nature's. So the flower girl Mary, and the newsies and the rest of these child beggars who lived among us, were losses society could tolerate" (63). Yet McIlvaine himself does little about the treatment of these children, admitting that he tries to avoid coming into contact with the boys who sell his daily newspapers: "I was not comfortable here, at the most shameful point of the newspaper business. [. . .] I saw only undersized beings on whose faces were etched the lines and shadows of serfdom" (114). For a treatment of the novel that reads it as a pessimistic view of the historical claims of children (and of women), see Gentry.

14   A whole essay needs to be written that situates Doctorow's depiction of time in *The Waterworks* in relation to its nineteenth-century context, for instance by setting the novel beside the philosophical engagement with temporality that Henri Bergson would produce from the late 1880s onward. Such an essay would also have to take into account Doctorow's other works that engage with similar themes, particularly the two novels that immediately followed *The Waterworks*, *City of God* (2000) and *The March* (2005).

Works Cited

Adams, Rachel. "The Ends of America, the Ends of Postmodernism." *After Postmodernism: Form and History in Contemporary American Fiction*. Spec. issue of *Twentieth Century Literature* 53.3 (2007): 248–72.

Anderson, Perry. *The Origins of Postmodernity*. London: Verso, 1998.

Anonymous. "Cemetery Workers Strike." *Owosso Argus-Press* (October 4, 1966). Online access. October 1, 2012. http://news.google.com/newspapers.

Aristotle. *Poetics*. Trans. Malcolm Heath. London: Penguin, 1996.

Artaud, Antonin. *The Theater and Its Double*. Trans. Mary Caroline Richards. New York: Grove Press, 1958.

Attridge, Derek. "Against Allegory." *J. M. Coetzee and the Ethics of Reading: Literature in the Event*. Chicago: University of Chicago Press, 2004. 32–64.

—. "Deconstruction and Fiction." *Deconstructions: A User's Guide*. Ed. Nicholas Royle. Basingstoke: Palgrave, 2000. 105–18.

—. "Derrida's Singularity: Literature and Ethics." *Derrida's Legacies: Literature and Philosophy*. Ed. Simon Glendinning and Robert Eaglestone. London: Routledge, 2008. 12–23.

Auster, Paul. *The Invention of Solitude*. 1982. *Collected Prose*. London: Faber, 2003. 1–150.

—. *Leviathan*. 1992. London: Faber, 1993.

—. "Memory's Escape: Inventing *The Music of Chance*. A Conversation with Paul Auster" (with Mark Irwin). *Denver Quarterly* 28.3 (1994): 111–22.

—. *The Red Notebook and Other Writings*. London: Faber, 1995.

—. "Unpublished Interview with Paul Auster" (with Chris Pace). *Blue Cricket* (February 21, 1993). Online only. October 1, 2012. www.bluecricket.com/auster/links/secret.html.

Austin, J. L. *How to Do Things with Words*. Oxford: Clarendon Press, 1962.

Bakewell, Geoffrey W. "Philip Roth's Oedipal Stain." *Classical and Modern Literature* 24.2 (2004): 29–46.

Barone, Dennis. "Introduction: Paul Auster and the Postmodern American Novel." *Beyond the Red Notebook: Essays on Paul Auster*. Ed. Barone. Philadelphia: University of Pennsylvania Press, 1995. 1–26.

Bates, David. "Crisis between the Wars: Derrida and the Origins of Undecidability." *Representations* 90 (2005): 1–27.

Bertens, Hans. *The Idea of the Postmodern: A History*. London: Routledge, 1995.

Bewes, Timothy. "Against the Ontology of the Present: Paul Auster's Cinematographic Fictions." *After Postmodernism: Form and History in Contemporary American Fiction*. Spec. issue of *Twentieth Century Literature* 53.3 (2007): 273–97.

Bradley, A. C. *Shakespearean Tragedy*. London: Macmillan, 1992.

Brault, Pascale-Anne. "Translating the Impossible Debt: Paul Auster's *City of Glass*." *Critique* 39.3 (1998): 228–38.

Brodkin, Karen. *How Jews Became White Folks and What That Says about Race in America*. New Brunswick: Rutgers University Press, 1999.

Bruffee, Kenneth. "Elegiac Romance." *College English* 32.4 (1971): 465–76.

—. *Elegiac Romance: Cultural Change and Loss of the Hero in Modern Fiction.* London: Cornell University Press, 1983.

Bryant, Jerry H. *The Open Decision: The Contemporary American Novel and Its Intellectual Background.* New York: The Free Press, 1970.

Buchanan, Ian. *Fredric Jameson: Live Theory.* London: Continuum, 2006.

Buell, Lawrence. "Observer-Hero Narrative." *Texas Studies in Literature and Language* 21.1 (1979): 93–111.

Burn, Stephen J. *Jonathan Franzen at the End of Postmodernism.* London: Continuum, 2008.

Bush, Clive. *The Dream of Reason: American Consciousness and Cultural Achievement from Independence to the Civil War.* London: Edward Arnold, 1977.

Coale, Samuel. "Didion's Disorder: An American Romancer's Art." *Critique* 25.3 (1984): 160–70.

Cohen, Josh. "Desertions: Paul Auster, Edmond Jabès, and the Writing of Auschwitz." *Journal of the Midwest MLA* 33.3–34.1 (2000–1): 94–107.

Cohen, Samuel. *After the End of History: American Fiction in the 1990s.* Iowa City: University of Iowa Press, 2009.

Coleman, A. D. "The Directorial Mode: Notes toward a Definition." *Light Readings: A Photography Critic's Writings, 1968–1978.* New York: Oxford University Press, 1979. 246–57.

Collado-Rodríguez, Francisco. "Back to Myth and Ethical Compromise: García Márquez's Traces on Jeffrey Eugenides." *Atlantis* 27.2 (2005): 27–40.

Connor, Steven. "Introduction." *The Cambridge Companion to Postmodernism.* Ed. Connor. Cambridge: Cambridge University Press, 2004. 1–19.

Conrad, Joseph. *Heart of Darkness.* 1902. Ed. Robert Kimbrough. New York: Norton, 1988.

Conti, Christopher. "The Aesthetic Alibi in *The End of the Road*." *Modern Fiction Studies* 58.1 (2012): 79–111.

Coppola, Sofia dir. *The Virgin Suicides.* Paramount Classics, 2000.

Dames, Nicholas. "Theory and the Novel." *n+1* 14 (2012): 157–69.

Davenport, Gary. "Looking Back to the Present." *Sewanee Review* 103.4 (1995): 645–52.

DeArmitt, Pleshette. "The Impossible Incorporation of Narcissus: Mourning and Narcissism in Derrida." *Philosophy Today* 44 (2000): 84–90.

DeKoven, Marianne. "Utopia Limited: Post-Sixties and Postmodern American Fiction." *Modern Fiction Studies* 41.1 (1995): 75–97.

de Man, Paul. *Allegories of Reading.* New Haven: Yale University Press, 1979.

—. "The Rhetoric of Temporality." *Blindness and Insight: Essays in the Rhetoric of Contemporary Criticism.* 2nd edn. London: Routledge, 1983. 187–228.

Derrida, Jacques. *Aporias: Dying—Awaiting (One Another at) the "Limits of Truth."* Trans. Thomas Dutoit. Stanford, CA: Stanford University Press, 1993.

—. "Autoimmunity: Real and Symbolic Suicides—A Dialogue with Jacques Derrida" (with Giovanna Borradori). Trans. Pascale-Anne Brault and Michael Naas. *Philosophy in a Time of Terror: Dialogues with Jürgen Habermas and Jacques Derrida.* Ed. Borradori. Chicago: University of Chicago Press, 2003. 85–136.

—. "Declarations of Independence." Trans. Tom Keenan and Tom Pepper. *Negotiations: Interventions and Interviews, 1971–2001.* Ed. Elizabeth Rottenburg. Stanford, CA: Stanford University Press, 2002. 46–54.

–. "Deconstruction and the Other" (interview with Richard Kearney). *States of Mind: Dialogues with Contemporary Thinkers on the European Mind*. Ed. Kearney. Manchester: Manchester University Press, 1995. 156–76.

—. *Demeure: Fiction and Testimony*. Trans. Elizabeth Rottenburg. Stanford, CA: Stanford University Press, 2000.

—. *Dissemination*. Trans. Barbara Johnson. Chicago: University of Chicago Press, 1981.

—. "Force of Law: The 'Mystical Foundation of Authority.'" Trans. Mary Quaintance. *Deconstruction and the Possibility of Justice*. Ed. Drucilla Cornell, Michel Rosenfeld, David Gray Carlson. New York: Routledge, 1992. 3–67.

—. *The Gift of Death and Literature in Secret*. Trans. David Wills. 2nd edn. Chicago: University of Chicago Press, 2008.

—. "The Law of Genre." Trans. Avital Ronell. *Acts of Literature*. Ed. Derek Attridge. London: Routledge, 1992. 221–52.

—. "*Le Toucher*: Touch/To Touch Him." Trans. Peggy Kamuf. *Paragraph* 16.2 (1993): 122–57.

—. *Limited Inc*. Ed. Gerald Graff. Evanston: Northwestern University Press, 1988.

—. "Marx and Sons." Trans. G. M. Goshgarian. *Ghostly Demarcations: A Symposium on Jacques Derrida's* Specters of Marx. Ed. Michael Sprinker. London: Verso, 1999. 213–69.

—. "Nietzsche and the Machine" (interview with Richard Beardsworth). Trans. Beardsworth. *Negotiations: Interventions and Interviews, 1971–2001*. Ed. Elizabeth Rottenburg. Stanford, CA: Stanford University Press, 2002. 215–56.

—. "Not Utopia, the Im-possible" (interview with Thomas Assheuer). *Paper Machine*. Trans. Rachel Bowlby. Stanford, CA: Stanford University Press, 2005. 121–35.

—. *Of Grammatology*. Trans. Gayatri Chakravorty Spivak. Baltimore: Johns Hopkins University Press, 1976.

—. *The Other Heading*. Trans. Pascale-Anne Brault and Michael Naas. Bloomington, IN: Indiana University Press, 1992.

—. "Passions: 'An Oblique Offering.'" Trans. David Wood. *Derrida: A Critical Reader*. Ed. Wood. Oxford: Blackwell, 1992. 5–35.

—. *The Politics of Friendship*. Trans. George Collins. London: Verso, 1997.

—. "Psyche: Invention of the Other." Trans. Catherine Porter. *Acts of Literature*. Ed. Derek Attridge. London: Routledge, 1992. 311–43.

—. "Remarks on Deconstruction and Pragmatism." Trans. Simon Critchley. *Deconstruction and Pragmatism*. Ed. Chantal Mouffe. London: Routledge, 1994. 77–88.

—. *Rogues: Two Essays on Reason*. Trans. Pascale-Anne Brault and Michael Naas. Stanford, CA: Stanford University Press, 2005.

—. *Specters of Marx: The State of the Debt, the Work of Mourning, and the New International*. Trans. Peggy Kamuf. London: Routledge, 1994.

—. "'There Is No *One* Narcissism' (Autobiophotographies)" (interview). *Points . . . Interviews 1974–1994*. Ed. Elisabeth Weber. Trans. Peggy Kamuf and others. Stanford, CA: Stanford University Press, 1995. 196–215.

—. "'This Strange Institution Called Literature': An Interview with Jacques Derrida" (with Derek Attridge). Trans. Geoffrey Bennington and Rachel Bowlby. *Acts of Literature*. Ed. Attridge. London: Routledge, 1992. 33–75.

Derrida, Jacques and Elizabeth Roudinesco. *For What Tomorrow . . . A Dialogue*. Trans. Jeff Fort. Stanford, CA: Stanford University Press, 2004.

Derrida, Jacques and Maurizio Ferraris. *A Taste for the Secret*. Trans. Giacomo Donis. Ed. Giacomo Donis and David Webb. Cambridge: Polity Press, 2001.

DeTora, Lisa. "Introduction: Real Americans, Heroes, and Home Fronts." *Heroes of Film, Comics and American Culture*. Ed. DeTora. Jefferson, NC: McFarland & Co., 2009. 1–16.

Dickstein, Morris. "The Complex Fate of the Jewish American Writer." *Nation* (October 22, 2002). Online access. October 1, 2012. www.thenation.com/article/complex-fate-jewish-american-writer-0.

Didion, Joan. *A Book of Common Prayer*. New York: Simon and Schuster, 1977.

Diemert, Brian. "*The Waterworks*: E. L. Doctorow's Gnostic Detective Story." *Texas Studies in Language and Literature* 45.4 (2003): 352–74.

Doctorow, E. L. *Conversations with E. L. Doctorow*. Ed. Christopher D. Morris. Jackson: University Press of Mississippi, 1999.

—. "E. A. Poe." *Creationists: Selected Essays 1993–2006*. New York: Random House, 2006. 9–20.

—. "E. L. Doctorow" (interview with John F Baker). *Publishers Weekly* (June 27, 1994): 51–2.

—. "False Documents." *Jack London, Hemingway, and the Constitution: Selected Essays, 1977–1992*. New York: Random House, 1993. 149–64.

—. "Left Out by Edith Wharton" (interview with Laurel Graeber). *New York Times* (June 19, 1994): 31.

—. *The Waterworks*. 1994. London: Picador, 1995.

Dotan, Eyal. "The Game of Late Capitalism: Gambling and Ideology in *The Music of Chance*." *Mosaic* 33.1 (2000): 161–76.

Duff, David, ed. *Modern Genre Theory*. London: Longman, 2000.

Dunst, Alexander. "Late Jameson, or, After the Eternity of the Present." *New Formations* 65 (2006): 105–18.

Eagleton, Mary. "Genre and Gender." *Modern Genre Theory*. Ed. David Duff. London: Longman, 2000. 250–62.

Eagleton, Terry. "Making a Break." *London Review of Books* 28.5 (March 9, 2006): 25–6.

Edwards, Erica. *Charisma and the Fictions of Black Leadership*. Minneapolis: University of Minnesota Press, 2012.

Eugenides, Jeffrey. "He's Not Like Other Girls" (interview with Geraldine Bedell). *Observer* (October 6, 2002). Online access. October 1, 2012. www.guardian.co.uk/books/2002/oct/06/fiction.impacprize.

—. "Jeffrey Eugenides" (interview with Jonathan Safran Foer). *BOMB* 81 (2002): 74–89. Online access. October 1, 2012. www.bombsite.com/issues/81/articles/2519.

—. "The Novel as a Mental Picture of Its Era" (interview with Bram van Moorhem). *3am* (2003). Online access. October 1, 2012. www.3ammagazine.com/litarchives/2003/sep/interview_jeffrey_eugenides.html.

—. *The Virgin Suicides*. London: Bloomsbury, 1993.

Felski, Rita. "Introduction." *Rethinking Tragedy*. Spec. issue of *New Literary History* 35.1 (2004): v–xx.

Fitzgerald, Francis Scott. *The Great Gatsby*. 1925. New York: Simon and Schuster, 1995.

Fleck, Linda. "From Metaphor to Metonymy: Paul Auster's *Leviathan*." *Critique* 39.3 (1998): 258–70.

Fredman, Stephen. "'How to Get Out of the Room that Is the Book?' Paul Auster and the Consequences of Confinement." *Postmodern Culture* 6.3 (1996): 50 pars.

Frisch, Andrea. "The Ethics of Testimony: A Genealogical Perspective." *Discourse* 25.1–2 (2004): 36–54.

Frow, John. "What Was Postmodernism?" *Time and Commodity Culture: Essays in Cultural Theory and Postmodernity.* Oxford: Clarendon, 1997. 13–63.

Fukuyama, Francis. "The End of History." *National Interest* 16 (Summer 1989): 3–18.

Gaines, Ernest J. *A Lesson before Dying.* New York: Alfred A. Knopf, 1993.

Geary, Daniel. "Racial Liberalism, the Moynihan Report & the *Daedalus* Project on 'The Negro American.'" *Daedalus* 140.1 (2011): 53–66.

Gentry, Marshall Bruce. "Elusive Villainy: *The Waterworks* as Doctorow's Poesque Preface." *South Atlantic Review* 67.1 (2002): 63–90.

Gibson, Andrew. "'And the Wind Wheezing through That Organ Once in a While': Voice, Narrative, Film." *New Literary History* 32.3 (2001): 639–57.

Gladstone, Jason and Daniel Worden. "Introduction: Postmodernism, Then." *Postmodernism, Then.* Spec. issue of *Twentieth-Century Literature* 57.3–4 (2011): 291–308.

Glaser, Jennifer. "The Jew in the Canon: Reading Race and Literary History in Philip Roth's *The Human Stain.*" *PMLA* 123.5 (2008): 1465–78.

Grassian, Daniel. *Hybrid Fictions: Contemporary American Fiction and Generation X.* London: McFarland & Co., 2003.

Green, Jeremy. *Late Postmodernism: American Fiction at the Millennium.* New York: Palgrave, 2005.

Gross, Theodore L. *The Heroic Ideal in American Literature.* New York: The Free Press, 1971.

Hägglund, Martin. *Radical Atheism: Derrida and the Time of Life.* Stanford, CA: Stanford University Press, 2008.

Halldorson, Stephanie S. *The Hero in Contemporary American Fiction: The Works of Saul Bellow and Don DeLillo.* New York: Palgrave, 2007.

Halloran, Vivan Nun. "Performative Mourning: Remembering Derrida through (Re) reading." *Postmodern Culture* 15.3 (2005): 29 pars.

Hassan, Ihab. "POSTmodernISM: A Paracritical Bibliography." *New Literary History* 3.1 (1971): 5–30.

Hayes-Brady, Clare. "'Obviously, Doctor, You've never Been a Thirteen-Year-Old Girl': Problematic Adolescence in *The Virgin Suicides.*" *'Forever Young'? The Changing Images of America.* Ed. Philip Coleman and Stephen Matterson. Heidelberg: Universitätsverlag Winter, 2012. 209–18.

Hedges, William. *Washington Irving: An American Study, 1802–1832.* Baltimore: Johns Hopkins Press, 1965.

Higonnet, Margaret. "Frames of Female Suicide." *Studies in the Novel* 32.1 (2000): 229–42.

Hoberek, Andrew. "Cormac McCarthy and the Aesthetics of Exhaustion." *American Literary History* 23.3 (2011): 483–99.

—. "Foreign Objects, or DeLillo Minimalist." *Studies in American Fiction* 37.1 (2010): 101–25.

—. "Introduction: After Postmodernism." *After Postmodernism: Form and History in Contemporary American Fiction.* Spec. issue of *Twentieth Century Literature* 53.3 (2007): 233–47.

Hungerford, Amy. "Don DeLillo's Latin Mass." *Contemporary Literature* 47.3 (2006): 343–80.

—. "On the Period Formerly Known as Contemporary." *American Literary History* 20.1–2 (2008): 410–19.

Hutcheon, Linda. *A Poetics of Postmodernism: History, Theory, Fiction*. New York: Routledge, 1988.

—. *The Politics of Postmodernism*. 2nd edn. London: Routledge, 2002.

Hutchison, Anthony. *Writing the Republic: Liberalism and Morality in American Political Fiction*. New York: Columbia University Press, 2007.

Irving, Washington. "Rip van Winkle." *The Oxford Book of American Short Stories*. Ed. Joyce Carol Oates. Oxford: Oxford University Press, 1992. 18–32.

Jacobus, Mary. "The Law of/and Gender: Genre Theory and *The Prelude*." *Diacritics* 14.4 (1984): 47–57.

Jameson, Fredric. *Archaeologies of the Future: The Desire Called Utopia and Other Science Fictions*. London: Verso, 2007.

—. *Fables of Aggression: Wyndham Lewis, the Modernist as Fascist*. Berkeley: University of California Press, 1979.

—. "Live Jameson" (interview with Ian Buchanan), in Buchanan. *Fredric Jameson: Live Theory*. London: Continuum, 2006. 120–32.

—. "Marx's Purloined Letter." *Ghostly Demarcations: A Symposium on Jacques Derrida's Specters of Marx*. Ed. Michael Sprinker. London: Verso, 1999. 26–67.

—. "Of Islands and Trenches: Neutralization and the Production of Utopian Discourse." *The Ideologies of Theory: Essays 1971–1986: Volume 2: Syntax of History*. Minneapolis: University of Minnesota Press, 1988. 75–102.

—. "Periodizing the 60s." *The 60's Without Apology*. Spec. issue of *Social Text* 9–10 (1984): 178–209.

—. *The Political Unconscious: Narrative as a Socially Symbolic Act*. London: Methuen, 1981.

—. *Postmodernism, or, The Cultural Logic of Late Capitalism*. London: Verso, 1991.

—. *Sartre: The Origins of a Style*. 1961. New York: Columbia University Press, 1984.

—. *Signatures of the Visible*. London: Routledge, 1992.

Kakutani, Michiko. "Of Death in Adolescence and Innocence Lost." *New York Times* (March 19, 1993). Online access. October 1, 2012. www.nytimes.com/1993/03/19/books/books-of-the-times-of-death-in-adolescence-and-innocence-lost.html.

Kaveney, Roz. "Dim Lights, Big City." *New Statesman and Society* (June 17, 1994): 40.

Kelly, Adam. "Beginning with Postmodernism." *Postmodernism, Then*. Spec. issue of *Twentieth-Century Literature* 57.3–4 (2011): 391–422.

Kierkegaard, Soren. *Fear and Trembling/Repetition*. Ed. and trans. Howard V. Hong and Edna H. Hong. Princeton, NJ: Princeton University Press, 1983.

Krell, David Farrell. *The Purest of Bastards: Works of Mourning, Art, and Affirmation in the Thought of Jacques Derrida*. Pennsylvania: Pennsylvania State University Press, 2000.

Kuklick, Bruce. "Myth and Symbol in American Studies." *American Quarterly* 24.4 (1972): 435–50.

Lewis, R. W. B. *The American Adam: Innocence, Tragedy, and Tradition in the Nineteenth Century*. Chicago: University of Chicago Press, 1955.

Lodge, David. *Consciousness and the Novel*. London: Secker & Warburg, 2001.

Long, Christian. "Running Out of Gas: The Energy Crisis in 1970s Suburban Narratives." *Canadian Review of American Studies* 41.3 (2011): 342–69.

Lyons, Bonnie. "Philip Roth's American Tragedies." *Turning Up the Flame: Philip Roth's Later Novels*. Ed. Jay L. Halio and Ben Siegel. Newark, DE: University of Delaware Press, 2005. 125–30.

Malpas, Simon. "Introduction." *Postmodern Debates*. Ed. Malpas. New York: Palgrave, 2001. 1–11.

Marler, Robert. "From Tale to Short Story: The Emergence of a New Genre in the 1850s." *American Literature* 46.2 (1974): 153–69.

Martin, Brendan. *Paul Auster's Postmodernity*. London: Routledge, 2008.

McGurl, Mark. *The Program Era: Postwar Fiction and the Rise of Creative Writing*. Cambridge, MA: Harvard University Press, 2009.

Melley, Timothy. "Bodies Incorporated: Scenes of Agency Panic in *Gravity's Rainbow*." *Contemporary Literature* 35.4 (1994): 709–38.

Merivale, Patricia. "Through Greene-Land in Drag: Joan Didion's *A Book of Common Prayer*." *Pacific Coast Philology* 15 (1980): 45–52.

Miller, Arthur. *The Theatre Essays of Arthur Miller*. Ed. Robert A. Martin. New York: Viking, 1978.

Miller, J. Hillis. *Speech Acts in Literature*. Stanford, CA: Stanford University Press, 2001.

Minter, David. *The Interpreted Design as a Structural Principle in American Prose*. New Haven: Yale University Press, 1969.

Mitchell, Jonathan. *Revisions of the American Adam: Innocence, Identity and Masculinity in Twentieth-Century America*. London: Continuum, 2011.

Moraru, Christian. *Cosmodernism: American Narrative, Late Globalization, and the New Cultural Imaginary*. Ann Arbor: University of Michigan Press, 2010.

Nealon, Jeffrey T. "Work of the Detective, Work of the Writer: Paul Auster's *City of Glass*." *Modern Fiction Studies* 42.1 (1996): 91–110.

Oberman, Warren. "Existentialism Meets Postmodernism in Paul Auster's *The Music of Chance*." *Critique* 45.2 (2004): 191–206.

Osteen, Mark. "Phantoms of Liberty: The Secret Lives of *Leviathan*." *Review of Contemporary Fiction* 14.1 (1994): 87–91.

Parrish, Tim. "Becoming Black: Zuckerman's Bifurcating Self in *The Human Stain*." *Philip Roth: New Perspectives on an American Author*. Ed. Derek Parker Royal. Westport, CT: Praeger-Greenwood, 2005. 209–23.

Posnock, Ross. "Purity and Danger: On Philip Roth." *Raritan* 21.2 (2001): 85–101.

Prosser, Jay, ed. *American Fiction in the 1990s: Reflections of History and Culture*. London: Routledge, 2008.

Punday, Daniel. "John Barth's Occasional Writing: The Institutional Construction of Postmodernism in *The Friday Book*." *American Literature* 77.3 (2005): 591–619.

Pynchon, Thomas. *Gravity's Rainbow*. 1973. London: Picador, 1975.

Rankine, Patrice D. "Passing as Tragedy: Philip Roth's *The Human Stain*, the Oedipus Myth, and the Self-Made Man." *Critique* 47.1 (2005): 101–12.

Redfield, Marc. "Pynchon's Postmodern Sublime." *PMLA* 104.2 (1989): 152–62.

Reed, Walter L. *Meditations on the Hero*. New Haven: Yale University Press, 1974.

Richardson, Brian. *Unnatural Voices: Extreme Narration in Modern and Contemporary Fiction*. Columbus: Ohio State University Press, 2006.

Richardson, Robert D. *Emerson: The Mind on Fire*. London: University of California Press, 1995.

Rosenthal, Michael. "What Was Postmodernism?" *Socialist Review* 22.3 (1992): 83–105.

Roth, Philip. *The Human Stain*. Boston: Houghton Mifflin, 2000.

—. *Reading Myself and Others*. London: Vintage, 2001.

Royal, Derek Parker. "Introduction; Or, 'Now Vee May Perhaps to Begin, Yes?'" *Philip Roth: New Perspectives on an American Author*. Ed. Royal. Westport, CT: Praeger-Greenwood, 2005. 1–7.

—. "Plotting the Frames of Subjectivity: Identity, Death, and Narrative in Philip Roth's *The Human Stain*." *Contemporary Literature* 47.1 (2006): 114–40.

Russell, Alison. "Deconstructing *The New York Trilogy*: Paul Auster's Anti-Detective Fiction." *Critique* 32.2 (1990): 71–84.

Ryan, Judith. *The Novel after Theory*. New York: Columbia University Press, 2012.

Safer, Elaine B. "Tragedy and Farce in Roth's *The Human Stain*." *Critique* 43.3 (2002): 211–27.

Saltzmann, Arthur. "*Leviathan*: Post Hoc Harmonies." *Beyond the Red Notebook: Essays on Paul Auster*. Ed. Dennis Barone. Philadelphia: University of Pennsylvania Press, 1995. 162–70.

Schama, Simon. "Gaslight, Necropolis." *New York Times* (June 19, 1994). Online access. October 1, 2012. www.nytimes.com/1994/06/19/books/doctorow-waterworks. html?pagewanted=all.

Schulman, Bruce. *The Seventies: The Great Shift in American Culture, Society, and Politics*. New York: The Free Press, 2001.

Segal, Alex. "Secrecy and the Gift: Paul Auster's *The Locked Room*." *Critique* 39.3 (1998): 239–57.

Shiloh, Ilona. "A Place Both Imaginary and Realistic: Paul Auster's *The Music of Chance*." *Contemporary Literature* 43.3 (2002): 488–517.

Shostak, Debra. *Philip Roth—Countertexts, Counterlives*. Columbia, SC: University of South Carolina Press, 2004.

—. "'A story we could live with': Narrative Voice, the Reader, and Jeffrey Eugenides's *The Virgin Suicides*." *Modern Fiction Studies* 55.4 (2009): 808–32.

Simmons, David. *The Anti-Hero in the American Novel*. London: Palgrave, 2008.

Simons, Jon. "Postmodern Paranoia? Pynchon and Jameson." *Paragraph* 23.2 (2000): 207–21.

Solotaroff, Ted. "Of Melville, Poe and Doctorow." *Critical Essays on E. L. Doctorow*. Ed. Ben Siegel. New York: G. K. Hall & Co., 2000. 137–43.

Strandberg, Victor. "Passion and Delusion in *A Book of Common Prayer*." *Modern Fiction Studies* 27.2 (1981): 225–42.

Theobald, Tom. *Existentialism and Baseball: The French Philosophical Roots of Paul Auster*. Saarbrücken: Lambert Academic Publishing, 2010.

Tokarczyk, Michelle M. *E. L. Doctorow's Skeptical Commitment*. New York: Peter Lang, 2000.

—. "*The Waterworks*." *Literary Review* 39.3 (1996): 435–6.

Varvogli, Aliki. *The World That Is the Book: Paul Auster's Fiction*. Liverpool: Liverpool University Press, 2001.

Wegner, Phillip E. *Life between Two Deaths, 1989–2001: U.S. Culture in the Long Nineties*. Durham, NC: Duke University Press, 2009.

Wellek, René and Austin Warren. *Theory of Literature*. Harmondsworth: Penguin, 1949.

Williams, Raymond. *Modern Tragedy*. 2nd edn. London: Verso, 1979.

Wise, Gene. "'Paradigm Dramas' in American Studies: A Cultural and Institutional History of the Movement." *American Quarterly* 31.3 (1979): 293–337.

Wolfe, Alan. *The Suicidal Narrative in Modern Japan: The Case of Dazai Osamu*. Princeton, NJ: Princeton University Press, 1990.

Womack, Kenneth and Amy Mallory-Kani. "'Why Don't You just Leave It Up to Nature?': An Adaptationist Reading of the Novels of Jeffrey Eugenides." *Mosaic* 40.3 (2007): 157–73.

Woods, Tim. *Beginning Postmodernism*. 2nd edn. Manchester: Manchester University Press, 2009.

Wutz, Michael. *Enduring Words: Literary Narrative in a Changing Media Ecology*. Tuscaloosa: University of Alabama Press, 2009.

Index

Printed in Great Britain
by Amazon.co.uk, Ltd.,
Marston Gate.